BORDERING ON INDIFFERENCE

Bordering on Indifference

IMMIGRATION AGENTS NEGOTIATING
RACE AND MORALITY

IRENE I. VEGA

PRINCETON UNIVERSITY PRESS

PRINCETON & OXFORD

Published by Princeton University Press
41 William Street, Princeton, New Jersey 08540
99 Banbury Road, Oxford OX2 6JX

press.princeton.edu

All Rights Reserved

ISBN 978-0-691-26208-6
ISBN (pbk.) 978-0-691-26209-3
ISBN (e-book) 978-0-691-26210-9

British Library Cataloging-in-Publication Data is available

Editorial: Rachael Levay and Erik Beranek
Production Editorial: Jill Harris
Cover Design: Karl Spurzem
Production: Lauren Reese
Publicity: William Pagdatoon
Copyeditor: Kathleen Kageff

Cover image: Loke Yek Mang / Shutterstock

This book has been composed in Arno

10 9 8 7 6 5 4 3 2 1

In memory of my mother, Juana Vega

CONTENTS

TABLES

BORDERING ON INDIFFERENCE

Introduction

I KNEW MARCOS PAYAN was my appointment as soon as he stepped in the coffee shop. It was the T-shirt that tipped me off—avocado green and a shade lighter than the Border Patrol uniform. It could have been his hair too. With it cut short and neatly combed to the side, he was either in the military or in law enforcement. I got up and introduced myself. I was right, but my initial satisfaction was tempered by his taciturn demeanor. He wasn't quite standoffish, but definitely uncomfortable. I had tried to usher him to the counter so I could buy him a cold drink, but he politely declined, explaining that agents could not accept gifts from the public because they could be misconstrued as bribes. I went back to the corner table I had secured for us and tried my best to look busy. He ordered a drink and waited at the counter.

A Border Patrol agent with about ten years of experience on the job, Marcos had agreed to meet with me as a favor to a mutual friend. He had been clear that this would not be an interview, but I still counted our meeting as a major win. For months I had made cold calls, sent unanswered emails, and guilted my friends into having awkward conversations with acquaintances all in the name of recruiting highly guarded agents for my research. Marcos's phone number was the fruit of one such effort.

When Marcos finally sat with me he tried to lean as far back as he could, an effort thwarted by the petite coffee-shop chairs. Maybe he was tired from the long shift he was coming from, or maybe he was regretting the meeting. Either way, our table felt like the size of a dinner plate, and I knew to get to the point fast. I explained that I was looking to understand immigration enforcement from the inside, and talking to agents was part of that effort. I clarified that all I needed was that he listen to my study plan and flag any issues.

Marcos thought that my main challenge would be getting agents to talk to me, something that resonated with my experience to that point. "Agents are really private about their job. . . . I don't even like wearing this shirt right now, but I just got off work." "What's wrong with the shirt?" I asked. "It makes me look like a Border Patrol agent." I started to laugh, then stopped myself. He flashed me a cautious smile and explained that "the agency doesn't have the best reputation" and that "a lot of people just think we're dream crushers." I tried to probe, but it was clear that he was done with that part of the conversation. I reluctantly transitioned to less controversial topics, like who I might ask for permission to interview agents.

The next time I spoke to Marcos was that fall. Somewhat surprised, but clearly pleased that I had gotten the study approved, he invited me into his home for the interview. The sprawling ranch-style house was only a few years old and located in a solidly upper-middle-class neighborhood. The comforts of his gainful employment were on display—a shiny truck in the driveway, a tastefully furnished living room, and a large and welcoming backyard. This was a far cry from the modest upbringing that Marcos had experienced as the child of working-class Mexican parents.

Marcos was proud of the life he had built with the Border Patrol job, but he admitted it had not always been that way. "At first, I really felt bad for a while. It was one of those things where it was like, oh my God, this person, they're just trying to make their living." Marcos understood this firsthand because members of his family had entered the United States without documentation. Marcos's grandfather had "just walked across the border" in the 1950s, and two decades later his father made his own clandestine entry hidden in a "huge, old pickup truck."

Marcos was neither ashamed nor proud that he descended from these men who had broken immigration law. It was simply part of his family history. If anything, this history had made him critical of immigration agents when he was growing up. Marcos had been "a little anti–Border Patrol" when he was younger, but somewhere along the line he had learned that the agency was a viable employment option for someone like him, a bilingual high-school graduate with a clean criminal record and the desire to move up in the world. Marcos could not pinpoint when his perception changed, but he took the job in the early 2000s during one of the immigration enforcement system's various growth spurts. The Border Patrol job came with a good salary, predictable raises, health and retirement benefits, and the sheen of being a federal agent. It was a no-brainer as far as making a living, but he still felt compelled to seek his father's blessing.

I know for me, the big thing that got me to actually apply for [the] Border Patrol was when I talked to my dad about it. And he told me, "Look, there's always going to be somebody there, whether it be you or somebody who is racist, somebody who does hate Mexican people or Latinos or what have you. . . . Why not it be somebody like you that actually knows what a lot of these people are going through?" And when he told me that, I was like, "You know what, that makes a lot of sense."

What made a lot of sense to Marcos was the unspoken promise of his racial/ethnic and immigrant background. It was the assumption that he, the son and grandson of formerly undocumented Mexican immigrants, could somehow be a force for good within an agency with a reputation for being bad. How exactly Agent Payan would be different from those without his background was left unspoken, but the idea that his presence was an improvement was assumed.

A decade into the work, Marcos's ideas about undocumented migration had remained stable in some ways. He still believed that most undocumented border crossers were like the men in his family, people who had been pushed out of their home countries by an array of hardships and pulled toward the United States by the prospect of work. He could even "relate" to immigrants because of his "roots," he told me. At the same time, Agent Payan's economic understanding of undocumented migration now stood alongside deep convictions about the importance of enforcement. He remained somewhat self-conscious of the work and did not espouse an outright ideological commitment to national sovereignty but explained his job in what he thought were more practical terms. Border control was a matter of keeping America safe from an array of loathsome characters. Economic migrants like his father and grandfather were not the issue—it was the cunning terrorists, the unscrupulous smugglers, and the violent drug traffickers he worried about. Agent Payan reasoned that he had to stop them all to catch the worst of them. This was just the way things were and had always been, he explained. "Along with my dad [and grandfather] . . . I'm sure a lot of horrible people came at the same time they did too."

Over time, Marcos became Agent Payan and acquired that most bureaucratic of perspectives on the job. He believed that his role was narrow and a straightforward matter of law and policy. At the same time, he began to feel that people misunderstood immigration agents, just as he once did. The public saw agents as "dream crushers" when all they were doing was apprehending people who could not prove that they had permission to be in the United States. He conceded that not all immigrants were criminals, but how could agents decipher between the *good ones* and the *bad ones* just by looking at them? He had learned that many of them were "liars" and "full of shit" anyway, so it was impossible to know who they really were without fingerprinting them. To fingerprint them, you had to arrest them first and call someone else to transport them to the processing station. At the station, it was a different agent's job to put "the bodies" through a legal process designed by someone way above both of their pay grades. The regulations—not agents—would determine where those "bodies" belonged. Some of them would serve time in prison, others would be detained while awaiting immigration proceedings, others summarily deported. At the end of each shift, Agent Payan would get in his truck, rest in his well-appointed home, and repeat it all the next day.

Yes, Marcos could "relate" to immigrants—he had a certain level of understanding for their plight, could even perceive a vague sense of connection and feel sympathy for some of them. In this way, he was living up to the assumption that his father made when he gave him his blessing to work in immigration enforcement: the idea that if there was going to be a Border Patrol, it would be better to have someone like his son there because he would understand what people were going through and not "hate Mexican people or Latinos." What neither Marcos nor his father accounted for in those early days was how the political-bureaucratic context in which Marcos would work, and the expectations of his role as an agent, would also shape and shift his views, perceptions, and behaviors. Marcos's background would acquire new meaning at work, would sometimes be a source of tension, and sometimes a source of possibility, but it would never be independent from his responsibilities as an agent. Marcos would continue relating to immigrants because of his roots, but that would not stop Agent Payan from doing his job.

Over the course of two years, I interviewed ninety immigration enforcement agents—both US Border Patrol agents and Immigration and Customs Enforcement deportation officers—working in Arizona and California. I spoke to a diverse set of agents, but most of them were Latinas/os like Marcos Payan, children or grandchildren of Mexican immigrants, many of whom grew up along the US-Mexico border they now policed.[1] *Bordering on Indifference: Immigration Agents Negotiating Race and Morality* tells the story of how these agents come into the work, how they are trained and socialized once on the job, and how that training and socialization impacts the way they reconcile the many moral and racial tensions of the work. Throughout the book I will draw contrasts and highlight similarities between Latina/o agents and their non-Latina/o peers, but the former will be our main interlocutors because these agents wield the immigration state's coercive power but are also members of the racial/ethnic group that is disproportionately targeted by that power.[2]

Even though readers will meet many agents like Marcos Payan, this book is not really about agents as individuals, nor is it only about the tensions they grapple with. *Bordering on Indifference* is about what Didier Fassin calls the moral economy of immigration control—the affective reactions and evaluative principles that are mobilized in relation to migrants and immigration. These norms, values, and sensibilities circulate in public space, through politics and bureaucratic and legal process, and they create the commonsense principles that agents use to make sense of their work and enact their professional role.[3]

I show that indifference is a major part of that moral economy. Michael Herzfeld defines indifference as "the rejection of common humanity . . . [and] the denial of identity, of selfhood" and argues that Western bureaucracies thrive on indifference, even as national myths celebrate hospitality.[4] Nowhere is the paradox between espoused inclusion and indifference more visible than in the United States, a country that presents itself as a nation of immigrants and celebrates *e pluribus unum* despite its settler-colonialist history and record of racialized exclusion.[5]

I examine the production of indifference on the front line of US immigration control, both as a bureaucratic strategy that agents use to look away from the most conflicting aspects of their work, and as a major product of their efforts to cultivate a moral sense of self. In doing so, I reveal how agents normalize socially and legally constructed categories, even when they are faced with evidence that contradicts the validity of these categories.[6] My analysis thus extends our knowledge of how the moral judgments, emotional reactions, and simplified heuristics of immigration agents working within and outside the United States function as mechanisms of compliance and stability in what Cecilia Menjívar aptly called ' bureaucracies of displacement.'"[7]

Thinking about indifference helps us unlock the bureaucratic dimension of immigration control. Not only are detention, deportation, and border control "spectacles" that enact illegality and trade in cruelty, but they are also less visible forms of "slow violence" that are carried out routinely under the guise of legal rationality.[8] *Bordering on Indifference* thus traces the development of what Hannah Arendt famously called the "banality of evil"[9]—it shows how immigration bureaucracies produce apathy and distance, perpetuating exclusion through culture, law, and process, no matter what their workforce looks like. At no point do the agents featured in this book appear as unthinking cogs in a machine, however. We see that agents like Marcos Payan and his colleagues are invested in being indifferent to the moral ambiguities and racialized character of immigration control because protecting the status quo pays—they get to keep their job—and because if undocumented migration is not seen as categorically *bad*, they run the risk of not being seen as *good*.

US Immigration Control:
Latinas/os on Both Sides of the State

Immigration control is a deeply racialized phenomenon throughout the world, and while its manifestations are varied, it is consistently people from the Global South who are targeted for detention, deportation, and border enforcement.[10] In the United States, it is Latinx people and Mexicans specifically who hold the unwelcome distinction of being constructed as the country's archetypal illegal aliens.[11] Seen as undesirable as citizens and disposable as labor,[12] Mexicans have long borne the brunt of America's nation-building efforts through conquest, settler colonialism, and immigration-based restriction and policing.[13] In addition to being othered in law, Mexicans have also been the poster child for the media and politicians' Latino threat narrative, which frames the group as an invading force that threatens American sovereignty and prosperity.[14] Consequently, the US-Mexico boundary has been framed as a liability to be managed and controlled, a fact that has produced a highly militarized and deadly border.[15]

While Mexicans dominate the American racial imaginary as it relates to immigration, the racialization of illegality has now expanded to include the broader Latinx population.[16] The category Latinas/os, which includes people from Central and South America but also the Caribbean, are overrepresented among those who are arrested, detained, surveilled, and deported by immigration authorities—this is the statistical reality that I am referring to when I say that the US immigration system is racialized. Agents, as well as some members of the public, may be tempted to explain racialized patterns through a logic of probability, that is, by saying that these racial patterns merely reflect the population of undocumented people in the United States or those arrested trying to cross the border. The government's own statistics belie that explanation.

For example, according to the government's population estimates, 63 percent of the undocumented population in 2018 was from Mexico, Guatemala, Honduras, and El Salvador. That same year, people from those four countries accounted for 92 percent of deportations conducted by Immigration and Customs Enforcement.[17] Enforcement outcomes are further patterned along gender lines. Men have a much higher chance of being deported from the United States than women.[18] The overrepresentation of Latinas/os in the government's enforcement statistics is not a direct reflection of who is out of status in the United States, but an outcome of laws, policies, and practices that disproportionately target the group.

Being the country's archetypal criminal and illegal aliens has had devastating, intergenerational consequences on Latina/o communities,[19] leading scholars to conclude that immigration enforcement functions as a gendered and racial project of social control.[20] In effect, the US immigration enforcement system is for Latinx people what mass incarceration has long been for African Americans.[21] Given this context, when Latina/o immigration agents go to work for agencies like the United States Border Patrol (USBP) and Immigration and Customs Enforcement (ICE), their experiences are marked by in-betweenness—they are state agents by profession, but also embodiments of the United States' main target as Latinas/os. This has remained true, even as these agencies have diversified.

As Kelly Lytle Hernández's seminal history of the Border Patrol showed, in the agency's early days immigration agents were primarily White working-class men looking to climb the economic and status ladder through the exclusion of Mexicans. Those White men were joined by a small but discernable number of middle-class Mexican borderlanders who distinguished themselves from working-class "Mexican browns" both racially and socioeconomically.[22] Decades later, the racial demographics of immigration enforcement agencies have changed dramatically. Today about half of the Border Patrol and one-third of ICE are Latina/o/Hispanic agents. Most of these Latina/o/Hispanic agents work in the southwestern borderlands, where the US government concentrates its attention.

The browning of the coercive arm of the US immigration bureaucracy follows the same trend as the diversification of the broader police profession. The number of women and minoritized officers working in immigration enforcement grew most notably in the 1970s and 1980s following the federal government's attempt to remedy racial discrimination in employment through targeted efforts to increase Hispanic representation in the federal workforce.[23] In fact, today the Department of Homeland Security is touted as a diversity leader in the federal government because of its prolific hiring of Hispanics into agencies like the USBP and ICE.[24]

The diversification (or rather, *Latinization*) of the immigration bureaucracy has not disrupted the legacy of racism within enforcement agencies like the Border Patrol.[25] In fact, the hiring of Latinas/os has been facilitated by the massive growth of the US enforcement apparatus, which has become more restrictive and criminalized over time. When Latinas/os go to work for the USBP and ICE, no matter their initial motivations, they embody state power and come to articulate ideas that reflect immigration agencies' ideological positions.[26] Latina/o immigration agents have thus implemented many of the border control and deportation policies that have had devastating impacts on Latinas/os in and outside of the United States. Some of those policies have even been conceived by Latina/o agents themselves.

Prevention through Deterrence (PTD)—the border control policy widely known for militarizing the US-Mexico border and, as Jason De León powerfully put it, weaponizing the desert against migrants[27]—was the brainchild of then El Paso Border Patrol Chief Silvestre Reyes. Prevention through Deterrence started as Operation Blockade (eventually renamed Operation Hold the Line), an initiative spearheaded by Reyes in response to El Paso residents advocating against Border Patrol agent excesses, which included chasing undocumented immigrants through their communities and even schools. The idea behind what eventually became PTD was to line up agents along the busiest crossing corridors with the intention of deterring migrants, instead of conducting apprehensions once migrants were already on US soil. The strategy did not deter undocumented crossings, but it did make them less visible in border towns by pushing migrants into remote areas. This, in turn, raised the stakes of crossing the border without documentation, which disrupted Mexican circular migration, growing the undocumented population in the United States and generating the conditions in which profit-seeking smuggling organizations now thrive. Worst of all, it also made crossing the US-Mexico border a deadly prospect.[28]

That the diversification of the USBP and ICE has not fundamentally changed the racialized character of immigration control challenges the common misperception that simply diversifying workforces will create more humane policing systems.[29] Scholars of representative bureaucracy have demonstrated as much. Representative bureaucracy theory is concerned with how demographic shifts in public agencies can improve minorities' experiences with the state. The driving mechanism for that improvement would be discretion, where bureaucrats (e.g., Latina/o immigration agents) who have an affinity with coethnic clients (e.g., Latina/o immigrants) would use their discretionary power to benefit those clients. There is a good deal of research showing the benefits of diverse workforces in institutions with helping missions, like education,[30] but in law enforcement the evidence is more mixed.[31]

Bordering on Indifference is less a case study of representative bureaucracy and more a cautionary tale for those who uncritically conflate institutional diversity with organizational change, especially in policing. My findings align with those who have argued that the idea of racial representation is based on the seemingly straightforward but, in practice, quite thorny premise that racial categories correspond to identities and competencies,[32] as well as a rather thin conceptualization of *representation*.[33] Bureaucracies can thwart group commitments, and this is especially true in racialized organizations, like the US immigration system, which constrain minority bureaucrats' individual agency through rules and regulations, as well as through racialized sanctions.[34] As Celeste Watkins-Hayes put it, "bureaucratic environments with histories of racial inequality and orientations that apply 'red tape' restrictively or punitively are likely to generate strong boundaries between racial minorities in bureaucrat-client relationships."[35] *Bordering on Indifference* contributes to the conversation on racial representation in bureaucracies through a case study that shows how diversity and repression can coexist in policing, an issue I return to in the conclusion.

Agents' Legitimation as a Window into the Moral Economy of Immigration Control

To be a federal immigration enforcement agent is to be a compulsory participant in what is a highly racialized, politically contentious, and moral debate about how the United States manages undocumented migration.[36] The public is divided, and the debate is divisive. On one side you have restrictionists, who frame undocumented migration as a crime and assault on national sovereignty. Immigrationists counter that the United States is Janus faced, not just tolerating, but even encouraging a certain amount of undocumented migration. In any case, they argue, migration should be managed humanely.

False dichotomies about the morality of undocumented immigrants permeate both sides of this contentious debate. As Emine F. Elcioglu put it, people with drastically different immigration politics are all vying for their own version of the "third-world migrant," a gendered and racialized construction that serves as the foil for both progressives and restrictionists. Progressives imagine the so-called third-world migrant as a feminized powerless victim while among restrictionists that image takes on a hypermasculine dangerous character that is a threat to Americans and state agents.[37] Latina/o immigrants serve as the archetypes for these debates, and the most restrictionist attitudes are linked to the image of the undocumented Latino man, imagined as indigent, with little formal education, working in a low-status job, and lacking English proficiency.[38] The agents I spoke to are critical participants in these normative contests, and their contributions are proscribed by their professional role—no matter how they might have thought about immigration before they got the job or what beliefs they might hold about immigrants in private. When at work they represent the restrictionist state.

As a result, interviewing agents about their work meant that I had a frontline view of how they engage in this debate on behalf of their employer. As representatives of the state, agents are both producers and consumers of the coercive bureaucratic ideologies that the USBP and ICE deploy to make the exclusion of migrants more palatable and to make the growth of the bureaucracy seem necessary and urgent.[39] While symbolic politics are central to immigration debates throughout the world, the performative dimension of US immigration control is especially pronounced at the US-Mexico border, a place that the US government has long defined as a threat to American sovereignty and its settler colonialist ambitions of a White America.[40] As Peter Andreas put it, successful migration management at the country's southern border has always been more about effective image crafting than about actual deterrence.[41]

As representatives of the immigration state, all agents are engaged in this incessant project of legitimation, but the pull toward justification is especially pronounced for Latina/o agents, who deal with layered legitimacy deficits. Not only are Latina/o immigration agents members of a "dirty work" occupation,[42] just like the rest of their colleagues, but they are also called to account for implementing immigration laws that disproportionately target and exclude *their own*. The intersection of race/ethnicity and professional role produces tensions for Latina/o agents, whether in the form of internal dissonance (as when Agent Payan said he felt bad for arresting people who came to the United States for work) or due to external sanctions, as when people call agents traitors for transgressing the expectation of solidarity against racialized immigration politics and policies.[43]

Bordering on Indifference reveals the moral economy of immigration control by capitalizing on frontline immigration agents' penchant for legitimation. As

previously defined, the moral economy of immigration control includes the
norms, values, and affects that circulate in public space and are reflected in
bureaucratic and legal process. In my analysis, moral economy is closely related to occupational culture in that both contain norms and values and even
heuristics that shape worldviews and provide behavioral prescriptions for
frontline agents.[44] I lean more heavily toward the concept of moral economy
because it emphasizes dynamism, pushing us to think about cultural values,
norms, and principles not as coherent systems, but as part of a broader constel-
lation of contested ideologies that are produced and circulated by states and
their agents to legitimize immigration control. As Didier Fassin put it, moral
economies are less about moralities as stable ideas and behavioral guides (although this is part of their function) and more about the political struggles
over immigration control as a normatively dubious state practice.[45] In examining the logics that agents believe vindicate them and their enterprise, I reveal
that indifference is key to how states police territorial borders and the symbolic boundaries of national belonging.

My focus on agents, an understudied group, adds a much-needed frontline
account to existing research on immigration control as an inherently coercive
and exclusionary form of state power that is applied in racially disparate ways.
Cecilia Menjívar's conceptualization of enforcement agencies as "bureaucracies of displacement" that uphold legal violence and structural inequalities
through state classification systems is key to my analysis.[46] Antje Ellermann's
conceptualization of deportation as coercive social regulation is central to how
I understand the moral ambiguity of immigration control at the implementation stage.[47] My focus on race is buttressed by Kelly Lytle Hernández's work
on the Border Patrol as a mechanism of racialized social control in the borderlands, as well as Tanya Golash-Boza's account of deportation as a tool of global
racial capitalism.[48]

I also build on the work of scholars who have studied immigration officials
as what Michael Lipsky famously called "street-level bureaucrats," or policy
implementers who are often thought of as low-level employees but have extraordinary power to determine legal and policy outcomes. Street-level bureaucrats' power comes from their autonomy from central authority structures
and, most importantly, their discretion or their ability to use their judgments
about how policies will be translated into work practices. Discretion is a constant in policy implementation because written mandates are necessarily in-
determinate, leaving bureaucrats to negotiate the myriads of situations and
people that they will encounter.[49]

Research on the implementation of immigration policy in the United States is epitomized by seminal works, including Kitty Calavita's *Inside the State*, that have shown how bureaucrats negotiate external politics, their mission, and organizational pressures to render immigration law to the public.[50] The picture we get from studying immigration bureaucrats—everyone from airport inspectors to customs and deportation officers, asylum officials, judges, and lawyers—is that they are neither apolitical implementers of others' wishes, nor completely autonomous actors.[51] Rather, they are constantly negotiating their mandates and moral judgments, which are informed by dominant constructions of immigrants as either deserving or undeserving, as well as their resources and constraints as they make decisions. These decisions fundamentally impact how immigration laws take shape, making it so that bureaucrats and the agencies they represent are not just policy-implementation entities—they make law.[52]

I too treat immigration agents as street-level bureaucrats, centering the power of discretion, ideology, and process to shape what sociolegal scholars call law-in-action.[53] However, *Bordering on Indifference* is not a book about the mechanics of implementing a specific policy, nor are decision-making heuristics its major focus. This is a book about the normative principles that pervade agents' work; it is about the normalization of exclusion, and it is ultimately about the making of indifference in institutions like the US immigration system. In this way, my work is in conversation with research that examines the moralities and bureaucratic rationalities of various professionals, not just immigration agents, but also corporate managers, welfare counselors, prison officers, and other law enforcers.[54] The processes that I am analyzing exist "upstream" from decision making, as Bernardo Zacka put it, so they can be difficult to perceive, but they are critically important because they protect the status quo in organizations.[55]

In studying these normative principles, I bridge policy implementation research with a broader discussion on how states engender indifference to various forms of inequality.[56] Bureaucratization is central to the creation of that indifference because bureaucracies are rule-saturated, hierarchically organized environments that encourage specialization and predictable progress toward specified goals.[57] This type of technical rationality can mollify moral instincts and thwart social group commitments in a variety of policy fields.[58] The social distance created by bureaucratic culture is especially pronounced in law enforcement organizations, like the USBP and ICE, where the archetypal *client* is constructed as an undeserving, immoral "bad guy."[59] My particular emphasis is on how these characteristics of bureaucracy help front-line agents look away from human suffering and perpetuate harm through law.

Although I center the racialized and moral dynamics that occur at the US-Mexico border, this book is part of a broader conversation about how globalization, shifting conceptions of penal power, and ever-expanding mechanisms of punishment are shaping immigration control throughout the world.[60] Scholars working in distinct national contexts have examined immigration control from the ground up, revealing cross-national patterns in how immigration bureaucrats are trained, how they exercise discretion and engage in emotional labor, and how they cultivate legitimacy for themselves and their employers.[61] This work reminds us that while country-level histories, laws, and immigration flows shape the moral economy of immigration control in distinct settings, the normative questions at the heart of detention, deportation, and border control are supranational.

Situating the Moral Economy:
Immigration as a Crime and Security Issue

Bordering on Indifference reveals the moral economy of US immigration control through the worldviews of frontline immigration agents. To understand those worldviews, we must first situate them within the historical, legal, and bureaucratic context in which they thrive.[62] That context is one where the US government treats immigration as a homeland security and crime control issue. This is a global trend, which is sometimes referred to as crimmigration,[63] the securitization of immigration,[64] the turn to governing immigration through crime,[65] or simply the criminalization of immigration.[66] I use these terms interchangeably throughout my analysis, but the term "crimmigration," which was coined by Juliet Stumpf in the early 2000s, most accurately captures the context in which US immigration enforcement agents work.[67] The USBP and ICE are hybrid agencies; they operate under the logic of criminal justice organizations, even though they are managing migration, which is an administrative process.

The global trend toward criminalizing immigration has distinct country-level historical and legal markers, but in the United States this phenomenon reflects a broader societal shift toward punishment and the "get tough" paradigms that have dominated American politics in a post–civil rights era.[68] As the government has declared wars on various social issues—first the War on Poverty, which was replaced with the War on Crime, then the War on Drugs, and now the War on

Terror—the government created a "repressive and exclusionist" society that has had disproportionately negative impacts on African Americans through mass incarceration and on Latinas/os through immigration enforcement.[69] It is true that *criminals* had been barred from entering the United States from the earliest days of immigration lawmaking and that illegal entry was criminalized as early as 1924,[70] but the criminalization of immigration as we know it today has been a decades-long legal and political project that reached new heights between the 1970s and the 1990s. Table 1 shows the laws that most fundamentally distorted the already-blurred boundaries between migration management and the punishment of crime in the United States.

The Immigration Reform and Control Act of 1986 (IRCA) looms large in the story of heightened immigrant criminalization. The act is most widely remembered as a legalization program that granted amnesty to 2.7 million qualifying immigrants, most of them Mexican. When President Ronald Reagan signed IRCA he hailed the legislation as the welcome product of a long and difficult bipartisan effort to "humanely regain control of our borders" while providing a path to citizenship for millions of undocumented people.[71] However, the legislation was a "three-legged stool" that also included provisions to toughen border control and sanction employers who knowingly hired undocumented workers.[72]

The sponsors of IRCA portrayed it as a comprehensive strategy to end unauthorized migration by cutting off the demand for undocumented labor and addressing the supply side through escalated border enforcement. The law fell short on the first goal but succeeded dramatically in its efforts to escalate immigration enforcement. The IRCA is responsible for a massive injection of funds toward border control specifically. The Border Patrol doubled in size because of IRCA, as spending for border control ballooned from $700 million in 1986 to over $1.46 billion by 1996.[73] This law set the groundwork for the Prevention through Deterrence program, which dramatically militarized the US-Mexico border, a process that had been happening since at least the 1970s.[74]

The act also contained legal provisions that have been subsequently expanded and used to grow the reach of immigration enforcement. For instance, the law contained a short but weighty provision called "Expeditious Deportation of Convicted Aliens." The brief section specifies that in the case of noncitizens convicted of a crime that makes them deportable, the attorney general should "begin deportation proceedings as expeditiously as possible."[75] This mandate made the deportation of "criminal aliens" an enforcement priority

TABLE 1. Key Immigration Enforcement Legislation, 1980s–1990s

Year/Legislation	Major Provisions
1986 / Immigration Reform and Control Act	Grants amnesty, creates employer sanctions, expands border control. Includes "Expeditious Deportation of Convicted Aliens" provision, which precipitates the creation of various programs to identify and remove noncitizens convicted of criminal offenses.
1988 / Anti–Drug Abuse Act	Creates category of "aggravated felony,"[1] calls for mandatory detention of those convicted of aggravated felony, disqualifies those convicted of an aggravated felony from eligibility for voluntary departure.
1990 / Immigration Act	Expands list of aggravated felonies,[2] makes people convicted of aggravated felony ineligible for asylum, limits judicial discretion to grant deportation relief, establishes a twenty-year ban for deportees convicted of an aggravated felony.
1996 / Antiterrorism and Effective Death Penalty Act	Expands list of aggravated felonies, makes convictions retroactive, requires mandatory detention of certain classes of noncitizens, expands classification of crimes of moral turpitude and deportation consequences for these crimes.
1996 / Illegal Immigration Reform and Immigrant Responsibility Act	Expands list of aggravated felonies, reduces sentencing requirement for categorization as aggravated felony to one year (from five), retroactively applies convictions, expands mandatory detention, establishes three- and ten-year bans for overstaying visa, creates 287(g), creates "cancellation of removal," creates "expedited removal" and "reinstatement of removal" procedure, changes "deportation" to "removal."

[1] Includes murder, drug trafficking, and firearms trafficking.
[2] Expanded to include money laundering, crimes of violence for which the term of imprisonment is at least five years.

that became more and more central to the immigration system's logics and practices over time.[76] As significant as IRCA's provisions were in setting the groundwork for the increased criminalization of immigration, the law was just the tip of the iceberg.

With the War on Drugs raging, legislators included increasingly punitive immigration provisions into laws that were not immigration focused. Congress passed the Anti–Drug Abuse Act of 1988, a law designed to increase criminal penalties for drug offenses. The law also created the now infamous "aggravated felony" for immigration purposes. Originally, only murder and drug or firearms trafficking constituted aggravated felonies, but Congress has consistently added to the list of crimes that qualify so that today the category includes everything from rape to receipt of stolen property. Aggravated felonies have been described as having an "Alice in Wonderland" quality since they need not be aggravated or felonious, but their lore looms large in the moral panic around criminal aliens.[77] The Immigration Act of 1990 further expanded the aggravated felony category to include money laundering and crimes of violence for which the term of imprisonment is at least five years. This act also made those who are convicted of an aggravated felony ineligible for asylum, established a twenty-year ban for deportees convicted of an aggravated felony, and limited immigration judges' discretion to grant deportation relief.

If IRCA, the Anti–Drug Abuse Act of 1988, and the Immigration Act of 1990 set the foundation for today's punitive immigration system, the 1996 Antiterrorism and Effective Death Penalty Act (AEDPA) and Illegal Immigration Reform and Immigrant Responsibility Act (IIRIRA) built the house. The AEDPA was passed on April 24, 1996, just days after the one-year anniversary of the Oklahoma City bombing. President Clinton was making good on the promise he had made just days after the bombing, to pass an antiterrorism bill that would keep Americans safe—not just from criminals, who had loomed large in the 1990s' law-and-order discourse, but also from terrorists. President Clinton warned that the bill he was signing that day made several "ill-advised changes in our immigration laws" that were unrelated to fighting terrorism. These provisions, he predicted, would "produce extraordinary administrative burdens" for the immigration bureaucracy, and he urged Congress to correct them in other pending legislation.[78] Congress did not heed President Clinton's warning, and when he signed the IIRIRA just five months later, he made no mention of the ill-advised immigration provisions that had been extended and expanded.

The AEDPA and IIRIRA distorted the boundaries between immigration and criminal law to the point that they are difficult to see. Together these laws dramatically expanded detention and deportation of noncitizens, while also severely limiting judicial discretion over immigration agents' decisions and restricting immigrants' relief options. For instance, AEDPA required the mandatory detention of all "criminal aliens," while dramatically increasing the number of people that met that designation. The act also expanded the list of crimes that qualify as aggravated felonies for immigration purposes, and it retroactively made legal permanent residents deportable for past crimes. The IIRIRA further expanded the list of offenses that would require mandatory detention and also empowered immigration agents to quickly deport people who committed fraud or misrepresentation through a process called "expedited removal." Many of these legal changes also apply retroactively, meaning that crimes added to the ever-expanding list of aggravated felonies trigger mandatory detention and deportation even if they were committed before 1996. The IIRIRA further eliminated judicial discretion to grant relief from deportation in cases where a person had been convicted of an aggravated felony, replacing previously available discretionary relief with a much narrower form of relief called "cancellation of removal." Together these laws solidified the shift to an immigration system that is "harsher, less forgiving, and more insulated from judicial review" than ever before.[79]

It is a common misconception that the Global War on Terror created the crimmigration system, a premise that this brief legal history dispels. As Jennifer Chacón aptly put it, the immigration system had been functioning as an adjunct to the criminal justice system for decades before the 9/11 attacks.[80] What did happen after 9/11 is that the already-distended immigration system grew exponentially as political and bureaucratic elites incorporated homeland security discourses into the already-punitive immigration system.

The Department of Homeland Security: A Twenty-First-Century Home for Immigration Control Agencies

The contemporary immigration bureaucracy's structure was created by the 2002 Homeland Security Act, an act signed with bipartisan support in the wake of the September 11, 2001, terrorist attacks. Then president George W. Bush had argued that the country's homeland security mechanisms were in disarray and no match for the "global terrorist threat" that was the country's newest enemy. To fight this cunning adversary, the president and his advisers proposed to streamline the country's homeland security functions into a cabinet-level department, with a direct line to the president. At the signing of the act, George W. Bush said, "To succeed in their mission, leaders of the new department must change the culture of many diverse agencies—directing all of them toward the principal objective of protecting the American people."[81] This was the biggest government reorganization since President Harry S. Truman signed the National Security Act of 1947, which consolidated military branches and created the Central Intelligence Agency, the National Security Council, and the Secretary of Defense.[82]

The immigration bureaucracy of the time, the Immigration and Naturalization Service (INS), was one of the twenty-two agencies whose culture had to be redirected toward the new goal of homeland security. Table 2 outlines the housing of the US immigration bureaucracy since 1891, when it was formed as such. The INS had long struggled with the colossal task of adjudicating immigration benefits and managing border control, detention, and deportation.[83] Proposals to separate service from enforcement had been recurrent throughout its history but were not achieved until the Homeland Security Act of 2002 created the Department of Homeland Security (DHS), which became operational on March 1, 2003.

Under the DHS, the US immigration bureaucracy is a multipronged entity that includes three main agencies with distinct functions: the United States Citizenship and Immigration Services (USCIS), Customs and Border Protection (CBP), and Immigration and Customs Enforcement (ICE). Like all DHS components, these agencies have homeland security as their core mission. However, the principal objective differs by agency. The USCIS is charged with service provision, which consists mainly of adjudicating immigration benefits, such as processing visa and asylum applications, facilitating legal status changes, and managing naturalization procedures. The enforcement side of the bureaucracy includes CBP, charged with immigration control at and between ports of entry, and ICE, charged with immigration control within the country's interior. While the lines between service and enforcement have always been blurry in US immigration control, the distinction is a helpful shorthand that points to different agencies within the broader system. My fieldwork was in the enforcement side of the bureaucracy, with CBP agents and ICE officers—it did not include USCIS officers.

Immigration enforcement, which was already favored in its predecessor, the INS, has grown dramatically within the DHS. Together, CBP and ICE accounted for 27 percent of the DHS's $52.2 billion budget in 2022; USCIS accounted for 5 percent. The CBP's 2003 budget of $5.9 billion had nearly tripled to $16.3 billion by 2022. Immigration and Customs Enforcement also

TABLE 2. Administrative Housing of the US Immigration Bureaucracy since 1891

Department of Treasury, 1891–1903
   Office of the Superintendent of Immigration (1891–95)
   Bureau of Immigration (1895–1903)

Department of Commerce and Labor, 1903–13
   Bureau of Immigration (1903–6)
   Bureau of Immigration and Naturalization (1906–13)

Department of Labor, 1913–40
   Bureau of Immigration (1913–33)
   Bureau of Naturalization (1913–33)
   Immigration and Naturalization Service (1933–40)

Department of Justice, 1940–2003
   Immigration and Naturalization Service (1940–2003)

Department of Homeland Security, 2003–Present
   United States Citizenship and Immigration Services
   Customs and Border Protection
   Immigration and Customs Enforcement

Source: Most of this material is sourced from the National Archives, "Records of the Immigration and Naturalization Service [INS]," https://www.archives.gov/research/guide-fed-records/groups/085 .html#85.1, accessed December 1, 2022.

benefited from this funding boom, growing its $3.3 billion budget in 2003 to $8.4 billion by 2022. Its Enforcement and Removal Operations (ERO), which is the arm charged with detention and deportation, grew from 2,710 agents in 2003 to 8,374 by 2022. The Border Patrol, whose growth had already been on an upward trajectory since IRCA, doubled in size between 2003 and 2022, from 10,717 to 21,759 agents.[84] The agents I interviewed are a fundamental part of the "formidable machinery" that is the US immigration system in the twenty-first century.[85]

This machinery is one where immigration is treated as a crime and security issue and where escalated enforcement efforts are propped up by what Rubén Rumbaut calls "zombie ideas," or old misconceptions about immigrants as criminals and unassimilable moochers.[86] This system is also undergirded by racialized moral panics that target Latinas/os specifically for exclusion, based on the logic of criminality and immorality.[87] In the post-9/11 context, these racialized tropes about Latina/o immigrants have merged with tropes about Middle Eastern terrorists coming through the unprotected southern border, the activation of a "brown threat" that motivates much support for increased

TABLE 3. Interview Sample Characteristics by Agency

	USBP	ICE	Total
Sex			
Male	47	25	72 (80%)
Female	13	5	18 (20%)
Race/ethnicity			
Latinx	41	13	54 (60%)
White	16	9	25 (28%)
Black	0	6	6 (7%)
Asian / Pacific Islander	2	2	4 (4%)
Native American	1	0	1 (1%)
Education			
High school diploma	9	0	9 (10%)
Some college	22	8	30 (33%)
Associate's degree	7	1	8 (9%)
Baccalaureate degree	16	9	25 (28%)
Master's degree	2	6	8 (9%)
Missing data	4	6	10 (11%)
Veterans			
Yes	22	17	39 (43%)
No	38	13	51 (57%)
Years with Agency			
1–5	7	4	11 (12%)
5–10	29	4	33 (37%)
More than 10	24	22	46 (51%)
Total	60	30	90 (100%)

enforcement under the color-blind guise of homeland security.[88] This is the ideological, bureaucratic, and legal context in which the agents I interviewed worked and that served as a backdrop for my conversations with them.

Description of the Research

Immigration agents are what social scientists call a "hard-to-reach" population, a group that is difficult to recruit into research studies. Some populations are hard to reach because they are in structural precarity; others are hard to reach because they can engage in organizational gatekeeping.[89] Immigration agents are the latter. In the methodological appendix I discuss how I gained access to federal immigration agents and describe some of the power dynamics inherent

TABLE 4. Latina/o Agents by Agency, Generation, and
Biraciality

	USBP	ICE	Total/Percent
1st generation	5	6	11 (20%)
2nd generation	24	4	28 (52%)
3rd + generation	7	0	7 (13%)
Biracial	1	2	3 (6%)
Missing data	3	1	4 (7%)
Other Latina/o	1	0	1 (2%)
Total	41	13	54 (100 %)

Note: 1st generation includes agents born outside of the United States;
2nd generation includes agents born in the United States to at least one
foreign-born parent; 3rd generation includes agents who are the grandchildren
of immigrants; biracial includes Latinx agents who have a non-Latinx parent;
other Latinx includes one agent with a Spanish-speaking Caribbean background.

to the process of "studying up," the term anthropologist Laura Nader used
when issuing a call to research power holders.[90] Here I provide the basic contours of my research.

Sample Description

I interviewed ninety immigration agents, sixty who work for the US Border
Patrol and thirty who work for ICE Enforcement and Removal Operations.
I interviewed these agents in Arizona and California, between the summer
of 2014 and the winter of 2016. These agents were primarily Latina/o and
White and predominately male. Almost three quarters of the Latina/o
agents were either immigrants (20 percent) or children of immigrants
(52 percent). The remaining Latina/o agents either were grandchildren of
immigrants (13 percent) or were of mixed ancestry (6 percent). I had missing generational data for four agents. Except for two agents, one with a
Spanish-speaking Caribbean background and another with a Central American parent, all the Latina/o agents were of Mexican descent (see table 3 for
sample demographics and table 4 for Latina/o agents' racial and generational status).

On average, the agents I interviewed had about a decade of experience in
immigration enforcement, although not necessarily with the agency they were
working with at the time of our interview. Several of the ICE officers started

off as Border Patrol agents or working at ports of entry. None of the Border Patrol agents had worked with ICE.

Based on my agreement with the Border Patrol I did not collect agent names, and I continued this practice with ICE. In previous publications I did not create pseudonyms given the risk of using one that corresponded to a respondent's real name. This approach is not sustainable given the book's narrative format, so I have randomly generated pseudonyms. I take great care to mask my respondents in several ways, by not overdisclosing and sometimes omitting details that would make them more identifiable. If there is any overlap between pseudonyms and real names it is purely coincidental.

Fieldwork Locations

I interviewed Border Patrol agents in two cities on the US-Mexico border. I use the pseudonyms Desert City, Arizona, and Mountain Valley, California, to refer to these locations. Most of the ICE officers I interviewed worked in Mountain Valley, although a few worked in a larger border city in California. I did not interview ICE officers in Arizona because I was unable to get access to ICE in that state.

Desert City and Mountain Valley are predominately Hispanic—specifically, Mexican—towns or cities in the American Southwest, in counties that are similar in size and demographics. When I began my fieldwork in 2014, the counties in which Desert City and Mountain Valley are located each had a population size of about two hundred thousand people; they were majority Hispanic (between 60 and 85 percent) and had a median household income of about $40,000. About 10 percent of the population in Desert City and Mountain Valley had a bachelor's degree in 2014, and both counties had a similar poverty rate between 20 and 30 percent.[91] These county-level characteristics had not changed substantially when I finished my fieldwork in 2016.

Approximately half of the ICE interviews were with officers who worked in another city that was much larger (over three million people), more diverse (about 40 percent Hispanic), and with a median household income twice as high as those of Mountain Valley and Desert City. The agents I interviewed there were more likely to be White or Black than the Mountain Valley ICE officers, who were primarily Latina/o. Given these differences in the location and since only three of the ICE officers from the bigger city were Latina/o, I do not delve into this city's context as deeply as I do for Mountain Valley and Desert City, where the bulk of my respondents worked.

Data Collection Period and Process

I conducted semi-structured interviews, meaning that I had a set of questions that I wanted to ask, but was open to discussing topics that were salient to agents themselves. My questions focused mostly on agents' work experiences, starting from the point when they became interested in the career and then delving more deeply into various aspects of their work. I conducted most of the interviews in Border Patrol or ICE buildings, including main offices, stations, detention centers, and local jails.

My 2014–16 fieldwork period coincided with a significant increase in asylum seeking among Central American forced migrants and a decrease in adult Mexican migration at the US-Mexico border.[92] President Obama was in office for the bulk of my fieldwork, although I did interview some ICE officers during the 2016 presidential campaign and during the transition to the first Trump administration. This political context heightened agents' penchant for legitimation, pushing agents to explain and yes, even defend themselves and their work as they spoke to me. Agents told me stories that they felt captured the nature of their job. They recounted memorable experiences and people that they felt communicated morals and lessons. They gave explanations they felt would clarify misunderstandings, justifications they thought might neutralize criticisms.

At first this worried and frustrated me. Over time I accepted that no matter how I presented myself, agents would treat me as a proxy for different segments of the public or *audiences* that they wanted to speak to.[93] Eventually, I came to relish their efforts as a window into the deeply hidden normative ideas that upholds their sense of legitimacy. Rather than pretend that my presence as an outsider was inconsequential to what agents told me, I use their reaction to me as a window into how they understand themselves vis-à-vis various publics.[94]

I discuss all of this in more detail in the methodological appendix, but for now it is sufficient to say that my interviews with agents were an excellent source of "accounts," especially when we discussed the most controversial aspects of their work. Accounts are statements that we, as social actors, issue to one another to explain behavior that is perceived to be "unanticipated" or "untoward," in the words of Marvin Scott and Stanford Lyman.[95] Accounts are a form of impression management that allow agents to repair threats to their positive self-image and that are given in response to some form of status degradation.[96] These linguistic devices "reveal nonconscious motives and meanings and . . . illuminate individuals' interpretations" in context.[97] Accounts contain the links between collective understandings and individual behavior. I use accounts as a window into that which is unspoken and taken for granted, a window into the moral economy of immigration control on the front lines.

A Note on Terminology

Throughout this book I refer to "Border Patrol agents" or "USBP agents," "ICE officers," and "immigration agents" when not making agency-level distinctions. These choices are intentional but may be difficult to follow for readers only casually acquainted with the US immigration bureaucracy. As mentioned above, the DHS parsed the immigration system into three distinct agencies: USCIS, CBP, and ICE. The agents I interviewed worked in the enforcement arms of the bureaucracy, CBP and ICE.

Within CBP there are multiple components, including the Office of Field Operations (OFO) and the United States Border Patrol (USBP). In public discourse USBP agents are commonly conflated or confused with CBP OFO officers, who work at ports of entry or at airports. An easy way to remember the difference between USBP agents and CBP OFO officers is that the former wear green, while the latter wear navy blue. I interviewed sixty USBP agents.

Within ICE there are two components: Enforcement and Removal Operations (ERO) and Homeland Security Investigations (HSI). Detention centers and deportations, among other immigration-related functions, are managed by ERO. The investigative and security functions of the agency are handled by HSI, and while it has jurisdiction over many immigration functions, that is not its emphasis. I interviewed thirty ICE ERO officers; most of them were either deportation officers or supervisory detention and deportation officers. I did not interview HSI agents.

Chapter Overview

Bordering on Indifference is organized as a processual account of Latina/o agents' growing investment in the moral economy of immigration control. It shows how Latina/o agents and their colleagues grapple with and reconcile the many racial tensions and moral ambiguities of their work. Each time agents succeed in resolving the contradictions they encounter on the job, indifference appears as both a resource and a product of their efforts.

Our entry into the world of immigration agents begins with chapter 1, an account of the four primary pathways into the profession. We learn that while many agents grew up *aspiring* to work in law enforcement, others pragmatically *drifted* into the job, some slotted in through the *military-to-policing pipeline*, and a minority were looking for a way to *serve* their country. These pathways—aspiring, drifting, military-to-policing, and serving—are racially patterned. Agents who drifted into the profession are mostly Mexican Americans who grew up on the border, the aspiring and military pathways are the most diverse, and only White agents said they came into immigration work to serve their country.

Distinct pathways into the profession all lead to one place: a police training program that teaches agents to think about immigration as a crime and security issue, no matter how they thought about the work before they came in. Chapter 2 maps the process of becoming an agent. I delve into the DHS's training program, as well as agents' experiences learning to think about immigration and migrants from a policing standpoint. We also see how agents use *manufactured ambiguity*, or the idea that agents can never be sure of undocumented immigrants' true identities or intentions, to close the gap between the "real police work" that they thought they would be doing and the administrative functions that pervade their work.

Chapter 3 discusses *caring control* and *disinterested professionalism*, two rationalities through which Latina/o agents make sense of the intersection of their race/ethnicity and professional role. Agents who engage in caring control frame themselves as humane and culturally competent agents who improve the qualitative character of migrants' custodial experience, while those who adopt a disinterested professionalism adhere to bureaucratic staples of neutrality and consistency across cases. Regardless of their approach, I argue that it is the immigration state that most benefits from Latinas/os' labor. Some Latina/o agents may be willing and able to deploy their Spanish fluency and cultural repertoire to be more effective regulators, increasing the state's capacity to control coethnics. Some agents are unwilling or unable to do that, but their presence as Latinx people is still useful to the government in a symbolic sense.

Chapter 4 delves into the moral ambiguities of immigration enforcement, examining how agents use denial to turn away from human suffering. Three forms of denial pervade agents' work: *denial of responsibility, denial of harm,* and *denial of the victim.* Agents deny responsibility by leaning on rules and laws, they deny harm by recasting their work as helping, or not hurting immigrants, and they deny the victim by implicating immigrants in their own suffering. Latina/o agents and other agents of color favor forms of denial that negate their responsibility, or the harm done by immigration control, while White agents tend to deny the victim and frame themselves as righteous distributors of immigration consequences. Denial strategies give agents moral license to perform immigration control, especially in moments of uncertainty.

Chapter 5 shows how agents' multilayered legitimacy deficits manifest as "moral taint," which is a stigma associated with work that is ethically dubious. Like all workers who deal with occupational stigma, immigration agents want to repair that moral taint, and they do so primarily by *concealing* their work and *refuting* what they see as misconceptions about themselves and their job. Since Latina/o agents deal with layered stigmas, they have an additional strategy: *defensive nationalism*. The product of concealment, refutation, and defensive nationalism is a sense of legitimacy that protects the immigration system's status quo from the ground up.

In the conclusion, I discuss lessons learned, especially in relation to workforce diversity in policing. I also discuss broader debates about whether it is possible to create "humane" immigration systems and end with three paths forward: uncoupling immigration and criminal law, divestment, and cultural change. I also encourage readers to think about borders and boundaries on a more macro scale, reminding us that it is the global system of bordered nation-states that begets immigration control and coercion. Any effort to make positive changes in immigration systems must contend with the counterpressure created by the very idea of national sovereignty.

1

Taking the Job

IMMIGRATION AND CUSTOMS ENFORCEMENT deportation officer Yesenia Siqueiros was never interested in immigration work. In fact, she had an aversion to it. The Border Patrol was one of the largest employers in the border town where Officer Siqueiros grew up, so she knew "there were always immigration openings." Well-meaning friends and family told her that her high-school diploma and command of English and Spanish made her the perfect candidate for the work. Yesenia conceded that the Border Patrol was a good job in an area where good jobs were scarce, but her position was a clear no. Her shyness seemed inconsistent with law enforcement, but there was also the matter of policing her own. "I'm not going to go after my own people. . . . That's not in my blood."

Yesenia wanted a career in education, accounting, or psychology. She enrolled at the local community college after high school, planning to get an associate's degree before transferring to a four-year university. But Yesenia soon learned that motivation alone would not be enough to complete a degree. For two years, she struggled to find classes that fit her full-time work schedule. She kept changing her major, hoping to find something with more course availability. She seemed to be getting nowhere, her frustration with college growing, while other aspects of her life were progressing. At age twenty, Yesenia got married and had a baby. Facing the responsibilities of adulthood, she remembered thinking, "I keep going to school, I'm never going to graduate. . . . It's just—I had a two-year-old now. . . . Okay, I'm going to apply."

Yesenia applied for a job at the local port of entry, sticking to her convictions about not chasing people. She would check border crossers' papers instead, just like people had checked hers her entire life. Actually, Yesenia thought, this might be an opportunity to improve people's experience with the immigration system. She had not had the best experience with immigration agents herself. A US-born citizen who lived on the Mexican side of the border for most of her childhood, Yesenia, like many border dwellers, viewed immigration agents with a combination of familiarity, fear, and intrigue, given their broad discretion and seeming unpredictability.[1] "I'm tired of being afraid of them. I'm going to become one of them and show people how females can be nice and respectful and have a good attitude and . . ." Yesenia chuckled at her earlier naïveté. "Yeah, like one person was going to change . . . how they're looked at."

Yesenia's application to work at the port of entry coincided with one of the CBP's post-9/11 hiring sprees. She was hired quickly, and the onboarding process was smooth. A "firm believer in signs," Yesenia interpreted this as an indication that she was on the right path. Six years into the job, she began working for ICE. She never did actively "chase" people; as a deportation officer she managed the cases of dozens of people who were in detention with nowhere to run.

Yesenia Siqueiros's entrance into immigration work arose from a series of pragmatic decisions made within a protracted set of opportunities. Her high-school grades did not qualify her for admittance to a four-year university. After a couple of meandering years at the local community college the responsibilities of adulthood changed her priorities. With an already-limited set of options further narrowing, she surrendered to the ever-present prospect of immigration work. Although she had never been interested in, and yes, had even actively resisted the work for years, the immigration state was there when Yesenia most needed it.

This chapter follows agents' pathways into the profession, exploring the deliberations—sometimes social, sometimes economic, sometimes philosophical—that they made before deciding to work for the USBP or ICE. Agents' reflections are patterned along racial/ethnic lines: Latina/o agents articulate instrumental motivations for doing immigration work, while their non-Latina/o counterparts express more varied reasons for entering the profession. Yesenia Siqueiros represents a large group of Latinas/os who *drifted* into the profession rather unceremoniously, when they "needed a career." These drifters were Mexican Americans who grew up along the border and were looking for a good job in the local economy. They joined a racially diverse set of agents who grew up *aspiring* to work in law enforcement or who slotted into the *military-to-policing* pipeline after their tenure in the armed forces. A small group of agents—all of them White—found immigration work when they were looking for a way to *serve* the country or for a more meaningful career.

These racialized patterns reflect my interviewees' origins and their level of education. Most of the Latina/o agents I spoke to were Mexican Americans who grew up in places like Mountain Valley and Desert City, border towns where poverty and unemployment rates are high and education rates are low. In these towns, many upwardly mobile Latina/o youth turn to the military or to law enforcement occupations for a leg up.[2] The Black, Asian, and White agents I spoke to were mostly transplants from different parts of the country, from the Midwest to the East Coast, and White agents were most likely to have a college degree. Unlike their border-dwelling Mexican American colleagues, non-Latina/o agents did not grow up steeped in awareness about immigration enforcement as a viable career—they came to learn about this job as an alternative to the traditional policing occupations they often aspired to.

Agents' reflections about their professional pathways may seem individualistic, but they are far from idiosyncratic. These reflections show that the browning of the immigration enforcement bureaucracy is another ironic turn in the country's long dependence on Mexican labor. As the US government flushed money into the coercive arm of the US immigration bureaucracy, America once again turned to the US-Mexico border for labor. But this time the workers America sought were not immigrants who would toil the agricultural fields before returning to Mexico, but their upwardly mobile descendants who spoke English and Spanish with similar ease and knew the border better than anyone else because it was home. These Mexican American border dwellers are more than willing to patrol the border, manage detention centers, and execute deportations if it means that they can live the American dream that drew their predecessors to the country in the first place. In effect, the federal government's fixation with *controlling the southern border* generates paradoxical combinations of threat and opportunity in border towns throughout the Southwest,[3] and it has created an "enclave" of Hispanic employment in the coercive arm of the immigration state.[4]

Drifting into Immigration Work

Agent Sergio Masciel was a supervisor in the Border Patrol's Public Affairs Office. Public Affairs agents, by virtue of their assignment, tended to be more comfortable than other agents in talking with outsiders like me. Agent Masciel was a notable exception. His demeanor was formal until we started discussing his pathway into the profession. At that point, he lit up.

Sergio delighted in telling me that he was a musician, a pretty good one at that. He had always dreamed of becoming a high-school music teacher, inspired by a particularly good instructor in his own life. He had pursued this passion after high school, attending the local community college to get the training he needed. Things went awry when he took a class with a professor who "didn't have the same passion for music" that Sergio did. Sergio needed more guidance than the professor provided: "We were kind of on our own to take the books, and I was looking at stuff I'd never seen before." The experience was a turning point, he said. "It pushed me away from it [even though] that is what I had wanted to do my whole entire life." Sergio eventually left the community college and took a job selling cell phones for commission. The money was good when he made sales, but not great when he didn't. Sergio applied to the Border Patrol when the situation became untenable and he needed "a more stable career."

To understand how people like Sergio Masciel can drift into immigration work even when they aspire to drastically different careers, we must understand the local opportunity structure in towns like Mountain Valley and Desert City. Protective service occupations—the federal occupational category that includes immigration agents but also correctional officers, police officers, and security guards—are more than twice as common in Mountain Valley and Desert City than in the rest of the United States.[5] This concentration of law enforcement jobs is not surprising, as prisons tend to be sited in small towns and rural communities with higher-than-average levels of poverty and racial minorities.[6] Immigration prisons are no exception. As César García Hernández put it, "we can think of immigration prisons as a jobs program" in struggling regions of the country.[7]

Mountain Valley and Desert City are towns that are textbook candidates for prison siting. They are predominately Hispanic/Latinx, with high unemployment and with educational attainment rates that lag behind state and national averages. In this way, the border towns I studied are like other rural communities where prisons function as an economic development strategy. The carceral economy in border towns differs from that in the interior of the country, however, in that, in addition to housing prisons, places like Mountain Valley and Desert City are also swept up in the government's fixation on the US-Mexico border.

The United States funnels its massive immigration enforcement investments toward the southern border in one way or another, creating jobs in this predominantly Mexican / Mexican American region of the country.[8] The government counts on border dwellers to staff the Border Patrol and ICE, as well as ports of entry and detention centers. In turn, many border residents depend on these employment opportunities. Immigration jobs are often the glorified "good jobs" in the border region, accessible to citizens with a high-school diploma and not much else.[9] As Border Patrol agent Camila Sarto put it, "Customs, Border Patrol, CHP [California Highway Patrol], those are good jobs because they all pay well. But other than that, I mean, it's hard. It's hard to find a job here."

When an ICE detention center closed in Mountain Valley, for example, local officials were concerned that the layoffs would exacerbate the area's high unemployment rate. Detention center workers protested in front of the center, drawing connections between their plight and those of the thousands of workers who had lost jobs when a slaughterhouse closed earlier that year. The detention center workers' ire reached the Democratic congressional representative for the region, who, in a local newspaper story, promised to repurpose the center and find new jobs for those who lost employment. In fact, a new and bigger detention facility was already being built just thirty minutes down the road. It opened later that year. Many of the agents I interviewed had worked security at the old detention center before they got hired by the USBP or ICE.

Pasqual Trigueros was one of those agents. Pasqual grew up in Mountain Valley, watching the Border Patrol agents who dotted his hometown, sitting in their air-conditioned trucks, wearing their too-dark sunglasses. Sometimes they nodded to him in acknowledgment, but mostly they looked ahead when he looked their way. He always wondered what the work was like, but that wonder was not to be mistaken with interest:

> Being local I always saw the Border Patrol. I always wondered what they're thinking when they're sitting in that car or while they're driving around the desert, but I never really thought I wanted to get into law enforcement. I originally wanted to be in the medical field—physical therapy, nursing, something like that.

The medical field was another large industry in the region. In fact, Pasqual had been completing the prerequisites to apply to a local nursing program while working as a part-time security officer when he met a recruiter who told him that the immigration detention center had openings.

The prison corporation that ran the detention center paid more than the security agency Pasqual was working for. It made sense to apply, and he did, thinking he would work at the detention center while he pursued the nursing degree. Over time, however, his responsibilities as a husband and father started piling up, and he began prioritizing work over school. Eventually, Pasqual left college and continued working for the detention center. Years later, he accepted that in security "there was no stability because it was contract work" and decided to apply to the Border Patrol. About nursing, he said, "It was something that really interested me, and it still does, but I just chose this. This is what happened to come into my path."

There is an idealized notion of career choice where people reflect on their interests and motivations, then go in search of a career that fits their dispositions. The reality is that the jobs or careers that people "end up" in are highly contingent on social and structural factors, like how much education and training they can access, how far they are able to go to acquire that human capital, and what is available to them in their current area. This is true for everyone, but especially for working-class youth of color whose career aspirations are strongly shaped by local opportunity structures.[10] The power of local constraints and opportunities is very evident in Latina/o agents' pathways into the immigration enforcement career.

Latinas/os' professional pathways contain interesting combinations of serendipity and predictability. Latinas/os who drifted into the work became agents not because of an interest in law enforcement or immigration, but because the job offered a pragmatic step forward in their upward mobility journey. Latinx people have the lowest levels of education and are the most common racial/ethnic group living in poverty in Desert City and Mountain Valley. Immigration enforcement jobs are some of the highest paying in the region and are accessible to those without a college education. Like two pieces of a puzzle that snap into place, border residents can slot into immigration jobs rather unceremoniously, even when their initial inclinations are elsewhere.

Border Patrol agent Paco Linal aptly described this *natural attraction* when he explained, "I realized I needed a career, and this was enough for me. . . . The [Border Patrol] job kind of gravitated towards me." A high-school graduate, Paco had been "working here and there," first at a manufacturing plant, then at two local grocery stores after the plant shut down. He thought he was doing well enough to move out of his parents' house and into his own apartment, but once he did, he appreciated that "minimum wage wasn't going to cut it."

Paco looked around his hometown and evaluated his options. Like others before him, Paco "didn't see a lot of opportunities besides something with law enforcement or nursing." Paco reasoned that he could go into nursing, a woman-dominated field that requires years of training, or law enforcement, a

male-dominated field accessible to those with a high-school diploma. Paco took
the practical route. "I realized I needed a career . . . this was enough for me."

The minimum qualifications for an entry-level job as a federal immigration
enforcement agent are relatively accessible. Applicants must be a US citizen, a
high-school graduate, and under thirty-nine years of age (with exceptions for
veterans), have a valid driver's license, and no criminal convictions. The starting
yearly salary for Border Patrol agents and ICE officers was between $39,000 and
$50,000 in 2014, when I began my fieldwork.[11] Already, that number is close to
$10,000 above the median annual household income in Mountain Valley and
Desert City in 2014, approximately $40,000 in both cities. However, that salary
drastically understates the difference between these towns' median income and
agents' salaries.

Federal immigration agents receive multiple benefits above their base wages.
Agents earn locality pay and premium pay for working Sundays, holidays, and
night shifts. They qualify for a special type of overtime called "administratively
uncontrolled overtime" (AUO), which can add up to one-quarter of yearly
salary to agents' paychecks.[12] Border Patrol agents and ICE officers also receive
yearly, noncompetitive salary increases for the first four to five years of their
career, and they get cost of living increases. Within five years of starting, immigration agents can be earning over $100,000 a year—more than double the
median salary in Mountain Valley and Desert City. Agents also have access to
a very desirable menu of health insurance and retirement programs. Stated simply, a job with the federal immigration bureaucracy is one of the best jobs available to border dwellers, with or without a college degree.

This combination of prevalence, accessibility, and gainfulness means that
immigration enforcement jobs function as a safety net in the border region.
For example, Efren Blanco turned to immigration work when the two companies he had built from the ground up stopped making money. When his stress
exceeded the financial benefits of running two transnational firms, Efren applied to the Border Patrol. "It's a secure job. You know? Where you have a
secure check every other week." Similarly, Marcelino Ramos turned to the
immigration bureaucracy out of "financial necessity" when his trucking business became one of the millions of small companies that went under during
the 2008 recession. Being from a border town in Texas meant that Marcelino
knew where to turn when he needed a job. He explained, "I was having a hard
time with my company. I wanted a little bit more of job security."

While Agents Blanco and Ramos entered immigration enforcement in du-
ress, others were simply looking for something better. Raul Amparan was

running a successful jewelry store, working part-time at a restaurant, and pursuing his dream of becoming a fire medic. While completing his requisite internship hours for his emergency medical technician (EMT) certificate, he learned that "the medics and the EMTs, they don't get paid much here." Raul described this as a "setback," but not one that took his eye off the fire medic job. This was until he found out his girlfriend was pregnant. He needed "a real job."

> I had no idea I was going to be a Border Patrol agent. . . . I was working two jobs, trying to get by like most of the people here, and then I found out I was going to be a dad. So I was like, "I need a real job." . . . So I applied for everything. I applied for the Border Patrol. I applied for corrections, for the police department. I didn't know the difference between federal, state, local. . . . They were hiring for BP. So I got called right away. . . . Within four and a half months I was at the academy. I saw it as "I need to provide for my daughter." And I knew that being a federal agent was going to give me great benefits, great pay, job security. I was going to give my daughter the best life possible.

Agent Amparan already had *a real job*—in fact he had two real jobs and was completing an internship to become a fire medic. Still, he lacked the security and benefits that a federal law enforcement position would afford him. When his life required the long-term stability of a career, he knew exactly where to go. A job in immigration enforcement not only was readily available; it also offered a major step toward the intergenerational prosperity he sought.

Whether facing financial pressure or seeking a more stable career, many Latina/o border dwellers turned to immigration control as plan B. Of the two immigration agencies discussed in this study, Border Patrol agents were particularly likely to describe *drifting* into the job. The Border Patrol has a much larger footprint than ICE, employing over twice as many agents as its counterpart.[13] The nation's border control apparatus casts a wide employment net, creating the conditions for Latina/o border dwellers to enter the profession rather unmethodically.

In drifting into careers in immigration control, Latina/o Border Patrol agents are like the working-class White law enforcement officers of decades past. These men wandered into law enforcement out of convenience or when other occupational pursuits did not pan out.[14] People who drift into policing tend to have lower qualifications and express less commitment and less work satisfaction than those who entered the profession more intentionally.[15] Indeed, Border Patrol agents who drifted into the profession had less postsecondary education than most other agents I spoke to. Although few agents made educational distinctions along agency lines, my conversation with Border Patrol agent Esteban Luar suggests that these do exist.[16]

When Esteban was at the academy a classmate told him that CBP's Office of Field Operations agents were the "dirtiest" and the Border Patrol agents were the "dumbest." Esteban, who was then in training to become a Border Patrol agent, bristled at the comment, but he ultimately conceded that his agency mates had the lowest education level of all the trainees.

> I'm taking offense to this. And he goes, "Look around." And I go, "Man, I can't believe—oh my God, you're right." And it's, you have to have a high-school diploma or a GED or its equivalent, where in some other law enforcement agencies, you actually have to have a degree. And so to have a place hire you, pay you approximately a hundred thousand dollars a year, and all you really have to do is learn Spanish and graduate from high school? It makes it very easy, very lucrative; it draws them in.

Few agents were explicit in making these intragroup distinctions to me, an outsider to the profession. I cannot weigh in on Agent Luar's generalization about Border Patrol agents' aptitude. What I can say is that for those agents who drifted into the Border Patrol, the work was a lifeline—a "plan B" in the face of a botched plan, or a fortuitous opportunity when there did not seem to be a plan at all. Their path into immigration work was different from that of their colleagues who grew up aspiring to work in law enforcement.

Aspiring to Work in Law Enforcement

Many of the agents I spoke to—Latina/o agents included—told me they always knew they wanted to do something in policing. Some wanted to go into a federal agency, like the Federal Bureau of Investigation, the Drug Enforcement Agency, or the US Marshals Service. These agents initially thought of their immigration job as a foothold but ended up settling in. Others aspired to policing jobs with a city or county. For these agents, immigration work proved an attractive alternative when local jobs either did not materialize or paid less than anticipated. Finally, a plurality of agents cast a wide net, applying for local, state, and federal policing jobs simultaneously. The immigration bureaucracy was simply the one that called first. These agents cannot be described as having drifted into immigration work, because their position in law enforcement was an actualization of their long-standing career aspirations.

Within these aspirational narratives, however, we see group-based patterns in how agents develop an interest in law enforcement. Non-Latina/o agents gave more varied, less regionally specific explanations for their professional interests. Some of them came from law enforcement families. Others told me they had always been athletic and wanted a job that kept them active or that kept them outside. Yet others developed an interest in policing while in college. In contrast, Latina/o agents seldom separated their desire to go into law enforcement from their experience growing up on the border, where the immigration state is not only omnipresent, but also actively recruiting.

The experiences of ICE officer Manuel Iglesias and Border Patrol agent Michael Trent illustrate these differences. Manuel Iglesias was a supervisory officer who had found rapid success with ICE, surely owing to his shrewd personality and the credentials to back it up. Given that he held a bachelor's in criminal justice and a master's in a related field, I was not surprised when Officer Iglesias told me he had always aspired to law enforcement.

I grew up in a border community, and I was always impressed with the professionalism. Growing up, it [the immigration bureaucracy] would always be at the school functions; they'd always bring the dogs over. And it was always kind of an interesting thing. So when I was trying to figure out what I wanted to do as a career, I always had federal law enforcement in mind.

Manuel Iglesias did not simply fall into a career in immigration control. He had nurtured an interest in law enforcement for years and pursued the credentials to work in the field. But his interest, in turn, was firmly anchored in the local opportunity structure in his hometown and shaped by the state's recruitment campaigns in the border region.

In contrast, Agent Michael Trent, a White man from the Midwest, had not heard of the Border Patrol until he moved to Arizona. He had tried to get into law enforcement for years, earning a college degree in criminal justice and applying for multiple local and county-level policing positions. When his applications failed to produce an offer, he moved to Arizona to pursue a different career. It was there that he learned about immigration enforcement as an accessible alternative to the policing positions he had been applying to. Agent Trent explained:

[What] I really wanted to do was be a police officer. I was all excited by community policing and all those things coming out of college. . . . I [applied and] made it to all these final one hundred here, final two hundred here. Nothing panned out.

Nothing in Agent Trent's narrative references his town's opportunity structure or childhood experiences with immigration agents. Instead, he tells me about the appeal of the field itself. This pattern, in which Latinas/os mentioned experiences specific to the border region, and other officers emphasized their interest in the law enforcement field itself, replicated itself across my study. The same opportunity structure that allows border residents to turn to immigration work as a safety net also shapes their career aspirations.

The concentration of immigration enforcement in border towns means that the figure of the immigration agent is familiar to residents. Time and again, Latina/o agents who aspired to work in law enforcement referenced the ubiquity of these jobs in the border region as they explained how they became interested in the work. Agent Santiago Ortega told me, "I grew up in a border town, and a lot of my neighbors were Border Patrol, and I always found it kind of interesting." Border Patrol agent Patricia Leon said, "There's so many Border Patrol agents here in this community. It just always caught my attention." For some Latina/o agents, immigration work was becoming somewhat of a family tradition. Three Latina/o respondents were children of immigration agents, two agents were married into the same family, and one agent counted eight cousins and one uncle who worked in immigration control in California, Texas, and Arizona.

White agents like ICE officer Carter Grayson, who grew up in a border state, but not along the border, lacked this familiarity with immigration jobs. Officer Grayson told me he knew nothing about immigration enforcement. "I always wanted to be a police officer. I actually wanted to be a US marshal." He took the immigration job as "a foot in the federal door" and ended up making a career out of it.

Many Latina/o agents referenced the local port of entry as the source of their interest in law enforcement. For instance, ICE officer Ezequiel Jerez said that immigration agents were a constant presence in his childhood. Schooled in Mexico until junior high, Ezequiel started crossing the border daily to attend high school in the United States. He saw CBP agents when he crossed the border in the morning, when they made presentations at his school, when they sponsored tables at the local block parties, and when they threw candies from their tricked-out SUVs in the Founders' Day parade. When he was making career plans, Ezequiel knew it would be something in law enforcement. "I'd see these guys running the canines; I want to be there." Ezequiel earned a bachelor's degree in criminal justice in preparation for the job he always wanted.

Border Patrol agent David Bustos also liked the dogs at the port of entry, but he was particularly drawn to the inspectors' uniforms. As a child, David crossed the port of entry frequently and for mundane things, as many border residents do. He thought the port inspectors looked sharp in their pressed uniforms. From his vantage in the backseat, the canine officers seemed to float in tandem with their dogs as they inspected the cars lined up to enter the United States. The first time Agent Bustos put on a Border Patrol uniform, it felt like the realization of a far-fetched dream: "I never imagined myself wearing this uniform. . . . I watched my parents, my uncles and aunts, my neighbors bust their ass picking lemon, lettuce, cauliflower, and I always thought, 'That is what is waiting for me.'" But David had held on to his ambitions. He did work the agricultural fields of the region, during and after high school, a job much of his family still held. But in the end he found his way into law enforcement.

Even though immigration policing imposes disproportionate material and symbolic burdens on border residents, regardless of citizenship status,[17] the state's scrutiny is unevenly distributed. Some borderlanders are "privileged actors" who can go about their daily lives knowing they will pass immigration agents' split-second risk assessments, being almost certain they can avoid the indignities of immigration policing.[18] In a predominantly Mexican border region, these privileges are based not only on citizenship status, but also on social class, phenotype, gender, types of documentation (e.g., border-crossing cards versus tourist visas), and even educational status.[19]

It makes sense, then, that Latinas/os' positive perceptions of immigration agents did not hinge on US-born citizenship. Ezequiel Jerez and David Bustos, both of whom were born in Mexico and lived there for most of their childhoods, came to admire the port of entry inspectors precisely because they crossed into the United States so often. Manuel Iglesias, the US-born child of Mexican immigrants, grew up watching immigration agents do canine and other presentations throughout his K–12 schooling experience. None of these agents experienced particularly privileged childhoods. David Bustos and Manuel Iglesias came from working-class immigrant families, while Ezequiel Jerez came from a working middle-class family in Mexico. To be clear, not all Latina/o agents had positive perceptions of immigration bureaucrats growing up.[20] The point is that the ones who did formed these positive perceptions as impressionable boys,[21] looking up to the commanding officers who were ubiquitous in the community.

The US government recognizes the opportunity to cultivate a future immigration workforce by courting border youth.[22] The CBP has one of the largest Explorer programs in the federal government. According to the CBP, these programs offer youth between the ages of fourteen and twenty exposure to law enforcement careers within their formative years.[23] Most of these programs are in border towns in Texas, Arizona, and California. Immigration and Customs Enforcement ERO does not have an Explorer program as of this writing, but its other arm, Homeland Security Investigations, sponsored its first program in 2013 under the Learning-for-Life affiliate of the Boy Scouts of America.[24] Tellingly, ICE chose San Juan, Puerto Rico, as the base for its inaugural cohort, perhaps the next best place after the Southwest border to cultivate bilingual Latinas/os for federal law enforcement.

The Border Patrol additionally maintains a well-developed public affairs arm that focuses on building inroads with local communities. As a participant in the Border Patrol's Citizens Academy, I got a firsthand look at how the government uses a broad base of public affairs programs to recruit border youth. The Citizens Academy is a six-week community engagement program that tells CBP's side of the border enforcement story; it is designed to persuade the public of the agency's virtue. I participated in two iterations of the Citizens Academy, one in Mountain Valley and one in Desert City. In the Desert City program, eleven out of the twenty-one participants were Latinas/os (including me); the rest were White. The age difference between these groups was stark: most of the Latina/o participants were youth who introduced themselves by declaring their interest in immigration jobs, while the White participants, mostly retired, expressed concern for the security of the border. One middle-aged Latina high-school counselor said she wanted to learn more about the Border Patrol because many of her students were interested in the career.

The recruitment function was even more glaring in the Mountain Valley Citizens Academy. All the participants were young (approximately eighteen to thirty years old) Mexican Americans from the local area who either were majoring in criminal justice at the local community college or were interested in doing so. Two of the participants had already applied to work in immigration control and were preparing for the hiring process. The agents called us "trainees." We were exposed to lighter versions of Border Patrol training activities, like tracking footprints in the desert and participating in simulated use-of-force scenarios, complete with mock weapons and bulletproof vests. At the end of the session, the agency announced our graduation in the local newspaper, declaring that the *trainees* got insight into the "rigorous training" Border Patrol agents receive. I cannot confirm how many of my fellow participants became immigration agents. From our conversations at the end, it was clear that the Citizens Academy only confirmed their interest in the career.

The immigration state's recruitment efforts entice Latinx youth away from their other, admittedly limited options, many of which carry higher cost of entry, and into the coercive arm of the state. Given this context, it is no wonder that many border youth not only aspire to a law enforcement career, but actively prepare for it. While most Latina/o agents did not have a degree, many had taken community college courses that would prepare them to work in law enforcement. Immigration and Customs Enforcement deportation officer Leon Camargo told me, "I always wanted to do law enforcement. When I was in college, I started off as an administration of justice major, and I wasn't sure if that was for me. . . . I changed my major five times. And at the end, I ended up back at administration of justice." Officer Camargo did not finish his undergraduate degree, because he got hired by ICE when he was still in college. "I got into the career I wanted to do so I kind of put school on the back burner."

The local community colleges' fact books reveal that Officer Camargo is part of a much larger group of border dwellers who are preparing for law enforcement careers. At Mountain Valley College, administration of justice was either the second or the third most popular major during the 2018–19 school year, depending on whether the students were pursuing a terminal associate's degree or intending to transfer to a four-year college. Nursing, which accounted for 15 percent of majors at the college, was the number-one major. At Desert City College, administration of justice was the second most popular major of the degrees awarded in 2018–19; it was surpassed only by the associate's degree in general studies.

Latina/o agents who grew up aspiring to a career in law enforcement are pragmatic dreamers. Their ambitions are rooted in what seems possible and probable, given the local opportunity structure and their preference for finding a good job in or close to their hometown. These agents are not unique in wanting to stay local. Many Mexican American border dwellers exhibit a strong attachment to the region, a preference that can limit their geographic mobility and circumscribe their employment searches.[25] Even when they leave home to go to the military, many of them are looking to return to their hometowns, where they become part of a much larger military-to-policing pipeline that staffs immigration enforcement jobs.

Falling into Immigration Work after the Military

For decades, the armed forces have actively targeted minoritized populations, along with working-class White populations, to maintain and grow military enlistment. Majority-minority communities along the border and throughout the United States are saturated with recruiters who sell military service as a strategy to pay for college, build discipline and job skills, and secure a better economic future.[26] Many of these recruitment campaigns are targeted to minoritized racial/ethnic groups. For instance, the "Yo Soy El Army" campaign encourages military service by signaling to Latina/o cultural values and framing Latinos as ideal "citizen soldiers."[27]

Working-class Latinx high-school students who have limited postsecondary options are military recruiters' main target in Southwest border towns.[28] In fact, in working-class high schools like the ones most of my respondents attended, Latina/o students are more likely to have contact with a military recruiter than with a high-school counselor.[29] Working-class Latinas/os' level of exposure to the military far surpasses that of middle-class White students; and with that increased exposure comes familiarity and comfort, increasing Latinx youth's propensity to enlist.[30] Between 2004 and 2017 the share of non-Hispanic Whites in the military fell from 64 to 57 percent, while the share of Hispanics increased from 25 to 36 percent.[31] Scholars have taken note of these patterns, criticizing the United States for leveraging a "poverty draft" against low-income, minoritized communities and creating a "culture of conscription" among Latinos specifically.[32]

Once in the military, Latina/o and other enlisted personnel become part of the military-to-policing pipeline. A study conducted by the Marshall Project shows military veterans are overrepresented among law enforcement officers. While only 6 percent of the US population has served in the military, 19 percent of police officers are veterans.[33] The immigration control bureaucracy is no exception to this trend. One-third of Immigration and Customs Enforcement officers and Border Patrol agents are veterans. Almost half of the agents that I spoke with had served in the military before working in immigration enforcement.[34]

Border Patrol agent Orlando Ortiz followed the seamless path into immigration enforcement that was forged by the border region's many military and policing programs for youth.

> When I was sixteen I joined the JTPA, and I was lucky that they sent me to the port of entry . . . to kind of learn some of the jobs that they did, and I loved it. . . . So after high school I joined the Navy, and after that I worked at the prison. I worked there for about a year, and I decided you know, this is my time. Customs wasn't open, but Border Patrol was.

Orlando's matter-of-fact description reveals the multiple institutions that drew him toward policing. The program that Orlando participated in at age sixteen was one of various employment and training programs for "economically disadvantaged" youth, funded through the federal Job Training Partnership Act of 1982 (JTPA).[35] One of the functions of JTPA was to expose youth to viable careers, usually in the form of paid placements during the summer months. Orlando "loved" his placement at the port of entry, which inspired him to enlist in the Navy after high school. Once his service was done, he returned to his hometown and slotted right into carceral economy in the region. Orlando had thought of his stint as a correctional officer as just that, a short-term position while he waited for a more permanent job at the port of entry. It was the Border Patrol, however, that was hiring when he was ready to make the move. His status as a veteran made it easy to secure a job he ultimately "fell in love" with.

Latinas/os are not the only veterans who glide directly from military service to immigration enforcement. Veterans of all backgrounds said they "fell into" the job after the military. As Border Patrol agent Eladia Marin explains, "I was in the military before, so it's an easy transition to another law enforcement career." This sentiment is echoed by Border Patrol agent Eric Chen: "I'm prior military, so as a federal job, there is already an enticement."

Several government initiatives recruit veterans into federal service, creating the "enticement" that Agent Chen mentioned. One such initiative is the Veterans Preference program, which gives veterans an advantage over similarly qualified nonveteran applicants. Veterans also benefit from an expedited hiring process that grants them credit for recent military fitness tests and medical examinations. Applicants who meet certain criteria can obtain waivers for polygraph examinations. Perhaps most critically, though, veterans who secure federal employment are eligible to count their military service toward retirement and leave accrual, a practice they refer to as "rolling over" benefits. This was a major motivator for agents to transition into federal law enforcement, as benefits do not transfer into private, state, or local policing jobs. Two ICE officers, Cole Walter and Nolan Wright, offer a pragmatic logic that is echoed by many of their peers. Officer Walter told me he works in immigration because "I was looking for a good government job I could roll over." Officer Nolan Wright of ICE put it bluntly: "I knew my military time wouldn't be wasted."

Veterans' path from military service to law enforcement also contains an element of social routine. Many veterans said they applied to the job, really without thinking much about it, as they were planning for postmilitary life. Agent Guillermo Bobadilla explained that he applied to work with the Border Patrol toward the end of his enlistment when he and his "Marine buddies" were plotting next steps.

> When you're in the military, pretty much your last year you start to decide what you want to do. . . . So [I was] sitting around with some Marine buddies, and we were talking about what we're going to do when we get out, and someone mentioned the Border Patrol, and I thought, "That's a good job. That's a good federal stable job."

Agent Bobadilla and his friends applied to the agency around the same time. He got the call a few months after his enlistment ended, while he was living back home with his parents. The job seemed like a step up from studying at the community college, so he took it.

Decades earlier, ICE officer Manolo Gil had a similar experience to that of Guillermo—a reminder of the pipeline's longevity. As a young Marine stationed at Camp Pendleton in the mid-1980s, Officer Gil heard radio ads announcing that the Border Patrol "was hiring and testing in San Diego." San Diego happened to be Manolo's hometown, and knowing this, his lieutenant asked him, "Would you take a group down there to do the testing for the Marines that might want to do that after they get out?" Officer Gil remembered, "I wasn't really intending to test, but I said, 'I'm here, why not?'" Officer Gil transitioned into the Border Patrol after the military and worked there for eight years before transferring to ICE.

Scholars have argued that Latina/o youths' decisions to enroll in the military then transition to enforcement agencies like USBP and ICE is a "choiceless choice" given their constrained options, the targeted recruitment, and the mutually reinforcing features of various militarized institutions along the border.[36] Consider the following exchange with Border Patrol agent Roberto Juarez, which lends support for this choiceless choice hypothesis. I asked him, "If you weren't in the Border Patrol, what other job would you be doing?"

That would be really tough. . . . It's pretty hard to have a good job here [in the border town]. . . . I know prior to even joining the military, I was trying to look into something like architecture and graphic design or something like that 'cause I really enjoyed drawing and buildings. But again, that would be something that's really tough here. Probably would be easier to get something in a bigger city. So yeah, that's a tough question.

Agent Juarez's inability to imagine an alternative, upwardly mobile career in his hometown vividly illustrates the limited opportunity structures along the border.

The well-oiled military-to-policing pipeline, coupled with the massive size of the US immigration bureaucracy, increases the chances that veterans will "fall into" immigration when looking for any job in law enforcement. Veterans looking to protect their benefits, as well as those looking for technical and cultural fit, find a familiar home in immigration control. Many veterans shared the sentiments of Border Patrol agents like Clay Perry, who clarified that what drew him to the job "wasn't so much fighting the immigration fight. It was more just having something different to do, being outside, something in law enforcement." They were different from agents who thought of immigration control as a way to serve their country.

A Way to Serve

Border Patrol agent Darlene Caldwell, a White woman in her early forties, was a second-generation law enforcement officer who had grown up watching members of her family in uniform. She always thought the job looked "pretty cool," but she had other options. After high school, she had gone off to college and earned a bachelor's degree in business. She worked in insurance for years, traveling the country and making a good living, and was not particularly unsatisfied with her life. That changed after the 9/11 terrorist attacks, when she became motivated to do something in service to her country. Her instinct was to enlist in the military, but her mother suggested the Border Patrol instead. Darlene found immigration work a suitable alternative to the military.

September 11th happened, and I wanted to do my part . . . possibly full-time military. And [Mom] said, "Ooh, you're getting a little bit old to go through boot camp." . . . She said, "You should consider the Border Patrol." . . . So I got online that night. I applied for the job. This was about January after September 11th of 2001. . . . Within eleven days of the one-year anniversary of September 11th, I was at the Border Patrol Academy. So that's why I decided to do it. [gets emotional]

I was taken aback by Agent Caldwell's surge of emotion. She was the first, albeit not the last, agent to get emotional during an interview, and I certainly did not expect it, given that I had only asked her about her career pathway. After giving her a second to compose herself, I asked if she had ever pursued law enforcement or the military before then. "Never." She explained, "but I just—September 11th truly affected my heart."

Agent Caldwell's pathway into immigration enforcement is not a story about economic pressure, a long-held desire to serve in law enforcement, or a seamless transition from the military. She had followed a relatively traditional middle-class pathway, going straight to college after high school and then entering the workforce in the field aligned with her degree. She considered a career in immigration enforcement only after she experienced a surge of patriotism that pushed her to serve her country in some capacity. Agent Caldwell represents a small group of agents—all of them White—who frame their entry into immigration enforcement as a service to their country. Each of them found the Border Patrol or ICE during their search for a more meaningful career or a *way to serve*.

Agent Oliver Booth's trajectory into the Border Patrol was like Agent Caldwell's. He "wanted to do something" for the country after the 9/11 attacks. At twenty-eight, however, his age seemed like a liability. A friend suggested the Border Patrol since he could speak Spanish.

I was right around twenty-eight years old. So I felt that I was too old to go into the military. . . . I had a buddy that said, "You speak Spanish? Why don't you go be a Border Patrol agent?" . . . I looked into it. And [it] turned out to be a pretty good thing, doing something, again, for my country—anyhow, something that paid decently also.

Agent Booth spoke fluent Spanish because he had been a missionary in Latin America as a member of the Church of Jesus Christ of Latter-Day Saints. Agent Booth and his friend knew that Oliver's Spanish ability would serve him well in the Border Patrol and that the pay was "decent." Even though he had not previously been interested in immigration work, he joined the agency when he was motivated to serve his country.

For ICE officer Grant Dawson, it was not age but sexuality that prompted him to consider immigration enforcement as an alternative to the military.

A college graduate, Officer Dawson had a comfortable office job when 9/11 happened. He was not considering a career change, nor had he ever been particularly interested in the military. The 9/11 attacks prompted in him "a sense of duty," and he "chose to serve."

> I looked at how did September 11th happen? Why did it happen? And I had a sense of duty. I chose to serve. I would've gone into the military, but because I'm gay, I would not; I was not going to lie about who I was. At the time there was the "don't ask, don't tell" policy. So I could serve openly here in ICE, so that's why I chose to come here.

The military's "don't ask, don't tell" policy made the military a nonstarter for Officer Dawson, a gay man. Working for ICE would allow him to fulfill his desire to serve without having to lie about his identity. He moreover saw a connection between the 9/11 attacks and immigration, which allowed him to understand a position at ICE through the lens of national security. Referring to the *hijackers* in the attack, he says, "Those people that were here, a lot of them were in violation of their status, yet they weren't on anyone's radar."

Another set of agents—people like Graham Porter—simply sought out the work as a more meaningful way to contribute to the national interest. Agent Porter explained:

> My thing was—this is the honest-to-God truth—I was doing finance, and I wanted to do something more in a service-orientated capacity. . . . It was one of those things. It sounds corny, but it was a big consideration. Like, okay, I want to look back and say, "Did I do something good for the world, or did I increase a stock price?"

A college graduate who gleaned success, but not satisfaction, working in finance, Agent Porter decided he wanted to do something he could be proud of. His search was broader than most agents who were looking for a more meaningful career, but it was the Border Patrol process that moved ahead the most quickly. Graham became increasingly interested in the agency, thinking that it ticked all the boxes, including "mix of indoor and outdoor activities," a must after spending ten years at a desk. Most importantly, he would be doing something he was proud of: "I'll be able to look back and say I did something in service for my country and my community."

Service to community meant something different to ICE deportation officer Ash Harding. Officer Harding grew up in the church, having attended private Christian school and then studying theology as an adult. At one point, he thought he would be a pastor, but he ended up "leaving Bible college" to serve in the military. As a practicing Christian, Officer Harding believed that the job as a deportation officer was "tailor made" for him because it allowed him to serve in a different capacity than he had before.

> I've always wanted to serve. I studied for the pastorate because I wanted to serve; I went into the military because I wanted to serve. A, it's a service career, serving the public, so I enjoy that part of it. B, it's an enforcement of our laws, our government, our system, which I'm a huge fan of. And C, I wouldn't have said this early on, . . . but for me, it's been the perfect balance between a career and a ministry.

Officer Harding was a deportation officer, not a religious guide for detainees. It was the meaning he ascribed to the work that set him apart from his colleagues.

People often ask me whether Latina/o immigration agents are selected for restrictionist immigration attitudes, nationalistic tendencies, assimilationist desires, or even internalized self-hatred. This question mostly comes from other Latinas/os and is delivered with more than a tinge of the race-traitor judgment that Latina/o agents are familiar with.[37] That was the same judgment that Yesenia Siqueiros, whom we met at the beginning of this chapter, communicated when she explained that she had never been interested in immigration work. She perceived that work as a matter of chasing her "own people," and that was not in her "blood," as she put it.

When people ask me this question I answer with some assurances and some caveats.

First, I provide the assurances. The bulk of the Latinas/os that I spoke to were pulled into immigration work by economic forces. My findings align with existing research on this matter. Josiah Heyman interviewed Mexican American immigration agents in the 1990s and found that they were largely working-class border dwellers who came into immigration enforcement when they were looking for mobility via civil service careers in the border region.[38] Decades later, David Cortez interviewed Latina/o ICE officers in multiple states in the Southwest and showed that their primary motivations for working in immigration control were still economic.[39] In this way, Latina/o immigration agents are like the many other minoritized workers who live out the promises and paradoxes of social mobility via employment in social control occupations.[40]

I have taken great care to demonstrate the force of Latina/o agents' instrumental motivations for working in immigration control. By instrumental motivations I mean that the job is a means to an end, the end being socioeconomic mobility and stability. I have argued that even those Latina/o agents who grew up aspiring to work in law enforcement are responding to the local opportunity structure along the border, where the immigration state is both a force of social control and an attractive employer. Those are the assurances. Now come the caveats.

The instrumentalist explanation that I have elaborated above applies best to the Latina/o agents who grew up in places like Mountain Valley and Desert City. The opportunity structure in these border towns is such that law enforcement jobs—everything from correctional officers to local and state police officers, to federal immigration control agents—are some of the best routes to upward mobility. That is not to say that they are the only jobs that border dwellers are choosing from. Jobs in agriculture, education, and nursing are also part of the occupational landscape in Mountain Valley and Desert City. However, law enforcement careers have a particular combination of qualities— prevalence (i.e., they are common), gainfulness (i.e., they have good salary and benefits), and accessibility (i.e., they have low educational requirements)— that make them both desirable and reachable for Latinas/os like the ones I spoke to. These were working-class people who had attended some college, but did not necessarily have a baccalaureate degree, and who were looking for a good job close to home. They were also subject to the normalization of militarism in these towns, as well as the very intentional recruitment campaigns by the immigration state and other law enforcement agencies. Latina/o agents who do not have this background and experience may have distinct motivations for entering immigration enforcement, a matter ripe for more research.

The non-Latina/o agents I spoke to expressed more varied motivations for entering immigration enforcement. There was some instrumentalism, especially among those looking to preserve their military benefits by going into federal law enforcement. Yet none of the non-Latina/o agents talked about this career choice as a matter of economic necessity, like many Latinas/os did. Overall, they articulated motivations that were more untethered from socioeconomic conditions in the towns where they grew up.

Like their Latina/o counterparts, the non-Latina/o agents' professional narratives also reflect their backgrounds. Most of them did not grow up along the border, instead hailing from varied parts of the country. They were more likely than Latina/o agents to have a college degree, which meant that they were choosing from a broader menu of professional options. They were more likely than the Latinas/os to have made a career change into immigration enforcement after years of doing something else. All of this may explain why non-Latina/o agents moved farther from home for the job and why they could be more philosophical about how they ended up in immigration control than their Latina/o counterparts, who were mostly from the border region.

Having laid out the empirical patterns, it is important to recognize that the question about selection is key on a conceptual level. This question gets to the heart of how we understand the relationship between dispositional factors and organizational influences on bureaucrats' behavior. It is a question about whether Latinas/os' and their colleagues' work behavior is a function of who they were when they entered the USBP or ICE (i.e., their dispositions), or whether their socialization into the culture of the profession is what matters more. The unsatisfying answer is that it is never just one thing—it is not dispositions or organizational socialization—but both, and these matter differently at distinct points in time. Organizational socialization factors may be strongest when bureaucrats are learning the ropes and may dissipate over time, but these factors are never independent of who the immigration enforcement officers and agents are as individuals or as members of groups.[41]

My position is that even though having a particular ideological bent is not a necessary condition for opting to work in immigration enforcement, it is reasonable to assume that selection also matters. Just as the Forest Service recruits a particular type of *man*, one with a "love of the woods" to conform to the organization's vision and purpose,[42] or a "country masculine habitus" to fight wildfires,[43] so too are the USBP and ICE most successful in recruiting a particular type of person. In the Southwest border region, that "type" of person may be a Latina/o with some college, but not necessarily a baccalaureate degree, who is looking for the best "good job" in the local economy. This may also vary by agency, as ICE officers were more likely to have a college degree and more likely to be military veterans. These mechanisms may be different from the ones that operate in the recruitment of others into immigration enforcement. These are important questions that are ripe for more research, but many are beyond the scope of my study.[44]

That agents do not have to enter as ideologues does not mean that they are naive or neutral to the work's politics and especially its racial dimension. The Latina/o agents I interviewed are reinforcing the racial hierarchy in the United States, and they are also reproducing the intra-ethnic boundaries that have long characterized Latina/o relations in the US borderlands and throughout the country.[45] This is true whether they think of their work in these terms or not. In this sense, Latina/o immigration agents are performing what political scientist Cristina Beltrán calls multiracial Whiteness, an ideology where Whiteness is a political color rather than a racial/ethnic background and one that lays claim to belonging through persecution of a variety of others, including immigrants.[46]

Thus, even if most Latina/o agents enter immigration work for instrumental reasons, that does not mean that dogma is absent throughout their career. Latina/o agents come to articulate ideological, nationalistic positions that are aligned with conservative politics, a phenomenon that is tied to professional membership and a political resocialization that is (re)shaping the politics of Latinx communities throughout the country, but particularly in the US-Mexico border region.[47] Their path toward indifference grows as they learn the ropes at work. Like other workers, Latinas/os and their colleagues eventually come to reflect and take on the common sense of their organizations, no matter their initial aspirations.[48] Officer Dario Saenz of ICE put it best: "We all kind of get into this, everybody has their own reasons . . . their own ideas. . . . But in the end, you have to be able to adapt." How people adapt to their role as Border Patrol agents and ICE deportation officers is the subject of the next chapter.

2

Becoming an Agent

BORDER PATROL AGENT MODESTO LARALDE was one of the many Mexican Americans who turned to immigration control when he "needed a career." A former electrician, Modesto had grown tired of the construction industry's ups and downs. He found the Border Patrol through a rather general job search. "I looked up online any federal jobs, and [the USBP] was one of the jobs that came up." Modesto admitted he did not know exactly what the agency did, but his father had once mentioned that immigration agents conducted raids at construction sites. Modesto thought that type of action-oriented police work "sounded cool," so he applied.

Once on the job, Agent Laralde learned that Border Patrol work was not what he thought it was. The worksite raids of his father's story had never materialized for him. He laughed, "I found out later . . . that was back in the '70s and '80s. . . . What I believed the Border Patrol did was totally different than what they actually did." To Agent Laralde, immigration enforcement had a way of feeling highly consequential and pointless, all at once. Satisfaction and efficacy were elusive in a job where agents were paid to control an unrelenting phenomenon, all as their "hands are tied behind our back."

> At times, you feel like it doesn't matter what you do. . . . We [are] given all this authority . . . but by the time it actually gets down to us, they've taken so much of it away. . . . You don't feel like you're making a difference. . . . It's very different than other jobs.

Agent Laralde's reference point was construction, where "there was always an end product" that one could evaluate, both for quality and for output. "You evaluate somebody on how well they did that product. You know? How much of that product, things like that. In the Border Patrol [you] can't really do that. There isn't really an end product." Not only was the goal of the Border Patrol somewhat unclear and largely unachievable, but the agency was also unpopular on a local level and with large segments of the American public. "You're not very appreciated for that job. . . . That's probably the hardest thing about it."

Agent Laralde diagnosed the problem as "politics." Conservatives approved of the Border Patrol's approach and believed the work to be necessary. But others—he did not specify what others—thought agents were "just beating up illegal aliens [and] that we shouldn't be enforcing the laws that we're enforcing." While he felt the deep imprint that politics left on his job, Agent Laralde also thought politicians' pronouncements were symbolic: "Whatever they decided as politicians rarely affects us. . . . A lot of it is just for votes." This was because agents' authority was rooted in law, and even that could be chipped away by bureaucratic vagaries. Agent Laralde's strategy was to focus on "personal victories," by doing his best to stop people from crossing through his several-mile stretch of desert. The alternative was to focus on the "thousands [of people] that came in" through the areas left unguarded, a decidedly less satisfying prospect.

Agent Laralde lamented that nobody was as committed to immigration enforcement as the agents themselves. "Nobody else cares; politicians don't care; the people don't care. They think my job is stupid anyway." Agents were just doing their best, he said, operating in a system that hired and trained them to do a job that they were not allowed to do. The rug had been pulled out from under their feet. "Most guys think when they leave the academy . . . that they are going to fix the whole immigration problem. You come in thinking, 'I'm going to do the best job I possibly can.' Then you come out and you realize a lot of stuff you're not allowed to."

This chapter explores the process of becoming an immigration agent. My respondents went into the job for different reasons. Some sought stability, others had long aspired to a career in law enforcement or were part of the military-to-policing pipeline, and still others yearned for a career with meaning. Distinct pathways lead to the same entry point in the process of becoming an agent: a law enforcement academy whose training involves deconstructing the recruits' civilian outlooks and developing the police*man*'s working personality.[1] At the Border Patrol and ICE academies recruits begin a journey toward becoming enforcement-oriented careerists,[2] whose preference for hyperregulation can manifest as "zealous administration" of immigration law.[3] I show that agents come to understand immigration through the lens of homeland security and crime whether they came in thinking about immigration in that way or not. They develop an enforcement mission that bumps up against the realities of migration and the limits of their bureaucratic function, leading to a sense of inefficacy that they attribute to politics.

The agents I spoke to will spend most of their careers processing people who fall somewhere on the forced migration spectrum, from economic migrants who cannot make a living in their home countries to asylum seekers who have been forced out by war, climate change, and other forms of life-threatening conflicts. Yet, they will do that job with the skills and outlooks of police officers looking to get the "bad guys" and under the constraints of their bureaucratic function, which is to usher immigration cases through a legal process.

Much of what we see agents doing in this chapter, therefore, is grappling with the multiple contradictions that pervade their work. The main contradiction concerns agents' *professional mission* as enforcement-oriented police officers and their somewhat reactive *bureaucratic function* as policy implementers. Agents want to enforce law in a categorical way, but they must carry out the decisions of other actors (e.g., executive leaders or immigration judges) regardless of whether those decisions cohere with their sense of mission. The second, related contradiction has to do with the good guy / bad guy dichotomy that permeates police culture, and the shortage of the archetypal bad guys in agents' day-to-day work.[4]

For the agents I spoke to, the archetypal bad guys are "criminal aliens": sexual deviants, gang members, drug traffickers, human smugglers, terrorists, and an array of felons. These criminal alien archetypes are raced and gendered as Latino men. Agents differentiate those "bad guys" from people who are "just illegal,"[5] or who have broken immigration law but do not have a criminal record. The issue for agents is that the archetypal bad guys of their professional mission are hard to come by. Their most common work routines involve carrying out their bureaucratic function, which is largely about processing illegality by ushering immigration cases along to the next phase of a legal process. For Border Patrol agents this might mean transferring asylum seekers in their custody over to ICE, while for ICE officers it may mean monitoring the cases of hundreds of detained people who are waiting to see a judge. To reconcile the contradictions between the highly stylized versions of police work that they were taught at the academy and what immigration work actually looks like, agents *manufacture ambiguity* about immigrants—about their identity and their intentions—and this lends agents' work the validity they seek. For Latina/o agents manufactured ambiguity has an additional purpose—agents use it to reconcile the tension between their racial/ethnic background and their work.

Developing a Professional Mission:
Learning to Punish Criminality at the Police Academy

Anyone, from the mildly curious job seeker to their most striving counterpart, can readily access recruitment materials and learn about what it takes to be a Border Patrol agent or an ICE ERO officer from the agencies' websites. The government's conflation of immigration with crime and national security is clear in its recruitment materials. On the ICE ERO hiring website, the agency says it is looking for people "to protect America from cross-border crime and illegal immigration that threaten national security and public safety."[6] For its part, the Border Patrol is looking for those who can "protect our nation by reducing the likelihood that dangerous people and capabilities enter the United States between the ports of entry." In exchange, the agencies promise stability, but also excitement and status. The Border Patrol says that "adrenaline rushes come standard" with the job, while ICE promises that its "complex law enforcement mission" yields the daily "satisfaction of securing this nation."[7]

Aspiring immigration agents who respond to these ads and make it through the application process will eventually attend an ICE or USBP academy. These are residential academies held at one of several campuses of the Federal Law Enforcement Training Center (FLETC), the government agency that provides police training to over ninety federal agencies as well as to some state, local, and tribal law enforcement organizations. According to FLETC, its training provides instruction that is "common to all law enforcement officers, such as firearms, driving tactics, investigations, and legal training."[8] Its partner agencies, like the USBP and ICE, provide training that is "unique to their missions." For immigration agents, that mission-based training includes instruction in immigration and nationality law and Spanish.

This is a critical point: the academies that immigration agents attend are standard police training programs, supplemented with additional materials considered relevant for their immigration function. Police academies are highly paramilitary, and they emphasize "high-risk, low-probability" topics, like use of force, and neglect "low-risk, high-probability activities," like how to effectively communicate with the public, how to build community connections, or how to de-escalate situations.[9] At their academies, immigration agents acquire the technical skills of a police officer—they learn how to take control of situations decisively, how to conduct field interviews assertively, and how to drive vehicles defensively. They learn that most critical and dangerous of all skills, how to use force. Immigration agents do learn about immigration law, but they are taught almost nothing about immigration as a social phenomenon. In effect, agents are trained to excel at the enforcement part of their mission, but their training does not prepare them to interact with the traveling public or to attend to the humanitarian issues they inevitably encounter.[10] This emphasis on policing characterizes both the Border Patrol and the ICE academies.

The Border Patrol Academy is a residential program held over twenty-four weeks on the Artesia, New Mexico, campus of FLETC.[11] Border Patrol recruitment materials describe this academy as "one of the most demanding federal law enforcement academies in the United States."[12] In a Border Patrol recruitment video, the government emphasizes the physical, tactical, and firearms training agents will receive as they prepare to face "dangerous or tense" situations in the field, including "active shooters and riot control." The video, running three minutes and thirty-seven seconds, mentions immigration law once, and even this is in the context of a ten-second clip in which aspiring agents are told that the "Law Program will ensure you understand our nation's immigration laws and how to properly and legally exercise your authority as a *law enforcement professional*."[13]

Agents seem to agree that the Border Patrol Academy is "hardcore" and "very military based," as Agent Raul Amparan put it. Agent Amparan describes being made to march and do push-ups on the first day he arrived at the academy, with people yelling in his face, throwing his bags around, and giving confusing directions. Border Patrol agent Camila Sarto told me that people warned her about the Border Patrol Academy when she was considering a job in immigration. She had heard that it was "way tougher than any other academy." The most informed assessment about the academy came from Border Patrol agent Jairo Morales, who had served in the military, then worked in local law enforcement before joining the agency. Agent Morales told me that the Border Patrol Academy was harder than the local police academy, but easier than military bootcamp.

The ICE ERO Academy is also a residential academy, but this one is held on the Glynco, Georgia, campus of FLETC over twenty-two weeks. This academy shares the basic structure of the Border Patrol program. Federal Law Enforcement Training Center instructors provide the law enforcement training that is common to all policing professionals, while seasoned immigration agents—in this case, ICE officers and attorneys from the agency's Office of the Principal Legal Advisor—provide ICE-specific training. According to

Frank Unger, a FLETC instructor who was interviewed in an ICE podcast, the ICE-specific lessons include "a tremendous amount of training and law. It's Fourth Amendment, it's constitutional law, it's immigration law, and removal law."[14] Recruits also engage in practical exercises that mimic an actual day in the life of a deportation officer, for instance by learning how to run record checks to find people, how to conduct law enforcement interviews, how to arrest and transport people, and so on. In an ICE news release about the ERO Academy, the government says that its focus is to ensure that their officers "understand the procedures involved in removal proceedings, from initial arrest to the execution of final order of removal."[15] Officer Leon Camargo of ICE said that the academy was "very similar to Border Patrol, just as difficult."

Police training is not only about providing recruits with technical skills—it is a penetrating experience of organizational socialization similar to military indoctrination.[16] Police academies are full of byzantine rites of passage that initiate recruits into the highly insular and moralized world of policing.[17] Recruits are degraded and shamed, their civilian ideas and assumptions ridiculed until they are excised, all with the goal of having recruits earn the idealized status of police officer.[18] The hierarchical structure of police training demands that recruits give up their autonomy in favor of becoming an expression of the "organizations' social self," and it produces wary, paranoid, and depersonalized officers.[19] It is during this training that police "recruits become increasingly authoritarian, conventional, moralistic, domineering, rigid and hostile towards the public."[20]

When immigration agents attend a police academy, they are becoming members of a distinctive cultural group—they come to see themselves as the "good guys" engaged in a morally righteous battle with the "bad guys." Police develop an exaggerated sense of duty, tend toward black-and-white categorical thinking, and cultivate a moralized perception of their work that makes them believe they could achieve their mission if only they were left alone to do their job.[21] A sense of cynicism and aggrievement is also common among police who feel not only unappreciated for the risks they take on behalf of the public, but also betrayed by police leaders whom they see as pandering to political interests instead of standing up for their rank and file. Officers' skepticism about the public produces a high degree of solidarity among insiders and distance between them and outsiders.[22] Even as agencies have incorporated ideas about community policing and have diversified the profession, these cultural tenets have remained remarkably stable across time and national context,[23] and they capture the orientations of many of the immigration agents I spoke to.

Adjusting to Their Bureaucratic Function:
The Administrative Processing of Illegality

After graduating from their respective FLETC academies and taking their oath to uphold the constitution, immigration agents report to their duty stations. By then, they have been taught the version of immigration that the federal government favors: immigration as a crime and a security risk. They have learned they stand between the disaster that is uncontrolled migration and American prosperity. They have developed a sense of mission, through what Border Patrol agent Alexis Echevarria called "indoctrination," which has molded them into being self-motivated agents who "go out there, own the zone, and [ensure] nobody gets through."

Once on the job, all agents must adjust to the reality of their work, which contrasts starkly with their training. A certain level of recalibrated expectations is par for the course in all professions but is particularly true of policing. Police work is often dramatized as a flurry of excitement and danger but in practice consists mostly of doing tasks like paperwork, traffic control, and responding to calls that officers may consider insipid, and waiting for something exciting to happen.[24] Immigration enforcement strays even further from the idealized notions of police work. This gap has long been on display at the US-Mexico border, where agents spend most of their career arresting, detaining, and deporting Latinas/os who are either responding to the US economy's insatiable thirst for labor or claiming asylum following various forms of displacement. This gap between agents' enforcement orientation and what the job looks like in practice was very salient during my 2014–16 study period.

I was in the field during a time when thousands of families and unaccompanied minors, mostly from Central America, but also from other countries, were seeking asylum at the US-Mexico border.[25] During this time, agents were doing less policing of their "typical" target: Mexican men who could be swiftly deported at the southern border; and their *administrative* duties increased. Instead of conducting tactical border surveillance—a task they relished— Border Patrol agents encountered asylum seekers, many of them families and unaccompanied minors, who turned themselves in or presented themselves at ports of entry. Many of these migrants declared fear of returning to their country, triggering a legal process that requires a Credible Fear Interview with a USCIS officer. The combination of many people needing to be processed and lack of personnel to do it overwhelmed the southern border stations, and the Border Patrol quickly fell out of compliance with its own short-term detention policy.[26] As a humanitarian crisis unfolded, agents complained of low morale and resented having to do care work when they signed up to do law enforcement.[27]

Asylum seekers are subject to mandatory detention under this country's criminalized immigration framework,[28] which increased the already-distended population of migrants incarcerated in ICE detention centers. Women and children were transferred to family residential centers or released through various Alternative to Detention programs, purportedly humanitarian alternatives, that involved keeping families behind bars or strapping parents with electronic ankle bracelets that private companies charged them to maintain.[29] Immigration and Customs Enforcement officers also arranged travel documents for migrants being deported via government-chartered removal flights to noncontiguous countries. To state the obvious, this was not what agents thought they would be doing. They were, moreover, performing these administrative tasks with the outlooks of police officers—the contrast between their professional mission and their bureaucratic function at its height.

The Shrinking Badges of ICE Officers:
From Policing to Docket Work

Officer Lorenzo Delgado of ICE described the recalibration to the reality of the job as a matter of shrinking badges. He told me, "Some people graduate from the academy, and their badge is like humongous. After a year of being in the agency, your badge tends to get smaller." For ICE officers, that badge shrinkage came with the realization that most of them are case managers, or more accurately, "docket workers." Docket work consists of monitoring the cases of people who are in ICE custody, whether in detention or nondetained programs. This, Officer Manuel Iglesias explained, is "the bread and butter" of being a deportation officer:

> A case lands on a docket when an individual gets arrested by whoever, whether it's ICE or CBP, Border Patrol, whatever it may be; they land on a docket. . . . And the deportation officer would then review the charging document, whatever that may be, Notice to Appear, Administrative Removal, Expedited Removal. They would look at it for legal sufficiency . . . if there was some uncertainties; consult with the immigration attorneys, with the chief counsel's office to ensure that the individual in question is removable in fact, and we are detaining them appropriately; file the charges with

the court; and if the case does go through the court system, follow the case through the court system, sometimes through the appellate court system; through the Board of Immigration Appeals; and further up to the Circuit Court of Appeals if it goes there . . . pretty much see the case through to administrative finality.

For deportation officers, the goal of all this docket work is, well, deportation. As Officer Iglesias explained, "The expectation [is] that this individual will be removed at the end." Officer Iglesias is not wrong: the role he and his colleagues play in the immigration system is specified in their job title. From a legal standpoint, however, removal is just one potential outcome—not the point—of immigration case processing.

Many people are involved in any one person's immigration case; not all of them share the deportation officer's goal for or understanding of the process. For instance, an ICE attorney is aligned with the deportation officer's objectives, but an immigration attorney is fighting for their client's relief,[30] while grassroots advocates work to release people from ICE custody.[31] An immigration judge may be somewhere in the middle of these ends, employing their own racialized and gendered ideas of deservingness in making removal decisions.[32] The point is that deportation officers cannot always live out their title. Their ability to deport is contingent on many factors, including the legal protections that immigrants are entitled to and officers' insulation from immigrationist forces that limit their executive capacity.[33] All of this can be very grating for mission-driven officers who "just want to do our job."

At times, deportation officers feel actively forced to do the opposite of enforcement. Officer Noah Webb of ICE laughed as he told me that the media portrays ICE as an expulsion machine, when agents instead feel like they are doing social work. "The media doesn't see this, but we've come to the point where we do a lot of social work. . . . A lot of guys are saying, 'Hey, this is what we were trained for, to do enforcement. Why aren't we enforcing immigration?'"

I was curious to sort this out with ICE officers. I agreed that their day-to-day work looked like case management, but their enforcement orientation was the opposite of social work's advocacy for the marginalized. I engaged ICE supervisor Luke Newman on this point:

IRENE: Hearing people describe what a deportation officer does, it sounds like case management.

OFFICER NEWMAN: That's a huge part of it.

IRENE: But you guys are socialized as law enforcement officers. . . . Social workers [do case management], but they are professionalized in a completely different way to think about their cases.

OFFICER NEWMAN: Yeah. Bottom line is my job is to remove you or effect whatever the court decides. So if the court decides you're going to be given a bond or if my boss decides you're going to get a bond or whatever, then that's my job from that docket management or social working point is to release you, whether I agree with it or not. Right? A social worker, they're totally there to help. . . . We're not here to help, but we're here to effect whatever the agency and the judicial system decides.

Officer Newman is cut-and-dry about his professional mission as he understands it; he is there to deport people. However, he also is clear-eyed about his bureaucratic function, in that he is also there to carry out the mandates of others who have power over individual immigration cases, like immigration judges, or presidents and bureaucratic leaders who can issue agency-wide mandates compelling agents to exercise discretion in particular ways.[34] It is this reactive bureaucratic function that agents find most grating as cops who just want to get the "bad guys."

While the detained and nondetained dockets represent the bulk of ICE deportation officers' work, other assignments better approximate what agents consider *real* police work.[35] ICE officer Jacinto Estrada chuckled as he explained, "If you get hired in a [detention] facility, it's going to be very, very different to that [recruitment] video you see. . . . And being in an office is more administrative work." Officer Estrada continued, "But, if you're hired for a field office, you'll probably be doing a lot of hands-on, fugitive operations so you'll need all this knowledge and training [just] in case." Immigration and Customs Enforcement officers might also work on task forces with other federal agencies, like the Drug Enforcement Agency. They could be assigned to the Criminal Alien Program, which identifies and takes into custody noncitizens who have been arrested by other law enforcement agencies. Many agents reasoned that these possibilities justified keeping up with their police training program, just in case.

An assignment to the ICE Fugitive Operations team, or "Fug Ops," would be one of the reasons to keep up with their police training. This assignment epitomizes the public's ideas of what ICE does as well as many officers' fictionalized notions of what being a federal agent would be. These are the ICE officers who conduct what the public recognizes as immigration raids in communities and homes, what ICE calls "enforcement actions." Officers working on these teams identify "immigration fugitives," then conduct surveillance on their "targets," planning for the most tactically advantageous encounter where they can take them into custody without compromising officer safety.[36] This is the stuff of *real police work.*

The problem for the mostly junior officers who are raring to do this kind of work is that Fugitive Operations teams represent a fraction of job assignments within ICE ERO. In 2016, there were 129 Fugitive Operations teams in the entire country. Most of these teams are small, with assignments based mostly on seniority.[37] Without discounting how traumatic these Fugitive Operations arrests are for communities on the receiving end, they are not as common as they are harrowing. For example, in 2016, when I conducted ICE interviews, the agency was removing approximately 1,250 people per week (65,332 that year). Only about 250 of these 1,250 people were arrested by Fugitive Operations teams nationwide.[38] In other words, over 80 percent of ICE removals began when ICE took custody from another law enforcement agency, a reminder of the immense role that local police play in federal immigration control.[39]

Some field offices may even lack a Fugitive Operations team. Such was the case in Mountain Valley, where ICE supervisor Luke Newman laughed when I asked him about the Fugitive Operations team in the area.

> People, to include my employees, they like to throw around that term "fugitive ops." "We're going to go on fugitive ops." What the hell are you guys talking about? The guy's not a fugitive. But they like that term, like we're in the movies. . . . But really nine times out of ten, what we do here, it's not fugitive ops. . . . But it sounds a lot cooler.

Fugitive Operations are the closest that ICE officers will get to conventional notions of police work. It is the type of work that best approximates their training, what police officers are taught to value and what they get status from doing. It is important to note, however, that not all agents aspire to do this type of work.

According to Supervisor Newman some of the agents under his watch were more oriented toward docket work than to the other aspects of the job. They would be perfectly content with a role where all they were doing was processing immigration cases and they never had to engage with the more enforcement-oriented parts of the job. Still, he needed them to be able to do both. He explained, "Some deportation officers would rather spend their twenty years of their career doing that [docket] work and never gearing up and having to go knock on somebody's door and put them in handcuffs in front of their kids." "At the same time," he continued, "I need that deportation officer [who] doesn't want to put handcuffs on somebody—I need them to know how to do it, how it feels to do." No matter their proclivities and preferences, all agents must be able to perform their role, which is to enforce, and to enforce with gumption. Officer Newman summarized it this way:

> We're the cops that arrest them, we're the cops that manage the case, and then I'm the cop that has to show empathy. . . . And then I'm the cop that has to put all my gear on . . . and get vehicles together and M4s, shotguns, all this stuff, . . . take you in handcuffs and shackles and deal with your family. Do all those things and safely get the mission done without me or my guys getting killed.

Even Officer Newman—who recognized that "fugitive operations" does not capture the reality of most officers' work—defaults to dramatized notions of policing and the ever-present risk of death in the profession when characterizing his job. In fact, immigration agents have some of the lowest rates of death and injury of all US law enforcement, but this does not dislodge the warrior mentality that is ingrained in agents' outlooks.[40] Agents' enforcement orientation is not at all surprising given that the USBP and ICE are policing agencies, embedded within a political-bureaucratic context where undocumented migration is understood first and foremost through a crime and security lens. But even if expected, this stark enforcement orientation has a certain irony to it.

Deportation officer Danilo del Rosario, a Filipino man, was one of the few ICE officers who were willing to accept the gap between the paramilitary underpinnings of their police training and the character of their daily work. He went as far as to mock his colleagues, shaking his head as he told me, "I look at these agents like, 'Shit, you're dressed like SWAT, and you're hooking up a non-crim?' Come on." That gap is even starker in the Border Patrol.

Border Patrol Agents:
At War with an Enemy That Does Not Fight Back

If docket work represents ICE officers' "bread and butter," as Officer Manuel Iglesias put it, "working the field" or being out "on the line" epitomizes Border Patrol agents' work.[41] Being "on the line" means surveilling the territorial border between the United States and Mexico. In the sectors I studied, this usually meant patrolling a several-mile stretch of desert landscape. This is what most Border Patrol agents do, most of the time. Agent Ezra Aniston put it this way:

> Here in the Border Patrol, we pretty much all do the same thing. We all pretty much get out there and patrol the border. It's not like we have three hundred people doing administrative duties every day and we have three hundred people going out into the field every day and we have three hundred people teaching class and being in training. It's not like that. Those [administrative roles] are the very small pockets we have.

The routine of the Border Patrol agents who I interviewed better approximated idealized conceptions of police work, at least as it related to their line duties. However, the gap between the fact and fiction of the work was most obvious when, after hours of patrolling the border in highly militaristic ways, they encountered not the treacherous "bad guys" but mostly compliant migrants. To comprehend this gap, we must first understand what the work looks like.

Border Patrol agents start their eight- to twelve-hour shifts by receiving their assignment at muster, typically held in a large room at station headquarters.[42] After muster, they visit the armory to pick up the weapons they are entitled to, based on their assignment. Agents assigned to roving patrol in a border city may carry only the standard handgun on their belt, while those assigned to remote areas of the desert may also carry long rifles. Next, agents check their vehicles to make sure their tires are aired up, their gas tanks are full, and, hopefully, their air conditioning works—a key source of comfort in the desert Southwest. Border Patrol agents are a common sight at gas stations in border towns, as many of them stock up on provisions before heading out to their "assigned zone."

"Sign cutting" is a critical part of what agents assigned to desert areas do on their shift. Sign cutting consists of looking for disturbances in the environment—mostly footprints, but also minuscule details like moisture on overturned rocks, clothing fibers on vegetation, or branches broken off desert brush. Border Patrol agents are proud of their sign-cutting skills, something that reminds them that technological advances have not entirely erased the importance of their human skills.[43] The most experienced agents can tell from the sign's characteristics roughly how many people they are tracking, whether it is a mixed group (men, women, and children) or mostly men, how long ago they entered, and which direction they are heading.[44]

Once an agent has "cut a group," they follow a standard protocol that consists of calling in the sign to a supervisor, and giving them the sign's description (i.e., a literal description of, e.g., a shoe print, when visible; migrants often attach material to the bottom of their shoes to disguise their sign) and the sign's coordinates. As agents often said, "cutting a group is where the chase begins." This is what an agent looks forward to on their shift—finding that a person or group has entered the country in their area. Agents often describe the chase as a game of "cat and mouse" or "hide-and-seek with guns," and they typically enlist their colleagues in a time-saving strategy called "leapfrogging" to see how far the group has gotten.[45]

It is not an exaggeration to say that Border Patrol agents talk about desert patrol as if they were on an adventure. When I suggested to Border Patrol agent Aaron Novar that none of that sounded appealing to me, he admitted that desert patrol could be "frightening," especially at night, but it was also "addicting." The addicting part was the adrenaline rush of hunting people.

> You can't beat that rush. . . . There's a famous quote by somebody that says until you've hunted man—was it Ernest Hemingway, I think? There's no hunting like the hunting of man. And once you've done that, you'll never go to anything else. And that's kind of what we do. We hunt people. Hunt them down and arrest them.

I was taken aback by Agent Novar likening border surveillance to hunting people. When he first said it, I thought that his comments captured the dehumanization of immigrants in the enforcement bureaucracy. I later learned that this Hemingway quote is somewhat of motto among police officers, generally, and has even appeared in law enforcement training materials.[46] Agent Novar's use of this Hemingway quote reminds us that the cultural outlooks of immigration agents are indicative of a much larger problem in American policing.

Once agents find who they are tracking, their main priority is "officer safety." Agents are taught to take tactically advantageous positions, to shout commands in Spanish, and to order people to sit down in a line with their legs in a V. They make people take a shoe or their shoelaces off to prevent them from running. During this process, agents are simultaneously positioning themselves behind the group, so that border crossers cannot see them but so that the agent can surveil them all. Agents watch for behavioral cues to identify potential "troublemakers," or people who seem less compliant. If an agent identifies one such troublemaker agents handcuff *him* to make an example and prevent others from "bucking up."[47]

Agents then search each person individually, looking for weapons. This task is not to be done alone. If agents have not already been joined by a partner, they will wait for their backup to begin the search. Agents also take basic demographics at this juncture, but they view detainee accounts with skepticism, assuring me that they do not truly know who they are dealing with until they are fingerprinted. Depending on the location of the arrest, either a transport vehicle will pick up the migrants or the arresting agent will transport them to the station for processing.

The outcome of this highly tactical, militaristic police surveillance and arrest process is almost always the same: undocumented border crossers are not the cunning criminals that agents have been trained to apprehend. Those interested in confirming the disjuncture between how agents are taught to approach immigrants—as criminal threats—and how these arrests usually go may find the National Geographic show *Border Wars* informative. The series shows how the US government sends agents to the border as if they were at war, only for them to mostly encounter an enemy that does not fight back.[48] Most agents concede to the disjuncture. One Border Patrol agent told me, "Ninety percent of people you catch are people that want to find a better way of life [that] they want to build for their kids." Another told me that most of the weapons they find on migrants were not weapons at all, but rather can openers and other sorts of "contraband" that migrants use to survive their arduous journey. Agents do find people carrying drugs, but most of these are so-called backpackers, who are often coerced into carrying bundles of marijuana on their back to pay their crossing fee to cartel-affiliated smugglers.[49] Even Agent Novar, who likened the patrol to hunting men, admitted the arrests he makes are "mostly administrative."

Neither ICE deportation officers nor Border Patrol agents get the satisfaction of living out the highly stylized version of immigration control that they are sold in DHS recruitment videos or taught at the academy. Immigration and Customs Enforcement officers are adjusting to becoming case managers, while Border Patrol agents are adjusting to being on the front line of a war with, as it turns out, asylum-seeking families, unaccompanied minors, and others in distress. Yet agents' own sense of professional validity depends on the existence of the "bad guys" requisite for their own "good guy" role.[50] The solution is to insist on the fiction of immigration control, and that involves creating *manufactured ambiguity* about immigrants' identities and their intentions.

Manufactured Ambiguity

Agents are charged with investigating, arresting, and deporting anyone who is out of status. Officer Jacinto Estrada of ICE put it bluntly, "You either have the documentation to be legally in the United States or you don't. . . . It's in black and white. The law is the law." Border Patrol agents were also clear on this. Agent Jerry Balt explained, "You catch them; you take them in. Even if they're American citizens, they still have to be inspected at entry." This categorical thinking is typical of police officers and of other bureaucrats with scarce resources who use a discrete set of action categories to process many cases.[51] The process of classification, of turning people into dehumanized action categories, is what statecraft looks like in practice.[52]

For immigration agents, that process of classification involves recognizing that many immigrants are not the "bad guys" they value arresting, then doing away with that realization and carrying out their policing procedures anyway. As mentioned before, agents do distinguish between noncitizens in their charge, differentiating between the cunning criminals and terrorists who epitomize the warrant and peril of their work, the less dangerous but still unwelcome "regular illegal immigrants," and the families and children that they are completely unprepared to deal with. These distinctions are moralized, in that some immigrants are the "worst of the worst," while others are not "bad" per se, but unwelcome victims of another nation's disorder—interlopers, but not the real bad guys.

In fact, most agents are willing to admit that most of the people they deal with are not the archetypal criminal aliens that animate their work. Border Patrol agent Justino Quijada explained, "It is a minority that we get people with criminal histories, anything from burglaries to child abuse to murder; most people don't have a criminal history." The rub is, and this is key, that agents argue that they "never know" who they are dealing with. "You never know" is a common dictum among police officers who see themselves as warriors who must always remain suspicious of the public and ready for things to escalate or devolve.[53] In immigration, agents use this "you never know" logic to manufacture ambiguity about where immigrants fall on the false dichotomy their employer has established for them: immigrants as either criminals or "just illegals." This manufactured ambiguity allows agents to buy into a sense of urgency to identify and contain immigrants who could be anyone.[54]

I told Agent Quijada I was unclear about this idea that agents "never know" who they are dealing with. I mentioned to him that many agents conceded that the migrants they deal with on a day-to-day basis are not the archetypal "bad guys," not the criminals they seemed to emphasize in the abstract. I wanted him to explain the logic of what I now call manufactured ambiguity. Agent Quijada admitted that, yes, most people who cross the border are coming to the United States for work, but at the same time, agents cannot know that unless they arrest them and take their fingerprints. He tried to explain the reasoning:

> The normal agent tracking a person through the desert, you can't distinguish. When you start following a group of people, if you could tell me who to follow, if you could tell me, "You know what? This guy coming across, by looking at his footstep, this guy has an AK-47 and he's bringing drugs into the country, that's this guy." "And then this guy, has no criminal history and is coming in to pick apples in Washington." I'm gonna go after the guy with the AK-47. . . . But we don't know who they are until we apprehend them; we can't distinguish that until we arrest them, roll their fingerprints.

Border Patrol agents explained time and again that migrants are inscrutable until their fingerprints are run through their databases. These immigration databases are linked to other federal repositories; a fingerprint search will yield a person's criminal record if they have one. It is through this process of linking immigrants' fingerprints to the state's records that noncitizens become legible to agents and sortable based on the state's classifications. Until those databases confirm that those migrants are not criminals, then agents assume they could be. In the Border Patrol's procedures, the logic is that migrants are assumed criminals until otherwise proven to be "just illegal." This manufactured ambiguity and agents' reliance on state records to prove migrants "true identities" allows Border Patrol agents to rationalize their compliance with policing procedures even when they recognize the gap between those procedures and the character of the situations and people they encounter day in and day out.

Border Patrol agents have access to this manufactured ambiguity because of the highly specialized nature of their work. An agent starting their shift may be assigned to a particular task, like being out in the field, doing transport, or staying in the sector headquarters processing unit. Depending on their assignments, they may have very goal-oriented and fleeting interactions with immigrants. Immigration and Customs Enforcement officers' docket work differs from Border Patrol agents' line work because the former have more information about people and thus less access to this manufactured ambiguity about immigrants' identities. Immigration and Customs Enforcement officers have a file on the people they are monitoring, a file that gives them extensive information about the person's immigration and criminal history, if they have one. Instead of manufacturing ambiguity about whether immigrants are "criminal" or "illegal," ICE officers manufacture ambiguity about what *immigrants might do* in the future and within the country's interior if officers do not remove them. This is a subtle but important difference.

Immigration and Customs Enforcement officers say that, by enforcing immigration law, they are preventing other types of lawbreaking from happening under their watch. For instance, ICE officer Grant Dawson told me that if someone is here without documentation—in agents' words, if they are "just illegal"—they may also be more likely to engage in criminal acts. Officer Dawson explained, "You say oh, well, they're not a criminal. But are they? Are they committing other things just by virtue of being here?" In addition, because ICE deportation officers are sometimes making release decisions, their "you never know" scenarios are rooted in risk-management logics about what might happen if they let the wrong person free. Immigration and Customs Enforcement officer Leon Camargo told me, "That guy from San Francisco that killed that lady . . . if I would've been that officer that released them, it's your fault that lady got killed." In effect, ICE officers subscribe to a slippery-slope argument about immigration lawbreaking leading to other forms of lawbreaking, despite ample research against this premise.[55] When ICE deportation officers say "You never know," they are referring to immigrants' actions, not where they fall on the false criminal alien / "just illegal" dichotomy that Border Patrol agents subscribe to.

The idea that agents "never know" who they're tracking through the desert, or that they "never know" what undocumented immigrants living in the United States will do next, is a manufactured ambiguity that lends coherence to their work given the gap between their training and the character of their day-to-day routines. Agents are grappling with a bewildering array of contradictory information: they are police officers who seldom deal with criminals; they are mission driven, but their mission is contentious and unattainable; and many are Latinas/os who are arresting and deporting people who look like them. In light of these contradictions, agents find reprieve in their employer's warning that they can never let their guard down.

That is why, despite the gap between the fact and the fiction of immigration work, officers did not think there was anything wrong with their training. Immigration and Customs Enforcement officer Nolan Wright was conclusive when I asked him about the possibility of bringing officers' preparation in line with their work. "I would not change the training. [We] still can't be complacent because you still never know what you're going to get. . . . You have to train for the worst."

Manufactured Ambiguity in Latina/o Agents' Experiences

Manufactured ambiguity is particularly valuable for Latina/o agents who struggle to reconcile the criminal-versus-illegal dichotomies that pervade their work. Latina/o agents shared stories from earlier stages of their career when they struggled with "feeling bad" about their work, but then had a conversion experience where someone who appeared as "just illegal" turned out to be one of the bad guys. Latina/o agents share these experiences with each other and even with family members as war stories that lend coherence to their work, considering its layered contradictions.[56]

Border Patrol agent Raul Amparan demonstrates how manufactured ambiguity allows Latina/o agents to reconcile the contradictions they experience as a function of their background. The son of Mexican immigrants, Agent Amparan was embedded in a familial and social network that included many foreign-born people, some of whom were undocumented. Because of his closeness to immigrants, he brought to the job a more complex understanding of the immigrant experience than is available to agents without his background. He knew that many undocumented migrants were people like his own parents, people who came to the United States for a better life. This was inconvenient knowledge that made him "feel bad" about his work, until he experienced something that confirmed you really "never know."

> When I came back from the academy, [in] the first group we ever apprehended . . . there was an older man, . . . and his feet were cut up, and they were bleeding. They caught him up in the mountain somewhere. And I felt so bad, I gave him my lunch; I gave him my water. You know? And on the way back, I was telling my training officer, I was like "I don't know if I can do this every day." You know? And he said, "Just give it a try, wait a little bit. See how you feel." I told him, "I think I might just go to customs." That was my initial thought. [We] went back to the station, and they would make us process them so we learned how to process. And it turned out that the same old man had raped a nine-year-old little girl. And when I asked him about it, he just kind of smirked and looked away. So I was pretty angry about that. You know? If I'm getting people like that off the streets—the most innocent-looking person can be the worst person ever.

This experience was the exception that proved the rule for Agent Amparan. That day, Agent Amparan learned that immigrants cannot be trusted. Perhaps most importantly, he also learned not to trust his own emotions. He learned to lean into the potential for immigrant criminality, even when illegality was most obvious.

The manufactured ambiguity that surrounds agents' ideas about who immigrants are or *could be* mirrors the lore that Harel Shapira identified when he studied the Minutemen, the militia that patrols the US-Mexico border. Shapira found that the mostly White male retirees who patrolled the border with the Minutemen were motivated by the prospect of catching an archetype called "José." This was a Mexican character who was unambiguously threatening, but for distinct reasons. There was the criminalized José whom Minutemen understood as a sexual deviant, a drunk, and a felon; and there was the virtuous, hardworking José who broke immigration law to feed his family.[57] Just like the Minutemen, the immigration agents I spoke to are really out to get the "criminals"—that is, the version of "José" that animates their professional mission—but they mostly encounter the more benign "José." What manufactured ambiguity allows agents to do is fabricate the archetype that suits their mission and their sense of legitimacy. Instances where a person who seemed "just illegal" but turned out to be a "criminal" are exceptionally useful in this regard.

Border Patrol agent Esteban Luar had a similar experience with a "sweet old lady" who reminded him of his grandmother. Agent Luar was conducting roving patrol on a highway a few miles from the border when his field training officer (FTO) noticed something suspicious about a vehicle they encountered on the road. The FTO told Agent Luar to pull the car over, and, even though Agent Luar was somewhat confused, he did as he was told. The woman who was driving the vehicle was very "sweet" and "nice" and was, in fact, transporting undocumented people. Agent Luar, still in training, was impressed by his FTO's ability to see that something was off with the car. The FTO later told him that the car had been "riding low" in the back, suggesting there was something heavy in the trunk. But the most instructive part of this experience came when Agent Luar fingerprinted the woman.

> [Her record] comes back for heroin smuggling, cocaine smuggling, marijuana smuggling, not just personal use but big amounts and everything else. She's been busted for anything and everything. And she has a rap sheet that's longer than you are standing up. And I'm just like oh my God. . . . She's dirty. And so from that point on, you don't trust anybody. You don't trust anyone until you roll them.

In addition to teaching Agents Amparan and Luar that criminals can lurk anywhere, these experiences of being fooled by [criminal] immigrants mark a before-and-after moment in their emotional life on the job. These experiences occur early on. Women and older people feature prominently in the stories Latina/o agents told me about learning that you "never know" and that they should not feel bad about their work. Stories that featured misleading characters who seemed to be "just illegal" but turned out to be criminals lent strength to the manufactured ambiguity that was so productive for agents—if elderly people and women can be the bad guys, then the bad guys do lurk in the most unexpected of places. You really never know, they reasoned.

The cunning criminals who animate US immigration politics have always more accurately reflected moral panics about racialized outsiders than the economic and humanitarian reality of immigration flows.[58] This is particularly true at the US-Mexico border, which serves as a stage for vote-seeking politicians to act out American anxieties about uncontrolled migration from the Global South and for bureaucratic elites to secure public support for increased enforcement, which in turn protects their livelihood.[59] In the American imagination, the country's southern border epitomizes the spectacle of undocumented migration, a state-produced version of the phenomenon that animates all sorts of characters, including armed drug cartels, violent gang members, unscrupulous human smugglers, cunning terrorists, and of course, some *regular migrants*.[60] But the fact of immigration control at the southern border bears little resemblance to this state-created fiction. Instead of fighting criminals, agents mostly process people who inhabit the various forms of liminal legality and illegality produced by the state.[61]

Deportation officers and Border Patrol agents work in the gap between their professional mission and their reactive bureaucratic function—a situation that is deeply unsatisfying for careerists who work in regulatory agencies.[62] As the coercive arm of the immigration state, agents are trained and socialized as police officers and taught that their raison d'être is to protect America by preventing the entrance and executing the removal of noncitizens deemed unwanted by the state. This mandate is in tension with their bureaucratic function, which is to implement immigration law and policy that does not always cohere with their mission.

As street-level bureaucrats, agents have a great deal of discretionary power, but they are not completely autonomous actors.[63] Agents are bound by law to do their part in ushering migrants' cases along the gauntlet that is the crimmigration system, and that often means carrying out the decisions of other actors regardless of whether those outcomes cohere with their enforcement mission. This gap between their professional mission and their bureaucratic function is one source of agents' frustration: a sense of disenchantment that they attribute to politics, when it is a function of their policy implementation role and the mismatch between their training and the character of their day-to-day routines. In short, agents want to punish criminality when what they are doing is processing illegality in a punishing way.

Still, agents do not see the issue in these terms. They believe that it is politics that are impinging on matters of law—that that is why they can't do their job. In insisting that it is the politics of the work that prevents them from doing their job, they are drawing an artificial line between law and politics. Politics gives birth to laws. Immigration law is not some divine object, but the product of that most irreverential of social contests between various interest groups and between vote-seeking politicians, all vying for their own vision of the problem and their solution to dominate the others. Of all laws, immigration is one of the most contested and normative legal systems because it is bound up in the racialized politics of national membership and sovereignty. Rather than victims of the political process, immigration agents are critical participants, both as an interest group themselves and as policy implementers whose decisions shape immigration-law-in-action. Agents say they are frustrated because politics "won't let us do our job," when a more sound conclusion is that their training programs are a mismatch for the phenomenon they purport to manage precisely because of the symbolic politics of immigration. That is, through political processes, the state has constructed immigration as a crime and security risk, institutionalized this version of the phenomenon, and created a training program that turns these state categories into agents' cognitive repertoires.[64] The state's police training program leaves agents woefully mistrained to deal with the lion's share of their work.

Agents' reduced sense of efficacy is characteristic of their cultural outlooks as police officers and not of the "formidable enforcement machinery" that is the US immigration enforcement system.[65] Immigration and Customs Enforcement deported over four million people between 2003 and 2016,[66] reflecting both a continuation of and a high point in the United States' long history of banishing noncitizens.[67] According to several of ICE's own "Enforcement and Removal Operations" reports, most people arrested by CBP agents at ports of entry or between them are "non-criminal immigration violators."[68] It is disturbing, but important, to remember that if agents were, as they say, "left alone" to carry out their work in the way they see fit, as they suggest they should be, the enforcement system would be more stringent than it already is.

All immigration agents contend with the gap between the fact and the fiction of immigration work, and they insist on its fiction because that is how their job makes sense. Understanding immigrants as potentially criminal, even when they are not obviously so, is a form of deliberate ignorance that facilitates agents' compliance with their policing mandates.[69] Indeed, the continuation of the US enforcement system as it exists today, as mirror of the criminal justice system, depends on agents going along with the state's version of immigration as a crime and security issue, despite their witnessing the humanitarian and economic underpinnings of the phenomenon firsthand. Going along is easier for some agents than for others.

Latina/o agents, especially those with close ties to immigrants, have a harder time accepting the false dichotomy that all immigrants are either criminals or "just illegals" who could be criminals. This is because it is harder to accept a generalization about a group when one has meaningful connections to that group. This is not to say that Latina/o agents are somehow immune to the identity-shifting force of becoming an immigration agent. Quite the opposite: Latina/o agents' acceptance of the state's definition of immigration puts them firmly on the path toward indifference and is a formidable example of institutional triumph over individual experience. In the next chapter we see how Latina/o agents contend with their own dissonance and others' antipathy when they grapple with the racialized implications of their work.

3

Between Caring Control
and Disinterested Professionalism

IMMIGRATION AND CUSTOMS ENFORCEMENT officer Ezequiel Jerez's assignment in the Criminal Alien Program meant that he spent most of his days
at the county jail, where I met him one weekday afternoon. The drab room
where we spoke must have been adjacent to intake holding cells because Officer Jerez's soft voice was often drowned out by the sound of slamming doors.
He spoke with a slight Spanish accent, evidence that he had learned English
in his teens when he started attending school in the United States. Before that,
Ezequiel had been schooled in Mexico, where he was born.

Officer Jerez stood out among his colleagues for his incisive reflections about
ICE officers' stringency. Within minutes, when most other agents were still reflecting on their pathway into the profession, Officer Jerez was describing his
philosophy on the job: "as a minority member of our community . . . I have the
opportunity to actually help that community." He wanted me to know that he
wasn't like the "rough riders" who "have this perspective where they enforce what
they believe needs to be enforced," signaling to the stubbornness that he found
so irritating about his colleagues. Instead, he saw himself as someone who had
"an opportunity . . . to help people understand how the whole removal proceedings work and inform them, you know, what are their legal options." He resented
that few officers shared his approach to the work. "Why do you think that is?"
I asked. "It's human nature, I think. We're always afraid of what's different. Our
own personal bias [affects] how we enforce the law."

The bias Officer Jerez disliked most was many of his colleagues' perception
that all immigrants were criminals. He knew that was not the case. In fact, he
explained, "there's two types of individuals . . . one, the criminal alien. That's
a criminal-minded individual who's going to rob you, kill you, and so on. The

other individual is the one who gets caught up in circumstances." Examples of "real criminals" were "rapists, child molesters, people that are coldblooded. . . . You turn your back, they'll kill you." The people caught in circumstances were those with charges like "domestic violence [where] things got out of hand" or those who "had a few drinks, got behind the wheel, got arrested for driving while intoxicated." Officer Jerez felt strongly that it was officers' responsibility to differentiate between these "two types of individuals."

While it was clear that Officer Jerez was committed to differentiating between "criminal aliens" and others, it was not immediately obvious what exactly he was doing to "help" people in his custody. When I asked him to explain, he told me, "I try to be as humane as possible, within the scope of my employment obviously." For Officer Jerez, being humane meant being courteous and thorough. It meant "informing" immigrants in his custody about the process and interfacing with their families in a respectful and empathetic way. What it did not mean was shirking the enforcement mission he was sworn to. "We still detain people, we still arrest people, we still remove people, but perhaps how we inform them, they can make better decisions, maybe have a positive outcome."

That positive outcome could be almost anything. It could be an appeased family member, who, after being informed by Officer Jerez, knew whether their loved ones had been deported or were in detention. The positive outcome could be a better understanding of the immigration system. Or it could even be a "criminal" being brought to tears because Officer Jerez caused them to reflect and "feel human again." This was his role, Officer Jerez explained. He could "have an impact" because he had the "ability to communicate with these people in their own language" and because he "understood the culture" and "their principles." This was important, he impressed on me, because "overall officers are not very humane."

This chapter examines how Latina/o agents make sense of their role vis-à-vis coethnic migrants in their custody. Some agents, like Ezequiel Jerez, see themselves as a humane alternative to harsh and callous colleagues, a benevolent presence in an otherwise repressive system. They argue that their ethnic background endows them with certain cultural and interactional skills, as well as Spanish-language abilities, that allow them to improve the qualitative character of the enforcement experience for certain deserving coethnics. To be clear, agents do not report using their discretionary power to halt an apprehension or deportation or to alter the legal consequences of a custodial encounter. Instead, they see themselves lightening an otherwise dark experience.

I use the term "caring control" to capture the oxymoronic character of Latina/o agents' purported humaneness. *Caring* refers to agents' reported efforts to improve the qualitative character of migrants' custodial experience through courteous gestures. Agents might adopt an affable persona with co-ethnics, signaling cultural familiarity through language and humor. They might also provide comfort items, like an extra blanket, clothes, or extra food. *Control* clarifies that Latina/o agents' courteous gestures do not disrupt the immigration system's punitive logics, nor do they alter the regulatory procedures agents are implementing. In fact, agents say that their ability to relate to migrants yields compliance benefits, as migrants are more likely to relax and follow the rules when agents are "nice" to them.

Latina/o agents' ability to deploy signals of cultural familiarity makes them more capable social control agents, allowing them to gain compliance through culturally informed compulsion. Caring control is thus a strategy of soft coercion that benefits both Latina/o agents and the state. By engaging in caring control Latina/o agents can feel good about their work, highlighting their civility relative to agents who are "not very humane," as Officer Jerez put it. At the same time, caring control benefits the state—the immigration system's procedures can continue uninterrupted, while its representative workforce can yield the government plausible deniability for its racialized policies and practices.

Not all Latina/o agents report engaging in caring control. Instead of using their racial/ethnic background to either improve coethnics' custodial experience or get compliance from them, some agents prefer "disinterested professionalism," a work approach that adheres to bureaucratic staples, like impartiality and procedural predictability. These agents say they treat everyone the same, no matter their background, and they are less willing to affirm that their racial/ethnic background endows them with certain abilities or responsibilities to coethnics in custody. While some of these agents simply cannot deploy the cultural and language skills that characterize caring control because they are later-generation Mexican Americans who are not fluent in Spanish, these distinct work approaches do not map neatly onto generational status. Many agents who preferred disinterested professionalism could but chose not to perform culturally informed courtesies because they felt it would compromise their authority.

Whether Latina/o agents engage in caring control or disinterested professionalism, it is the immigration state that most benefits from their labor. Some Latina/o agents may be willing and able to deploy their Spanish fluency and cultural repertoire to be more effective regulators, increasing the state's capacity to control coethnics. Some agents are unwilling or unable to do that, but their presence as Latinx people is still useful to the government in a symbolic sense. In both cases, the immigration state benefits from Latina/o agents' labor.

Caring Control: A Humane Approach

Agent Guillermo Bobadilla had tried to get his cousin Pablo to apply to the Border Patrol when they were both recently discharged military veterans. At the time, Agent Bobadilla was trying to get a technical degree at a community college, and Pablo was an unemployed job seeker. Agent Bobadilla remembered telling his cousin, "Pablo, man, you were in the Marines. . . . The Border Patrol is hiring. They pay pretty good." Pablo's answer was a clear no—he considered a job with the Border Patrol an affront to his racial/ethnic background and the broader Latina/o community. "I can't do that, man. I can't do that to my people." Agent Bobadilla was taken aback for a moment, taking his cousin's conviction as a jab against his own Latinoness. By the time he told me the story, though, he had become accustomed to this type of thing. Sitting back in his chair, with a posture somewhere between annoyance and exasperation, he explained,

> It's like, come on. I'm a realist. I can do the job because if I would've said I don't want this job . . . somebody else would be doing my job. . . . How is that person going to behave? Is that going to be someone who's racist . . . someone who mistreats people?

A "realist" who didn't see borders going anywhere, Agent Bobadilla reasoned that his presence in the Border Patrol was itself shielding immigrants from mistreatment and racism. Agent Bobadilla imagined himself actively preventing abuse by checking his colleagues if he ever saw something inappropriate. He said he had never personally witnessed any abuse, but he was privy to the rumors. "I heard there was this one guy who spit in some lady's face. I heard a Border Patrol agent did that. If he would've done it in front of me, I don't know."

At an earlier point in his career, Agent Bobadilla admitted that he would have been unable to stop something like that from happening. "When you're brand new, you don't want to say anything 'cause you're new." But he wasn't new anymore and felt he was "comfortable enough" to intervene. Agent Bobadilla clarified that he was speaking hypothetically, but if he ever saw abuse he would not stand idle. "I never saw an agent hitting an alien. But if I did, I would say, 'Look, you're done, man. I'm going to tell on you.'"

None of the agents I spoke with admitted to witnessing or engaging in the violence that has been shown to be a "systemic problem" in the Border Patrol.[1] They spoke in hypotheticals about abuse, admitted that violence happened in the past, or were willing to concede that it could still happen among a few "bad apples," but those were exceptions. It is possible, probable even, that agents were simply unwilling to admit to the existence of violence to an outsider. It is also possible that agents witnessed what outsiders would categorize as violence but did not recognize it as such themselves because they have normalized violence as regular police practice. The point is that in their telling, Latina/o agents offered the absence of violence as evidence that it was their presence that was preventing those "problematic things," as one agent put it.

Regardless of how Agent Bobadilla saw his work, his interactions with migrants occurred against the backdrop of his agency's history of racial violence and of all the politics of being a Latinx person in immigration enforcement. His cousin was not the only one who reminded Agent Bobadilla of his polemic position. Immigrants themselves often inquired about his ethnic background, sometimes with what seemed like genuine curiosity, other times with cutting judgment. In fact, this was such a common occurrence among Latina/o agents—immigrants asking them if they were Mexican and sometimes following with a "let me go"—that they accepted this was just part of the burden they would carry. Border Patrol agent Efren Blanco told me, "You can't take it personal. It's part of the job." But agents like Guillermo Bobadilla, who saw themselves as forces for good, resented the question. When immigrants reproached him for being a Mexican policing *his own*, he took the opportunity to remind them of the alternative.

> One time an alien said, he goes, "Oh, are you Mexican?" And I go, "Well, my parents are." He goes, "Are you a traitor?" And I go, "What do you prefer, that I arrest you and give you some food, give you water, or that a White guy arrests you and fucks you up?" And he goes no, "No, I prefer you, Officer."[2]

Even though Agent Bobadilla knew he would "treat people with respect," he still had to deal with their reprobation. In effect, Latina/o agents' racial/ethnic background served as an entry point—one of the rare entry points—for immigrants to assert their agency and challenge the power differentials between themselves and agents.

Bureaucrats hold most of the power in interactions with clients, or people making claims on the state. In this asymmetrical relationship, clients perform deservingness to trigger favorable discretion.[3] This relationship holds in immigration enforcement; agents expect immigrants to perform passivity, and when they perform defiance instead, they are seen as problems to be controlled.[4] In Agent Bobadilla's encounter above, intra-ethnic solidarity expectations are the basis for this person's defiance. By asking him "¿Eres traidor?" this person was essentially condemning Agent Bobadilla for not meeting expectations of solidarity that he is subject to as a Latinx person—in effect, he is calling him a bad Latino.

Instead of ignoring the person's reprobation, as many agents might do, Agent Bobadilla acknowledges the contradiction and seeks to reframe it. When he retorts by asking whether this person would prefer a Latino traitor who will give him food and water or a White agent who would be violent with him, Agent Bobadilla is weaving a complex web of rationalization. He is grappling with the gap between how he sees himself, as a force for good, and how others see him, as a race traitor, while also seeking to regain his authority by reminding the immigrant that he can choose how he wields his power. Facing this false choice, the person says, "No, I prefer you, Officer." Agent Bobadilla regains his authority and his own sense of goodness.

Whatever their altruistic ideas about the job, by joining the USBP and ICE Latina/o agents are signing up to enforce immigration laws that have long targeted Latinx people, and they are called race traitors for doing so.[5] For ICE officer Spencer Kay, that race-traitor dynamic is analogous to the reproach he gets as a Black man in law enforcement.[6] "I've been called Uncle Tom. . . . They've had people tell them that they were traitors to their race and other very derogatory things.'

These sanctions are not exactly shocking to Latina/o agents, who sometimes hold those very ideas themselves. For example, we met ICE officer Yesenia Siqueiros in chapter 1, where we learned that she resisted working in immigration enforcement in part because she did not want to chase "my own people." She eventually took a job in immigration out of necessity, as she put it, but years into the job she had come to understand her work in a different way. "I understand why we have control. It's not easy . . . but someone has to do it, and, in my view, you can do it with grace and with compassion." Officer Siqueiros saw herself as someone doing a hard job with benevolence, but others saw her differently, and they made it known.

When migrants asked Officer Siqueiros, "Aren't you Mexican?" she understood what they were doing—in her words, they were trying to take her on a "guilt trip" she just did not have time for. It was so predictable that Officer

Siqueiros was not even offended, just annoyed. When she decided to engage, she did so by reminding people that she was trying to improve things through respect:

> So people telling me that, I would ask them, "Am I being disrespectful to you?" "No, actually, you're not." I go, "Exactly. That is my way of contributing to this. Being professional, being respectful, letting you know how you broke the law."

In addition to emphasizing her respectfulness in dealing with migrants, Officer Siqueiros told me that people who tried to guilt her for her job simply did not understand Latina/o agents' role in immigration enforcement. She believed the government's efforts to hire agents who grew up on the border, a proxy for Mexican-origin people, was "a smart move" because they "understand the race."

> It's important to know what you're dealing with because if you don't, then everything looks suspicious, everything looks wrong, everything looks bad. So I think that was a smart move for them to do.

For Officer Siqueiros, "understanding the race" meant being able to decipher the local nuances, more effectively distinguishing between things or people that were suspicious and those that were normal. This skill, she thought, provided a major benefit not only to the government, but also to Latinx people who might avoid the unwarranted scrutiny of agents who simply did not know the ebbs and flows of Mexican border communities.

Respectful treatment is one benefit that Latina/o agents see themselves providing migrants; affability is another. Many Latina/o agents told me that they adopted an affable persona, signaling familiarity with [Mexican] immigrants, mostly through humor, but also through more subtle, lighthearted exchanges. For example, an agent might acknowledge a migrants' soccer jersey and playfully tell them that he roots for the rival team. Another agent might joke with migrants that they will be processed and removed quickly so they can get back to the task of crossing again, referencing what scholars have called the "cat and mouse game" of undocumented migration control.[7] Latina/o agents who reported adopting this affable persona told me that they do so to put migrants at ease.

Agent Mauricio Burgos was one of these agents. Agent Burgos was a tall, slim man with tawny brown skin, almond-shaped eyes, and thick, straight black hair. Aside from his height, he said he fit stereotypical notions of what it means to "look Mexican," an overgeneralized racial construction that boils down to being brown and having a visible trace of indigeneity.[8] Agent Burgos's look meant that he could not avoid the "Are you Mexican?" question, but unlike his colleagues who were annoyed, he used it as a platform to "break the ice."

> A lot of times . . . they go oh, "Officer, can I ask you a question?" "Yes, of course." "Are you Mexican?" "Well, of course. Don't you see the cactus on my forehead?!" And that makes them laugh. Sometimes just to break the ice, especially with little kids, I go, "We're going to walk to this truck." I go, "Who can tell me what it says here?" "US Border Patrol." I go, "No, Free Taxi—since you are lost, we're going to rescue you."

The "nopal en la frente" or "cactus on the forehead" metaphor is typically deployed as a pejorative to refer to someone who looks Mexican but is not culturally Mexican, whether because of assimilation or because of an assimilationist desire that pushes them to deny their culture. Here, Agent Burgos uses this metaphor somewhat ironically, since it is the type of thing that a coethnic might use to rebuke him for this job. By using this metaphor in a self-deprecating way, Agent Burgos turns it on its head. He is using it to "connect" and make people laugh, thereby putting them at ease. He thought this was especially important for the "little kids."

Spanish was a particularly critical mechanism that facilitated what Latina/o agents portrayed as lighthearted exchanges with the migrants in their custody. The importance of Spanish fluency to caring control can be appreciated in its presence and in its absence. Agent Donato Tobar was a later-generation Mexican American who did not grow up in an immigrant household and was not fluent in Spanish. He regretted that he simply did not have access to the interactional repertoire that his earlier-generation colleagues did. He saw how other agents talked to immigrants "to get their spirits up and just to make them laugh," but that was difficult for him to do. "It's harder because I can't carry that conversation." He still tried to "calm them down, especially if it's a kid," but he can't "go the extra mile to try to have a conversation because it's just hard."

In contrast to Agent Tobar, who lacked the cultural reference points and language to put immigrants at ease, Agent David Bustos felt he had a special ability to "bullshit" with immigrants because he spent his formative years in a working-class Mexican neighborhood. Not only could he "relate" to Mexican immigrants, but he was also himself a Mexican immigrant. He knew that coming into Border Patrol custody was not a lark; he appreciated that people were afraid of agents. It was that fear that he was trying to dispel by using "reverse psychology."

I use reverse psychology to say, "Hey, have you heard that joke?" And then I'll tell them the joke, and I'll make them laugh, and I leave them in the cell laughing. Then when it's time for food I say, "Let me see what the chef sent."

Note that Agent Bustos is talking about making people laugh in their cells, as he is feeding them things like bologna sandwiches, frozen burritos, crackers, and juice—standard fare in immigration and other prisons. Even though he argued that his relaxed and jokey persona put migrants at ease, he admitted that his lightheartedness could come off as flippancy.

We treat them well. . . . When they would arrive, I would give them their lunch. I would say "What's today? Tuesday? Today we have Chinese food, let's go." And then I would come back with Cup of Noodles, and I'd say, "Look, I told you it was Chinese food." And one time one person got mad, [and he told me] "Why are you making fun of us?" But I didn't even say anything. The rest of them that were in there told him, "Calm down, dude, Bustos is just doing that so that the day will go by faster, so we can laugh. He's not being malicious." Yeah, I had a good rapport with the guys.

Agent Bustos told me this story to convey his humorous approach for putting immigrants at ease. However, what this story also demonstrates is that for people who are going through the gauntlet that is the US crimmigration system, agents' jokes may feel like ridicule. That is exactly what Mary Bosworth and Gavin Slade found in their study of immigrant-staff interactions in a detention center in the UK. Staff thought they were engaging in light banter to establish rapport, while detainees interpreted their jokes as mockery and teasing.[9]

Indeed, many parts of what Latina/o agents consider humanitarianism will sound farcical to some readers. It is important to know, however, that these agents' ideas are not unusual among Latina/o law enforcers. Other scholars have found that helping "la gente" was a major motivator among Mexican American police officers who thought they would be "compassionate" and avoid excessive force against Latinx people.[10] Prospective Latina/o officers in Arizona also imagined themselves using Spanish and cultural knowledge to improve immigrant-police relationships.[11] There is also evidence that Latina/o police officers remain less cynical than their White counterparts once on the job,[12] meaning that they see the public as more deserving of help and are less likely to endorse the narrow crime-fighting orientation that produces violent policing.[13]

In fact, most police officers have altruistic ideas about their job,[14] but minoritized officers are particularly likely to believe that they can help their community through this work.[15] The Latina/o agents who engage in caring control appear to be part of a larger group of minoritized law enforcers who believe their presence will change policing for the better.

Such was the case for Agent Aaron Novar, who joined the Border Patrol in the 1990s as a "foothold" job while he sought a position in another federal agency. Agent Novar had a hard time adjusting to the Border Patrol because he was interested in crime control, but he mostly encountered economic migrants. Often, he would arrest people on his shift, take them to be processed and returned to Mexico, and then run into them again on the next shift.

> It took me a while to adjust to that, to be honest with you. [A friend] is the one that kept me in the patrol. I had about three years in when I started talking about jumping ship. I wanted to go back to the police force because that's all I know. . . . He's the one that told me, "Look, there's not very many Hispanics in the Border Patrol. Not very many of us. You can't effect change from outside. You have to be part of the change."

The idea that Agent Novar could be part of the "change" appealed to him. The Border Patrol was like the "wild west" when he started, and there were all sorts of "questionable things, like rumors of people getting beat up." I was curious to know why his friend's appeal to his Hispanic background made him stay, so I asked what it was like to be a Hispanic agent in that context:

> It's kind of hard, to be honest with you. Growing up here . . . you grow up anywhere in the Hispanic community, *la pinche migra*. You don't want to be part of that. Those guys are mean; those guys are evil. . . . You always live with that. . . . And this is what I tell the Hispanic officers. You don't want to come at it from an enforcement perspective. . . . You have to approach it from a humanitarian standpoint.

For Agent Novar, a humanitarian approach meant employing a lighter touch with people who came to the United States for work. It was those noncriminal, economic migrants who deserved humanitarianism, in his estimation. This demonstrates that the light touch that characterizes caring control is conditional—only migrants that agents consider deserving can benefit from this approach. As the agents we meet next make clear, that light touch is also functional. Caring control makes more compliant targets.

Caring Control: A Path to Compliance

In the ten years Officer Marta Vela had been with ICE, she had learned a great deal about how to interact with immigrants. She believed herself to be a skilled interviewer, an aptitude she had developed during her previous experience working at the port of entry. There, she had learned to "always be on top and fast," to go "back and forth, back and forth" with migrants until she was satisfied they were telling her the truth or she caught them in a lie. Marta was careful not to give "criminals" an inch because she felt they really knew how to manipulate agents and evade questions. But Marta would not be manipulated. She was so effective that colleagues would ask her to do their interviews when they were intimidated by "criminals." "They're like, 'Oh, shit, why don't you talk to them?'" And she did. Marta felt that, as a woman, her interviewing skills were particularly important because they helped her stay in control.

Marta had another side to her, though. She could also be empathetic, especially toward economic migrants, people who were "just coming to work . . . and trying to improve." She did not take satisfaction in deporting those migrants, she told me. Even though she still did it, she did it with a bit more tact. Instead of forcefulness, Marta used compassion to get cooperation:

> Some people are just crossing the border, and they're caught at the border. They've never been incarcerated; they've never done anything. They're not criminals. . . . They're afraid. So you have to know, differentiate, learn who you're going to be more stern with and who you're going to try to make them feel that you feel sorry for them or compassionate. So you can get some cooperation.

Marta's compassion toward economic migrants—however strategic—was rooted in her background. The child of immigrants, she criticized other Mexican Americans who did not speak Spanish. "They're very quote-unquote Americanized, and they're very, very brown." she sneered. "I perceive it as being ashamed. . . . It's a little bit embarrassing."

Even though she had a strong ethnic identity, she was certain that she could not have accomplished anything in Mexico, coming from a working-class background. She was grateful to have grown up in the United States and did not feel she owed Mexico anything. Multiple dynamics—her gender, her ethnic background, her parents' migration experience—factored into how Officer Vela differentiated between immigrants and how she treated them. Her compassion was reserved for the "noncriminals," a tool that she could use to get these migrants' cooperation.

By hiring locals and other Latina/o people who can communicate with migrants in Spanish, use common cultural reference points, and even translate their cultural knowledge for their non-Latina/o colleagues, the government increases its capacity to regulate Latinx migration.

For instance, Officer Lorenzo Delgado told me that what distinguishes a "very clever" agent from a less clever one is the ability to "identify what's the truth and what is a lie." Having grown up "in the ghetto," as he referred to his hometown on the US-Mexico border, meant that he was able to decipher cultural and local nuances in these communities. He used this knowledge to educate his colleagues, to the benefit of the state as a whole:

> When I train other officers in the field, I teach them about surroundings, what to look for. Gates, dogs, family members, you know. Mexicans are a very strong community, and we bond together, and we tend to protect our family. So I kind of let people know that not every individual you encounter in the field is going to be honest with you.

Officer Delgado's background is a benefit that accrues to his colleagues when he shares his cultural expertise with them. In this way, officers like Lorenzo Delgado serve as resources for other agents and ultimately increase the government's capacity to control Latinx communities.

Not all Latina/o agents see it as their responsibility to teach their colleagues how to do the job. Agent Zacarias Arambula was dismissive of his White colleagues' inability to strike the casual tone he located easily in his own background. At over six feet tall, with a burly frame and a voice that matched his physical appearance, Agent Arambula was hard to miss. In fact, he basically recruited himself into my study; he walked into the office where I was interviewing another agent and jokingly asked what we were discussing and why he wasn't part of the conversation. He was clearly a people person, so it is unsurprising that he described his interactions with immigrants as "laid back." But Agent Arambula's approach to work was not simply a function of his personality; he felt that it was due to his background. The way he talked about his interactions with migrants captures how Latinas/os use familiarity to gain compliance.

> I sit back and watch the way an American guero or White guy . . . [will] treat or interact with the alien people; [it] will be different. Then you'll get the Mexican guys that will interact with them like they're just talking with

somebody over a beer. As long as there's respect, as long as you treat them cool, they're cool. . . . If you talk to them like humans, you talk to them like men, they're going to abide by the rules and not run. . . . But then you get the robot come in, and "sientese, manos arriba," do this. Chill. Come on, man.

Agent Arambula thought of himself as a preferable alternative to a White agent, but not because he acknowledged that migrants saw White agents as the archetype of racial violence. Instead, he thought his background made him a more effective agent. Agent Arambula cringed at how White agents robotically issued commands, a sign of their cluelessness about how to talk to Latina/o immigrants. He thought the "Mexican guys" were much smoother, being able to interact with migrants with the casualness of a man having a beer with someone they know. If you could relate to immigrants in this way, Agent Arambula reasoned, they would abide by the rules.

Agent Arambula was effectively talking about racial/ethnic differences in what law enforcement refers to as officer presence, a concept in the use-of-force continuum.[16] All law enforcement officers are taught about the importance of officer presence, a hypermasculine construction of police authority that is supposed to inspire respect and compliance by merely existing.[17] Agent Arambula suggests that Latinos' cultural and Spanish fluency makes their officer presence particularly effective in interacting with coethnic migrants.

> The White guys, the Americans . . . their Spanish is "Sientete." [mocking wrong Spanish pronunciation of "sit"] They're all, I guess you could put it, they're all one-liners. Arnold Schwarzenegger. "Sit down. Look straight ahead." But that's the officer presence. If they instill fear, if they instill control that way, then the aliens are going to be like [raises hands as in retreat], you know? But you gotta come in and be, it's just like, "Quiúbole? [Mexican slang for "what's up?"] Where you from?" Talk to them. Baseball. Different types of officer presence. But I'll change real quick if I need to; I'll be that guy.

Note that officer presence, whether casual or robotic, is ultimately about control. According to Agent Arambula, White agents control migrants through one-liners that instill fear, while Latino agents can achieve control through casualness rooted in Spanish and cultural familiarity. All agents are seeking the same outcome—compliance—but they have distinct tools at their disposal, which they deploy based on their perceptions of safety and immigrant deservingness.

Other agents also notice their Latina/o colleagues' special ability to deploy culture and language in service of their control goals. For ICE officer Danilo del Rosario, a Filipino American man, it was language that was the key: "Hispanic American agents are more than capable because they know the language. You can be the biggest and toughest agent, but if you can't speak, you can't habla, you're done." Officer del Rosario spoke Spanish himself, a remnant of Spanish colonialism in the Philippines, where he grew up. As a result, he, too, could reap some of the rewards of his fluency. He said it was hard to communicate with detainees "if they don't like you," but because he spoke their language and "treated them like humans . . . they've actually thanked me." That Officer del Rosario emphasized Spanish is itself another reminder that Latina/o immigrants represent the archetype of illegality in US immigration enforcement.

Spanish facilitates understanding, but not exactly in the empathetic sense. Speaking Spanish lowers agents' threat perceptions because agents can decipher and read immigrants and stay in control. Agent Orlando Ortiz "saw the other side of not speaking the language" when he arrested a group from southern Mexico who spoke a dialect he did not understand.

> We've even dealt with people from Oaxaca that speak Mixteco. . . . That makes us feel kind of awkward. And I told them, "Hey, you know what, I understand that you guys speak another dialect, but when you're here with me, you speak Spanish." Because most of them, they do speak Spanish. But when they're there in the group, they'll start speaking Mixteco. And I said, "You know what? Respect me, and I'll respect you. Speak Spanish, and that way I know what you guys are doing. It's for your safety and my safety."

Immigration agents, like all police officers, are preoccupied with danger and officer safety.[18] Understanding what migrants are saying, in Spanish, means that Latina/o agents can relax, and in doing so, they can adopt a more casual stance with migrants they find unthreatening.

Even though Latina/o agents talk about their "humaneness" as altruism, the stories they describe demonstrate that caring control is conditional and functional. Agents embody the state's coercive power, and they can wield that power by cooperation or by force. Caring control is the "you catch more flies with honey than with vinegar" method of enforcement. It is a tool that some Latina/o agents can use to placate their targets and yield compliance when they find their targets deserving of that courtesy. Caring control is thus not a default or unqualified professional philosophy, but a restricted dispensation, a discretionary act that agents can offer or withhold based on their perceptions of safety and narrow judgments of migrants' deservingness.

Disinterested Professionalism

Border Patrol agent Pascual Trigueros's bearing was somewhere between cautious and standoffish. I had a hard time imagining him as a nurse, even though that is what he aspired to be as a child. The son of working-class Mexican immigrants, Agent Trigueros had served in the military before returning to the border town where he grew up. He then pursued a nursing degree that did not materialize. Life had gotten in the way, but he was pleasantly surprised at how good of a fit the Border Patrol had been for him. The camaraderie was his favorite part of the job. As a "naturally protective person," watching his partners' backs and "making sure that everybody comes home" at the end of the workday came easy. What was not effortless was dealing with people's misconceptions about his work. He felt the Border Patrol was "pigeonholed" as "just arresting people" when the job was much more complex. He was also a first responder, not just a cop. "I've seen people dehydrating. I've come across people . . . that have been abandoned by their smugglers, no water. They're like, 'Hey, do you have anything to eat?' I'm like, 'I have some of my lunch here if you want some.'"

Of course, criminals could get dehydrated and hungry too, so it was important to Agent Trigueros to "never judge a book by its cover," evidence of the manufactured ambiguity we learned about in the previous chapter. Agent Trigueros had to stay vigilant for the law enforcement part of the work; a complacent agent was an unsafe agent, and that was not going to be him. Between Agent Trigueros's intensity and his reservedness, I was not surprised when he told me he did not joke around with migrants, nor did he think it was helpful to do so. He admitted that, as a Latino, migrants sometimes acted familiar toward him. "They might feel that, I guess if you want to call it, relationship, because the Spanish would be a lot easier to communicate with me." But Agent Trigueros did not reciprocate that familiarity. Yes, he spoke Spanish, and he was the child of Mexican immigrants. However, his preferred work approach was rooted in neutrality: "I just treat everybody the same. Not friends—I'm not enemies; I'm not anything. I treat them professionally."

While many Latina/o agents use their language and cultural competencies to ease migrants' custodial experience and gain compliance from them, other agents reject that approach. Instead of caring control, agents like Pascual

Trigueros adopt a disinterested professionalism that adheres to basic bureau-cratic standards of neutrality and consistency across cases. In theory, this is a good thing, in that we want bureaucrats to be disinterested professionals who treat everyone with respect and uniformity. However, as Latina/o people who are working in the highly racialized organization that is the US immigration bureaucracy, these agents' disinterestedness negates the normative expecta-tions that migrants impose on them as coethnics.

Roberto Juarez's experience demonstrates this dynamic.

Border Patrol agent Juarez was Mexican on both sides of his family. But, unlike most of his Latina/o colleagues, whose phenotypes were as varied as the broader Latinx population, Roberto looked White. He had blue eyes and light brown hair, his skin perpetually flushed by the constant heat of the South-west borderlands, where he grew up and now worked. Because Roberto was a White-passing Latino, he could see firsthand that migrants interacted with the "White guys" differently than with the Latina/o agents. Migrants seemed to be more talkative with the Latinas/os, more willing to ask for things, a pattern that Agent Juarez found undesirable.

> I know oftentimes they might see me at first and say, "Oh, this is a White guy coming over here," but when I start talking to them . . . they'll quickly realize, hey, this guy's Spanish is pretty good. I think he's Mexican. [laughs] And once they figure that out, they kind of try to be a little more talkative and maybe even joke around saying, "Well, if you're Mexican, let me go. Come on, man." I'll quickly squash that.

Agent Juarez thought that reciprocating migrants' casualness would diminish his authority and relinquish his control. He explained, "If you let them joke around, then that's kind of a bad way of setting the tone. Because when you want them to do something, they might say, 'Well, is this guy joking with me, or is this guy being serious?'" Agent Juarez felt that his safety was contingent on him staying in control of the situation, and of migrants, so he stayed neutral, professional, and serious. Occasionally, but only when he was sure he was safe, Agent Juarez might explain to migrants, "I know exactly where you're coming from, but I have a job to do, and I'm going to do my job." He did that job in a professional and disinterested way.

The caring control approach that agents in the previous section articulated is qualitatively different from the disinterested professionalism that agents like Pascual Trigueros and Roberto Juarez performed. It is important to note, how-ever, that both work approaches are in service of the same basic goal: to stay in control so that agents can detain and process migrants who lack the state's permission to be in the country. Agents can take different approaches to maintaining their authority and achieving their goals. Some get the job done by being courteous and jokey; others get the job done by being neutral and straight-faced. What differentiates caring control from disinterested professionalism is a complex mélange of situation and agent-specific judgments about their safety and migrants' deservingness.

For Border Patrol agent Ramona Lanzo, her gender was the key factor in shaping her persona toward migrants. Agent Lanzo had never been a pushover, but she did not have any law enforcement experience before starting her work with the Border Patrol. The academy had been a major shock, especially given her prior experience in retail. Soon enough, she dropped her customer service mode and settled into the "strong personality" she had always had. Agent Lanzo told me that she always did her job "fairly" and "respectfully," but she also had to show migrants who was boss:

> As females . . . you can't be complacent and relaxed. . . . No, you have to take charge and you have to show them that you're the authority, you're there to perform your duties, and you're not gonna slack off. . . . I have a strong officer presence.

Agent Lanzo's insistence on being strong demonstrates that agents' social locations shape how they perform their authority. Women like Agent Lanzo who work in predominately male settings tend to compensate for their power deficits by following rules strictly, and sometimes even overperforming their authority. More generally, workers who lack power in an organizational hierarchy legitimize their presence by adhering strictly to the expectations set forth by their employers, something that can backfire as their reliance on rules may cause others to question their authority. Shannon Portillo calls this phenomenon the "paradox of rules," and it impacts women, minoritized bureaucrats, and younger officials in positions of authority in public administration.[19]

I was thinking about the paradox of rules when I engaged Officer Vela in a somewhat touchy conversation. I asked her why, if Latina/o agents told me that they were either neutral or humane, there was a common perception among border residents that they were actually more harsh than the non-Latina/o agents.[20] As a border resident herself, Officer Vela said she understood what people were talking about. Her theory was that those Latina/o agents were trying to avoid the impression that they would give "preferential treatment" to other Latinas/os.

I think those are officers . . . they either want to prove their authority . . . or they're so afraid of showing preferential treatment to their own race that they don't want to be perceived as weak or to do that. I think that's the major one. They don't want to be perceived as "everybody else I'm strict [with] but when it comes to them, I'll give [them] a break" kind of situation. So I think it was that.

Officer Vela went on, surmising that some agents' inability to handle their colleagues' or employer's perception that they could be biased toward coethnics led them to overcorrect. They either were more severe or went completely blank, adopting a dry persona that made them look worse than they were. "Some people just don't know how to deal," Officer Vela explained.

Taking a position on whether Latina/o agents are objectively harsher or whether their disinterested professionalism is perceived as such by coethnics is beyond the scope of my study. The coethnic migrants who are subject to Latina/o and other agents' authority—not agents themselves—are the best resource to answer this question. What we do know is that racial minorities expect a higher level of empathy from minoritized bureaucrats than from Whites,[21] and they have higher expectations for respectful treatment from minority law enforcement officers.[22] Institutional boundaries, as well as professional socialization, limit the extent to which minority bureaucrats can or want to meet these expectations, which means that minority bureaucrats are often condemned for the same behavior that is considered normative for Whites.[23] These distinct expectations remind us that racialized emotional labor is a real but "unseen burden" among minoritized bureaucrats in various policy fields.[24]

Thus, it is possible that Latina/o agents' disinterested professionalism may be read as harshness because they are not meeting the normative expectations that migrants impose on them. However, it is also possible that they are objectively harsher. That is what Manolo Gil told me when I posed the same question to him that I asked Marta Vela. Why, if agents say they are humane or disinterested, is there a common perception among coethnics that they are harsher than non-Latinas/os? Officer Gil said this question was of "deep interest" to him, both as an ICE officer and as someone who was himself born in Mexico.

I think that the general layperson would probably think that those with a Latino background, Hispanic heritage, would probably be easier on the illegal aliens that are of Hispanic heritage. But I have found that to be actually the opposite. I really think they're tougher, they're more difficult. . . .

You know part of it, part of it is you speak the lingo, you speak the language, so you can actually get inside.

What Officer Gil is saying is that yes, Latina/o agents can be "tougher" because their cultural and language familiarity can help them get deeper than agents from other backgrounds can get. He is suggesting that Latinas/os play an important role in policing coethnics, precisely because their background makes them more effective.

Caring control and disinterested professionalism are distinct sides of the same coin—they are both windows into how Latina/o agents grapple with and incorporate race/ethnicity into their professional role. Agents who adopt a caring control approach are more willing and perhaps able to deploy an affable persona and cultural competencies at work, while those who adopt a disinterested professionalism either cannot or prefer not to. While there are some agent characteristics that cluster in each approach, these should not be thought of as cut-and-dry typologies.[25] Rather, caring control and disinterested professionalism are better understood as contingent options that can be deployed based on various agent-level social locations (e.g., gender, generational status, time on the job), agents' evaluations of their level of control over the people in their custody, and their moral judgments of migrants' deservingness.

For instance, the Latina Border Patrol agents I spoke to adopted a disinterested professionalism as their default approach. This is so, they explained, because adopting the relaxed, affable persona that often characterizes caring control may put their already-precarious authority at risk. As women in law enforcement, they cannot afford to "joke around" with migrants whom they perceive as potentially dangerous, nor can they afford to send the wrong message to their colleagues who may already see them as physically weaker and sometimes less mentally and emotionally tough. The caveat here is that the Latina Border Patrol agents I interviewed did report engaging in the practices I call caring control vis-à-vis women and children. Latinas reported that they provided comfort items or extra or better food, or engaged in small gestures that they believed brought some solace to the families in their custody. Therefore, the same agent who engages in disinterested professionalism as a matter of course could also deploy caring control based on agent, migrant, and situational factors, but only when agents feel they are safe and in control.

It is important to clarify that caring control and disinterested professionalism do not fall neatly along Latina/o generational lines either. There is indeed an element of caring control—the deployment of cultural competencies in Spanish—that may be unavailable to later-generation Latinas/os. And—to the extent that caring control helps ease agents' insecurities about their job and that earlier-generation agents may have more insecurities—it is reasonable to expect that earlier-generation Latinas/os may be more likely to engage in caring control than in disinterested professionalism. However, I spoke to later-generation Mexican Americans, like Agent Tobar, who could not speak Spanish, but engaged in caring control and tied that "humaneness" to their racial/ethnic background. I also spoke to children of Mexican immigrants like Agent Trigueros who chose to "treat everybody the same," even though he could speak Spanish. Fleshing out the impact of Latinas/os' generational status on their approach to work is an important question ripe for continued study. Since three-quarters of the Latina/o agents I interviewed were either immigrants themselves (first generation) or children of immigrants (second generation) I cannot draw strong generational conclusions myself but encourage others to continue examining this question.

I want to be very clear that I am not treating caring control and disinterested professionalism as reliable indicators of agents' behaviors on the job, because agents have an incentive to frame themselves as disinterested or humane.[26] Still, I do want to mention that there are some indications that the practices I call "caring control" may in fact exist. For example, Amada Armenta and I found evidence of these "nice" immigration agents, who give an extra juice box, or an extra blanket, in the border-crossing narratives of Mexican immigrants.[27] Also, in Heide Castañeda's book on mixed-status families, she cites a young man named Michael who explained that he wanted to become a Border Patrol agent to be like the agent who was "super nice" to his mother when she was in detention. The agent snuck his mother extra food, and Michael thought he could be like that, an agent who had "compassion" and "understanding" because of his background.[28] Josiah Heyman, who conducted interviews and observations with Mexican American immigration agents, found that they enforced the law with "tact and kindness" or "cold aggressiveness" based on whether agents thought immigrants were poor and peaceable or dangerous and immoral.[29] Procedural justice scholars who are interested in the relationship between receiving fair and respectful treatment from legal authorities and people's perceptions of the legitimacy of law may be interested in further researching these patterns.[30]

Of course, it is also possible that instead of improving migrants' experiences with the state, Latina/o agents may degrade these experiences by being harsher than non-Latina/o colleagues to prove their solidarity to coworkers or to prove their commitment to the enterprise of immigration control. That I did not document this pattern does not mean it does not exist, but possibly rather that agents were unwilling to tell me about it. Another possibility is that the agents who adopt the neutral stance of disinterested professionalism may not meet the normative expectations that migrants have for them, like the expectation that Latinas/os may be more empathetic given their (presumed) commonalities. Their neutrality, a staple of bureaucratic rationality, could be read not as a matter of professionalism, but as an affront to the expectations imposed on them. All of these are questions ripe for more research.

Finally, some readers may understand caring control as evidence, or at least a budding possibility of it, that diversifying a police force like the US immigration system may make it more humane. My position is more nuanced. What Latina/o agents are doing when they engage in caring control is using their discretion to be "nice," within a context of systemic violence and discrimination. Therefore, far from evidence of change in the US immigration bureaucracy, caring control is a window into the bureaucratic and cultural processes that sustain indifference in racialized organizations, regardless of what their workforces look like.[31] Caring control is Latinas/os' "racial task," an example of the "ideological, interactional, and physical labor racial minorities perform in mostly White work settings" that perpetuate rather than disrupt racial hierarchies.[32] It is also an example of how police weaponize the language of empathy to maintain state power, ultimately thwarting resistance and critique and mollifying people into voluntary compliance.[33]

Whether nicely, neutrally, or harshly, what we do know is that Latina/o agents are doing the job. Surely anyone would prefer to interact with a respectful and thorough legal authority than with a rude one. Intuition and an entire literature on procedural justice has told us as much.[34] However, we should not think about caring control or disinterested professionalism as fundamentally different from a harsher work approach. Whether with *mano suavo* or *mano dura*, as Greg Prieto put it, Latina/o agents do their work—they are apprehending, detaining, and deporting coethnics and anyone else subject to their authority.[35] How they deal with the morally ambiguous situations they run into during the course of their work is the subject of the next chapter. There we will see how agents of all backgrounds rely on denial to turn away from the human suffering they witness and help reproduce by "just doing the job."

4

Denying Responsibility

THERE HAD NEVER BEEN A DULL MOMENT in Border Patrol agent Mauricio Burgos's thirty-year career, but his administrative post was different from his time in the field. Those times could be unpredictable, ranging from "mundane to very exciting." He was happy to tell me his "war stories," like the night he responded to a triggered motion sensor on an ominous desert night, only to find that a wayward cow had been responsible for the alert. The adrenaline rush that came with arresting people who were carrying drug bundles was like nothing else, and his experience trying to grab as many "bodies" as possible during the bonsai runs of the 1990s was something he would never forget. It was in the context of this conversation that Agent Burgos told me a story that captured a different side of his work. This story was neither mundane nor exciting—it was something else entirely.

"It was during the winter, and I was tracking a group of four. I could tell there were a couple kids in the group." Agent Burgos radioed his supervisor, who told him someone would give him a hand as soon as the shift changed. Fine, he thought, "I'll stay on them." He tracked the group, following their footprints for three hours until they seemed to stop. He got out of his truck and there they were, a family of four just two miles from the nearest highway. They had almost made it. Agent Burgos remembers being taken aback by how old the man looked.

> I remember a man, his wife, and his two kids. And the man, I honestly thought he was the grandfather, the father of the lady. But that was her husband. . . . He looks like he's sixty. He was maybe forty-two or forty-three. So I knew that he must've had a rough life.

Agent Burgos started his requisite apprehension interview, asking the father for his biographical details. The man wanted to explain himself.

The thing is, there is nothing for us in Mexico. Only here [in the United States] are we able to survive with work. Look, Officer, if you let us go, no one will know, no one is here for miles and miles; there is no one.

Agent Burgos told the father that he could not let them go, but the man insisted. His effort to differentiate himself from "criminals" conveyed his understanding of how the United States perceives and treats undocumented immigrants. "I know that you can do it. Look, we are not bad; we are not criminals. I have always been an honest person." Again, Agent Burgos resisted the ask. What happened next took Agent Burgos by surprise, the memory or the task of retelling it producing a physical response. He sucked his teeth and shook his head ever so slightly as he continued:

He gets on his knees, and he begs. And his kids started crying. I go, "Man," for him to actually [pause] 'cause you know, I know how Mexicans . . . the machismo is something that especially in front of your kids—you never beg in front of your kids. You never do that. And for him to be doing that. "Please . . ."

Again, Agent Burgos resisted, this time reminding the father of his professional responsibility, as well as the risk to his employment. "Sir, I can't do that. You are not here legally, and I took an oath, and even if no one knows besides you, me, and your family, I will know, and I cannot do that. It is against the law, and I would lose my job." The man continued pleading: "But I will not say anything." Agent Burgos finally says, "This is against the law, and I cannot do it. You say you are an honest man, and I want to think and believe and demonstrate that I too have honor." The man got up, his entire family now crying. Agent Burgos continued taking their information so that they could be transported to the processing unit and then returned to Mexico.

That story stuck with Agent Burgos for many years. Yes, he told me, a lot of times "they plead with you" and communicate "we didn't have enough; the kids don't have enough." He believed them; he was not blind to the inequalities between Mexico and the United States. He sometimes felt bad, could sympathize, empathize even, knowing that if he were in the father's shoes, he would also try to do the same thing. But those acknowledgments could only go so far. Neither the scarcity that had pushed this family to trek the Sonoran Desert nor Agent Burgos's recognition of their plight could overcome the significance of law or Agent Burgos's role in enforcing it. "What do you do?" he wondered aloud. "A lot of people see us as villains."

This chapter is about how immigration agents reconcile moments of moral ambiguity in their work. By moral ambiguity I mean specific experiences where agents were uncertain about the rightness of their actions or where they were aware that outsiders would see their actions as wrong, even if legal. The practice of immigration control is replete with such moral ambiguities,[1] stories like Agent Burgos's where the criminal alien archetypes that undergird agents' sense of purpose are missing, replaced by people whose humanity agents have trouble repudiating. Moral ambiguity can produce emotions that run counter to agents' exclusionary mission.

I use emotion as an analytical tool to uncover the affective and symbolic landscape of these instances of moral ambiguity.[2] Immigration control is often presented, both by agents and by politicians, as a self-evident and rational matter of law when it is actually a contested normative space where the racial and moralized conceptions of the *national us* and *foreign them* are challenged and reified. Focusing on emotion opens that normative space up for analysis.

Many readers may be skeptical about the authenticity of agents' emotional expressions and of the affective dimension of the stories they recounted to me. That skepticism is well founded. I have written about how immigration agents' emotional displays can be strategic legitimation narratives that are functional both for agents and for the state, an issue I return to in the next chapter. Nevertheless, focusing on the authenticity of emotion is a distraction from the broader point of my analysis: agents figure out a way to resolve moral ambiguities and comply with their mandates.[3] By demonstrating how agents struggle with what we might call "moral emotions" like sympathy, guilt, and shame—whether they feel them or are aware that others expect them to feel them—I reveal how agents resolve the most loaded aspects of their work.[4]

When agents are faced with situations of moral ambiguity they turn to denial. Denial is commonly understood as a refusal to admit the truth or to accept some unpleasant reality, but this is not only a psychological response to discomfort. The sociology of denial is concerned with how collective, organized, and official forms of denial maintain structural inequalities and protect perpetuators and witnesses from accountability for atrocities and other harmful acts.[5] Organizations, like the US immigration bureaucracy, invest a great deal of resources in elaborate myths and ideologies that justify their existence and give their employees license to do harm.[6] In this chapter we see how agents use denial to look away from human suffering and perform coercion on behalf of the state.

Agents engage in three forms of denial: they *deny responsibility* by relying on the power and morality of law; they *deny the harm* of immigration control by recasting their work as helping, or at least not hurting immigrants; and they *deny the victim* by implicating immigrants in their own suffering.[7] These strategies allow agents to recalibrate incongruous emotions and accept their role as witnesses, if not architects, of human suffering.

These denial strategies are gendered and racialized. Latina/o agents and other agents of color tend to *deny responsibility* and *deny harm*, while White agents are most likely to *deny the victims* of immigration control. These patterns reveal that race/ethnicity and gender shape the extent to which agents evaluate their work as immoral or at least ethically dubious, as well as how they reconcile their role vis-à-vis the human suffering they witness and produce as frontline policy implementers.

Notwithstanding the important group-level distinctions that I will elaborate below, at the end of the day, all the agents I interviewed were committed to their work. When I talk about denial, I do not mean to frame agents as naive or reluctant participants in immigration enforcement. They were mostly proud of their work, but especially so when they could arrest and deport the "bad guys." The stories of moral ambiguity that agents recounted can thus be understood as moments that most challenge their moral authority because the bad guy that is the requisite foil to their good guy role was missing. The denial strategies we will see in this chapter are a window into the rationalizations that allow agents to face, then look away from, some of the most atrocious consequences of immigration law, like the state-sanctioned separation of families and the rejection of the needy.

Denying Responsibility: "Nothing I Can Do"

OFFICER HUGH: Yeah. That was a tough one. Why do you want to end on that kind of note?

IRENE: I don't want to end on that kind of note; I really don't.

OFFICER HUGH: And now I feel ashamed that happened. I want you to redact that part.

IRENE: Okay. You want me to redact that story?

OFFICER HUGH: I don't even want that. I'm ashamed. You asked me a question, but now thinking about it, I'm thinking, wow, I think we could've did better than that. . . . Once they ran it up their chain of command, it's out of my hands. But if they had called us and said this is the situation, I could've said, "Hey, let's just process them as a family unit." You know? Simple as that. But you know, that was a person that was doing their job.

Immigration and Customs Enforcement deportation officer Sam Hugh grew visibly upset, his baritone voice coming down to almost a whisper as he shifted in his seat in the small government office where we sat for the interview. He had met me outside the building hours earlier. When I saw him walking toward me, a tall Black man wearing black slacks and a charcoal-gray polo, I almost didn't recognize him as my interviewee—he was dressed more like a golfer than a deportation officer. Officer Hugh and I made the requisite small talk about the beautiful spring day we were leaving behind as he escorted me past metal detectors, up a rickety elevator, and through a maze of hallways that all seemed to end in the same gray metal door. Each door easily submitted to his badge but protested loudly as it shut behind us.

The interview had been going well. Conversation flowed naturally to the point where I asked him to recount a memorable experience or person he encountered during his career. Officer Hugh first told me about the time he ran into a former detainee out in public. The man had thanked him for showing his wife kindness while she was in ICE detention. Officer Hugh admitted that he didn't remember the man or his wife, but he told the story with pride as it portrayed him the way he saw himself: as someone who does a difficult job in a fair and humane way and, sometimes, even goes out of his way to provide momentary comfort to people in need. The second memorable story was the exact opposite. It involved a young child and a grandmother—it had been Officer Hugh's job to pry the child from the woman as they clung to each other, sobbing and screaming. "I can still see the grandmother," he said as we locked eyes for too long. I sensed that he expected me to say something comforting, or at least that is what the situation called for. Something like, "Well, you did your best," but all I could mutter was "I can't imagine. My mom is watching my three-year-old right now." "Yeah," Officer Hugh interrupted, composing himself. "That was a tough one."

Bureaucracies like the US immigration system are characterized by a hierarchical authority structure, specialized roles and procedures, and a proliferation of rules that are supposed to be implemented dispassionately by trained officials.[8] The compartmentalization of roles and responsibilities allows any one bureaucrat to distance themself from their role in the harm done by certain policies. In effect, bureaucratic rationality sets the stage for everyday people to engage in harmful actions on behalf of the state.[9] This is what we see in the case of Officer Hugh and the other immigration agents we meet in this chapter.

Officer Hugh said his instinct was to keep the child and grandmother together, instead of processing the child as an unaccompanied minor. Another agent also appealed with him not to conduct the separation. "I'll never forget, a female officer who was working on the case, she pleaded with us, 'Is there a way that you can not do this?'" But Officer Hugh felt that it was not his place to reverse course. If he had been involved earlier in the process, he lamented, then he would have done something differently. But someone else, someone earlier and perhaps higher up in the chain of command, had already decided how this case would go. "At that point, nothing I can do. Like, hey, it's an unaccompanied kid." Officer Hugh's task was to take the child from the grandmother so the bureaucratic process could continue, and he did it because it was his job.

It is common for street-level bureaucrats to limit their responsibility for unfavorable outcomes by denying discretion and imposing certain restrictions on their own power.[10] The image of the obstinate bureaucrat is a major part of the American imagination—the unmoved DMV agent serving as the epitome of the rule-bound government employee. Most everyone who has objected to some unfair outcome, a rule that seems arbitrary or otherwise amiss, has been met with a dreaded "I don't make the rules" or "I'm just doing my job." In this way, immigration agents like Officer Hugh are one case in a larger universe of policy implementers who use rules and regulations to distance themselves from work actions when those actions bring them criticism from the public.[11]

The issue with that mundane distancing strategy of putting restrictions on their own power is that immigration agents' job is particularly coercive and morally ambiguous.[12] When Border Patrol agents stop people from entering the United States—especially when they are fleeing poverty, persecution, war, or environmental disasters—they may be following the law, but they must contend with the human face of global inequality. When deportation officers enter a community to remove a noncitizen, they may be acting on behalf of the government, but they are also separating them from their loved ones and the place they call home. For Officer Hugh, the shame he communicated to me was due to the wrenching act of physically separating the child from their grandmother, a coercive act of state power and violence, that even if "legal" in the black-and-white sense did not feel morally "right."[13]

Immigration agents are subject to what Arlie Hochschild called "feeling rules" for the profession, or norms for what emotions are considered appropriate to express.[14] In policing, those rules are hypermasculine. Police officers are trained to be assertive, even aggressive, to express distance and even rightful anger, to take control and stay in control.[15] Rather than sympathy or shame, rationalities like suspicion, disbelief, and ignorance are more familiar to immigration agents and are more well aligned with their training.[16] Immigration and Customs Enforcement officer Danilo del Rosario, whom we met in chapter 2, confirmed as much.

> Being in this type of profession, it's a type A, macho. A lot of these guys don't have any feelings. [laughs] They don't. They don't. And if you exhibit any type of feeling, you will be looked down upon, and kind of marginalized, so to speak. So yeah, we keep our feelings in check, and we're very objective.

Given these expectations, what are immigration agents to do with emotions that are incongruous with the hypermasculine feeling rules of their profession? What are they to do when, as ICE officer Magi Garza put it, their "humane side comes out" during an inherently coercive act like deportation or a border arrest? Officer Garza has a strategy to deal with the self-doubt—she "reverts back to what's legal." If a person has broken immigration law and her job is to enforce law, then she is doing the right thing by deporting them.

> There has been times that we have deported—it can be males or females— doesn't matter—just getting them out when they have family here. So that humane side comes out. Like, "Oh, se te ponen chinitos" [gets goosebumps]. Like, "Oh, what am I doing?" But then again, you revert back to "Okay, what's legal?" You know. It's legal or illegal? Okay, you know what? If it's something not legal, that's what we're enforcing. And that's how you try to look at it.

The implicit assumption in Officer Garza's rationalization is that law is moral, which is a common misconception. The United States is famous for committing *legal immoralities*, like the mass removal of indigenous people from their lands, the internment of Japanese people during World War II, and perhaps the epitome of a legal immorality—chattel slavery. Most people would recognize that even if these government actions were legal, they were not moral as in right. Of course, agents would not put immigration control in the same category with chattel slavery, internment, or indigenous people's displacement. Agents would remind us of the importance of national sovereignty, security, and respect for law, and insist that what is legal is what is right. Conflating legality with morality is how agents can face the human suffering produced by immigration law and retain a sense of rightness. Nevertheless, that strategy of leaning into the inherent morality of law can prove inadequate sometimes.

That is why, despite Officer Magi Garza's best efforts, sometimes her emotions got the best of her. She told me about one such time.

> I always remembered this one that I didn't, I just didn't feel—actually, I cried that time. We went after a person that it was a final order. His case was done. It was just early in the morning, and it's just, oh, it's just like [pauses] the kids were getting ready to go to school. So the family cried, and [her voice breaks with emotion] it's just like [makes ugh sound]. So that was hard. And he even cried. But he knew that his case was done. And he was like, "I just want the best for my kids." . . . I don't know what happened to him.

I asked Agent Garza if she had cried in front of her colleagues, during the deportation. She scoffed at the thought. "Not in front of them, of course." She told me she cried in the car, while she was transporting the man. "He was sitting in the back. He didn't see me. I just tried to, you know, be as normal as possible. But it did get to me." I asked what it was about the work or about herself that had produced this level of emotion. She wasn't sure but knew that she wasn't the only one of her colleagues to have been overcome by emotion at one point or another. It might vary based on "level of sensitivity," she surmised. She also thought that perhaps her emotion was gendered. "Maybe like as a female, maybe you feel more; I don't know." But at the end of the day, all she could do was "put it in balance" and remind herself "this is your job; this is part of your job. . . . You're just doing what's legal."

The stories of moral ambiguity agents told me almost always feature women, children, or families. The gendered aspect of these stories is no surprise since women and children leverage the most serious threats to the legitimacy of contemporary immigration control systems in the United States and abroad.[17] In fact, these stories are racialized and gendered on both sides of the bureaucratic encounter. Latina/o agents told me mostly stories of children and of the care work they engage in or felt compelled to engage in to cope with their uncomfortable feelings. Latina agents were particularly likely to retell stories that featured them working through the ambiguities of "caring" for unaccompanied children.[18]

Agents denied their responsibility for the particularly contemptible practice of detaining—or incarcerating—children by shifting the blame to their
parents. Border Patrol agent Camila Sarto demonstrates.

> Last year . . . we were having all these kids come in from Honduras and
> Guatemala. And we had a lot of unaccompanied children. And I had a little
> girl that was my daughter's age, like four. And she grabbed me from the leg.
> And she told me, "I'm afraid. Can you be my mom?" And I was like, oh my
> God, you know? It brought back memories of my kid. . . . As an agent, I had
> to take a break and be like, "I'll be right back." That's tough.

Agent Sarto had to take a moment to compose herself, and in reflecting she
concluded that the (ir)responsible party was the child's parent. She remembered thinking, "How can a parent send their child alone?" Another Latina
Border Patrol agent, Ramona Lanzo, had a similar reaction to a little girl from
El Salvador who had this "tremendous love and energy." Agent Lanzo remembers feeling conflicted, feeling the urge to "keep her," while also feeling a
righteous anger against her parents for sending her to the United States with
a stranger, a strange man for that matter. "How do you let a child go through
this?" she thought aloud. "I couldn't believe her parents would just—," she
trailed off. The gendered aspect of these stories reminds us that emotional
performances (or lack thereof) are shaped not only by institutional arrangements, but also by broader racial and gender schemas and expectations.[19]

Agents' sympathy for immigrants is limited, both by their commitment to
enforcing the law and by their inability to truly empathize with immigrants. Sympathy is about feeling sorry for someone else's situation, while empathy is about
putting oneself in another's position.[20] Agents Sarto and Lanzo struggle to
achieve true empathy with migrants, especially when it comes to children. In
moments of ambiguity that feature children, agents become particularly judgmental and make parents (ir)responsible for the inequalities and limited options
that pushed them into the dire situation of making claims on the US immigration state. For example, ICE officer Leon Camargo told me about a woman who
was caught trying to enter the United States with fraudulent documents.

Officer Camargo had been on temporary assignment at the port of entry
when a primary officer sent this woman to secondary inspection. It was there
that Officer Camargo learned that the woman had been previously deported
by ICE and was trying to come back into the country to be reunited with her
children. After her deportation, a relative had taken informal custody of them,
but that person could no longer care for kids.

The woman pleaded with Officer Camargo to please let her in, to look the other way, to pretend like the documents were real. He remembered her appeal: "I just need to get across. My kids are there. I left them with a *tia* [aunt], but she can't take care of them anymore." Agent Camargo felt sorry for the woman; he remembered she was "bawling" and thought, "I wish I could help." Yet, at the same time, he could not understand her choices. He told me that as a father, he couldn't fathom putting his kids through that. He remembered thinking, "How could you leave your kids like that? I don't understand. You have to bite your tongue."[21]

When I asked Agent Camargo, "What do you do in that case?" he asserted matter-of-factly, "You do nothing. The law says you gotta go back, [so] you gotta go back." The law was clear, he reasoned, even if the woman's desperation was hard to witness. In the end, Agent Camargo took the woman's tragedy as evidence of the difficulty of his job. "Those are the hard things we have to go through. . . . You know? 'Cause they're human. They're human. It is what it is."

Even when it is not children who are being detained or deported, they feature prominently in agents' stories of moral ambiguity. Officer Clementina Lardin told me a story about a man who had an outstanding order of deportation because he missed his court date. It so happened that ICE showed up at his house during family dinner.

> The grandma lived there, and the kids, the mom, the dad. We came knocking on the door, and they were so polite, and we came in, and we were like, "We're looking for the dad." And he was like, "Yes, I haven't appeared," and they're like, "Okay, we're going to deport you." . . . And he's like, crying; the kids are crying; the wife's crying; the grandma's crying. And we're just kind of like, "Oh my goodness." And then they wanted to go into a prayer. And they gather in a circle, and they start praying right before we were like—we felt sorry for the little kids because the little kids are like, "Don't take my dad."

Officer Lardin told me, "Maybe for a few days, I felt bad," but like her colleagues, she did not see a role for herself in the family's misfortune. Her sympathy had a certain distance and was tinged with apathy about her role in the whole matter. She was simply following directions from someone else, trying to find the people who were on a list that she had been handed. She explained, "It's just kind of like one of those things like what can you do? They're on our list,[22] and you have to go get them."

Agents who deny responsibility are framing themselves as subjects of an authority more potent than they are. The authority is most often the law, but it can also be the list of names, the agent who made decisions before then, the supervisor, and so on. As bureaucrats, these agents are indicating constraints on their discretion, but also trying to generate sympathy for themselves by pointing the finger elsewhere.[23] Note that agents are not justifying their actions, but instead they are explaining themselves. This distinction between explanation and justification is key to understanding immigration agents' denial strategies.

According to Marvin Scott and Stanford Lyman, explanations are accounts where the actor admits the action committed is bad or wrong, but they deny their responsibility.[24] Justifications are the opposite; these are accounts where actors accept the responsibility for the behavior in question but deny its pejorative connotation. The Latina/c agents I spoke to are prone to explain and excuse their work actions, where their White colleagues justify them. In fact, all the agents who told me stories where they appeared powerless to the rules and laws were either Latinas or men of color. The agents we meet next are also Latina/o, and they are also explaining, not justifying, their actions. This time, they are not relying on rules but on a strategy of redefinition. Agents do not appear as powerless in the face of another authority when they deny harm; instead they see themselves as helping immigrants through their work or at least not really hurting them.

Denying Harm:
"It's Just They're Being Held Back a Little Bit"

Border Patrol agent Wilfredo Escarra was surprised by the surge of guilt he felt the first time he arrested someone. It was early on in his career. He had just left the Field Training Unit, the last stage of on-the-job training that agents get before they go out on their own. Agent Escarra had made a bet with his classmates that he would be the first one to apprehend someone on his own, and he won. Agent Escarra remembered feeling "excited" about his first solo arrest, a rite of passage he had beat his peers to. "But then, later on, I was like 'Oh man.' I felt horrible about it."

Agent Escarra's guilt was not about the arrestee himself, but about his own family and ethnic background. At home that evening he had the realization that, "Oh my God, these are my people, even though I'm American, born in the United States." Agent Escarra explained that his parents had crossed the border without documentation too. "If it wasn't for them getting away, I would probably not be here. So it was difficult for me." When faced with that uncomfortable realization, the difficulty of the job given his own background, Agent Escarra found that it helped to put things in perspective. He told himself that Border Patrol arrests are merely a setback for immigrants, not the end of the world.

> They're probably going to try again. Just because they were apprehended right now doesn't mean they're not going to try again. It's not the end of the world for them. I didn't crush their dreams. It's just they're being held back a little bit.

Agent Escarra also reminded himself that he wasn't harming people or "doing anything bad to them." He was simply taking them back to the station and then "back to their country," where they could try again later and "probably get away."

Agent Escarra does not frame himself as a powerless implementer of the law that causes immigrant suffering; instead he seeks to deny or at least minimize the suffering itself. Denial of harm is the second strategy that agents deploy in the face of moral ambiguity. This strategy has two manifestations: agents *downplay* the very real implications of being arrested and deported, or they *recast* their work as helping immigrants. Agent Escarra downplays the gravity of Border Patrol arrests, while ICE officer Lorenzo Delgado recasts the case work he does during the course of a deportation as a service to immigrants.

As a Mexican American who grew up along the border, Officer Delgado understood immigrants' fear of enforcement agencies. He remembered hearing about "El Diablo Verde," or the Green Devil, as a child and asking his mother, "What is that, Ma?" His mother told him it was "La Migra," and even though the young Lorenzo still did not understand, he moved on. "I was a young kid," he told me. "The good thing is . . . this job that I have now, the position I hold now, is where I can help." I asked Officer Delgado how he helps immigrants in his current position; I had not heard of such a post within ICE. He explained that he makes sure to do "all the proper research" to see if the people he is deporting qualify for derivative citizenship.[25]

Derivative citizenship is a legal mechanism that allows the foreign-born children of US citizens to acquire citizenship through their parents. Immigration and Customs Enforcement officers check for derivative citizenship of people in their custody if they make a claim to citizenship or if they spot something in the case details that suggests the person could be eligible. In essence, ICE is doing their due diligence to avoid removing a US citizen—this is not a service. Officer Delgado takes that legal requirement and turns it into a form of "help" for immigrants. He continues,

Sometimes . . . I'll get thanked. You know? "I appreciate you going to the full extent and finding out that my son does derive citizenship." . . . So like I said, most of the time, you're helping the family, but you're also not destroying the family.

Officer Delgado's effort to frame deportation case work as helping, or at least "not destroying," immigrant families is an example of how agents recast their work in a more positive light. Emphasizing that they do decent and humane work is a common legitimation strategy among immigration officials, and while framing deportation as assistance may seem nonsensical, it is not unheard of.[26] For example, Amada Armenta found that local police who were deputized to enforce federal immigration law said they were helping immigrants by being kind or providing information that would ultimately help them regularize their status, when they were actually putting them into the deportation pipeline.[27] Immigration and Customs Enforcement supervisor Andrea Lopez provides another poignant example of how agents can recast immigration control as helping when they are faced with uncomfortable emotions.

Officer Lopez was a supervisor when I interviewed her, but she had paid her dues out in the field. As a Spanish-speaking woman, she had always played a central role in enforcement operations because her colleagues felt she would "defuse things." That meant she was always the first to interface with migrants whom ICE was looking to deport. "So if anybody was going to get blasted, it was me," she laughed, awkwardly. Thankfully, she said, most operations were routine and relatively scripted. She monotonously illustrated: "Your case is open. It's a final order of removal. You did not show up. You lost your appeals. We need to close this case." Those were the mundane, everyday cases. Occasionally, though, there was an experience that was neither dangerous nor routine— something that "sticks with you." She told me about one such instance.

One time, it was right before Christmas. . . . The case was on a lady; she could've been your mom and my mom, you know? She was an older lady. . . . She was there. So we were like, "Oh, we've come for you." "No, but we thought our case—." I said, "No, your case is done, appeals and appeals, they're all denied . . ." And she had her apron, and she had her masa [dough]. She had all, everything—she was making tamales. She was starting to make tamales. You could smell when you walked in all the stuff she had cooked. Like the carne [meat] and everything. I was like, "Oh my God."

When Officer Lopez told me that the woman could have been her mother, or my mother, she was momentarily grappling with the rehumanization of her "target." The Latina mother making tamales at Christmas time was familiar to Officer Lopez, as a cultural archetype but also a very real person—Officer Lopez had a Mexican immigrant mother herself. Officer Lopez was forced to contend with that momentary empathy.

Empathy is grounded in likeness; it is easier to imagine ourselves in another person's position if we perceive them to be like us.[28] This is why dehumanization is a core aspect of immigration control. Immigration agents can process more people, more expeditiously, if they perceive those people as unlike *us*, as immoral criminals or mere bodies that need to be processed for removal.[29] The American public can also accept the harshness of immigration control when the outsiders are seen as "categorically unequal."[30] In effect, Officer Lopez was struggling with the recognition of the humanity of this woman as she engaged in a state action—deportation—that depends on lack of recognition between agents and immigrants.[31]

There is some denial of responsibility in Officer Lopez's response. She explained to the woman that her case was done, the appeals had not worked, a judge had ordered her removed. In effect, Officer Lopez is explaining to this woman that she is powerless to reverse others' decisions. However, what Officer Lopez did next is what reveals the denial of harm.

Officer Lopez explained to the woman that once ICE deported her, she would be completely off their radar, and by implication, she was free to come back. She remembered trying to convey this indirectly: "Look, ma'am, your case is open. Until we go take you back to Mexico and close this case, we'll continue to come. Once your case is closed, we don't even know who you are." In effect, Officer Lopez was telling the woman in a somewhat vague and befuddling way that once ICE deported her, she could return to the United States, and there would be no way to track her. Officer Lopez reflected, "If she came back or not, I don't care. That case was closed. I felt so bad. I felt so, so bad. . . . It just killed me because we're all human after all."

Faced with the ambiguity of deporting this "older lady" along with the deep conviction that she would do the job, Officer Lopez figured out a way to protect her own sense of morality. Reliving the situation, or aware that others—including me—might not understand her position, Officer Lopez looked uncomfortable. She reiterated that she felt "so shitty" and like "a strike of lightning" would hit her for her part in that deportation, communicating shame and guilt. Her way of dealing with those feelings was to downplay the harm of deportation. Officer Lopez found solace in framing the woman's removal as a way of helping her get rid of ICE and continue with her life without the threat of deportation. At the end, she told me, "She's probably here. She probably came right back to finish the tamales. . . . That case is closed for us."

Ignorance is a constitutive practice of the state and a way that bureaucrats avoid responsibility for the harm done by various forms of immigration control, including deportation, detention, and border arrests.[32] Ignorance and its cousin, indifference, are built into the very idea of national sovereignty. The state can extend sympathy for others' misfortunes in an abstract way but bears no real responsibility for fixing *their problems*. The way Officer Lopez recast the woman's deportation as helping is a strategic use of ignorance, an act of imagination where she was not harming the woman who reminded her of Latina mothers everywhere, but instead was helping her get ICE off her back.

Denying harm and denying responsibility are forms of explanation. These are examples of agents implicitly conceding to the injustice of these instances of immigration control—namely instances involving people they find deserving of sympathy—and then explaining that they were powerless to do anything different or recasting their actions as helping. In the next section we will see White agents dealing with similar situations of moral ambiguity in a very different way, through justification. White agents deny the very idea that migrants are deserving of their sympathy and frame themselves as righteous deliverers of a merited punishment.

Denying the Victim:
"They . . . Put Themselves in That Situation"

Immigration and Customs Enforcement officer Carter Grayson resented media portrayals of ICE as cruel. "I don't like breaking up families," he clarified. If while on an enforcement action he found "an abuelita [grandmother] making breakfast," he wouldn't "sweat her." I asked how he would determine that, how he would decide whom to question and whom not to question. "Spidey sense," he responded. When my silence signaled that I needed more information, Officer Grayson clarified that he could separate the good guys from the bad guys.[33] Still, I probed, was there ever a time where media portrayals of ICE going into houses and "tearing families apart" felt accurate? "No." Officer Grayson responded, "The closest I can think of, there was a woman."

Officer Grayson could not remember exactly what the woman's conviction was but remembered it was "fairly significant." She had been deported ten years earlier, then returned to the United States and assumed another identity, "the identity of a US citizen," Officer Grayson said. She had four young children by the time ICE came to her apartment complex, found her vehicle, and waited for her to come out. Eventually, the woman got in her car to leave, and Officer Grayson and his colleagues "moved up," blocking her car in. Startled, the woman began to yell.

> Three or four kids hear their mom, come out of the apartment. These are all kids under the age of twelve. . . . She really made the situation a lot worse than it should've been. I felt badly because here are these kids that you know, they just see these guys coming in and arresting their mom. At the same time, she initiated it, really. She stirred the pot. . . . And so all of a sudden, we're these terrible people that are pulling her from her kids. And it's like, "Well, you got convicted of a felony. You committed fraud against the United States government. You come back . . . and it's our fault?"

Like his colleagues who deny responsibility and deny harm, Officer Grayson also tries to put distance between himself and the woman's suffering. But there is something different in his approach. Instead of putting restrictions on his power by referencing the law, or trying to reframe the deportation itself, Officer Grayson emphasizes the woman's responsibility for her own suffering. He said he "felt badly" for the kids, but it was their mother who worsened a bad situation with her "yelling and fussing." This is the denial-of-the-victim strategy.

White Officers were most likely to adopt this form of denial. Where Latina/o agents try to deny their responsibility or the injury of immigration control—strategies that implicitly accept but try to distance themselves from the harm they are perpetuating—White Officers embrace a role in which they are righteous facilitators of the consequences that people *deserve* for their wrongdoing. Immigration and Customs Enforcement officer Shane Klatt provides a powerful illustration of this distinction.

Officer Klatt remembered the two little girls with their pink backpacks. It was early in the morning, and their dad, ICE's "target," was walking them to school. "Fuck," he thought. The team would have preferred the children not to be around, but it wasn't as if they could cancel the operation and come back at a better time. There was no better time. They stopped the father but passed on handcuffing him for the girls' sake. Officer Klatt asked the man if someone was home so they could take the children back. "We wanted those kids to at least be able to say good-bye to their dad."

Officer Klatt says he could really sympathize with the family's dreadful situation. He too was a father and could imagine what it would feel like to be forcefully separated from his kids and his wife. He couldn't help but get "emotionally involved." Sure, he admitted, there were some agents who "didn't care," but that was normal—"you're going to have that everywhere." He explained that most agents "carry these burdens emotionally. . . . There are memories, moments you sit there, and I wouldn't say you feel bad about it, but you really can empathize."

Officer Klatt's distinction between "empathy" and "feeling bad" demonstrates how race/ethnicity shapes agents' emotional responses to moral ambiguity. Officer Klatt said he could empathize with the family's situation, as in he could imagine himself in their shoes. But he did not go as far as to "feel bad" for the work. Feeling bad is the product of engaging in behavior that violates our own sense of rightness or the expectations that others have for us as members of social groups.[34] As a White man, Officer Klatt does not feel bad because he is not subject to the same moral reprobation that his Latina/o colleagues are.

Without racialized expectations of empathy, White agents are free to resolve the same moral ambiguities that Latina/o agents try to explain by instead justifying. Again, explaining involves admitting the act in question is bad but trying to deny accountability, while justifying is about admitting responsibility but denying the act's pejorative connotation. As White immigration agents justify the human suffering in immigration control, they can even go as far as to adopt the role of righteous punisher—a strategy that the Latina/o agents I interviewed stayed away from. Officer Klatt illustrates:

At the end of the day, guess what? You were the one who didn't go to court; that was on you. You know? You came here illegally. . . . You jumped to the front of the line; you got caught; you got called on your bullshit. You put yourself in the situation. They even put themselves in that situation. I don't physically go down to Mexico, El Salvador, Honduras, Brazil, grab somebody and go, "Here you go, motherfucker, establish your life here; go have kids so I can remove you. As soon as you get comfortable with that shit, I'm going to pick you up and send you out here." We don't do that. They make that decision.

Agents embed a retributive conception of justice in the denial-of-the-victim strategy, framing themselves as deliverers of merited penalties for breaking immigration law. The subjects of those merited penalties are Latin American migrants, as Officer Klatt demonstrates when he rattles off countries like Mexico, El Salvador, Honduras, and Brazil. These are countries whose nationals have historically been ordered removed from the United States at rates that surpass their population average.[35] In this way, Officer Klatt reminds us that when immigration agents see themselves as punishers, it is Latin American migrants whom they are punishing.

Agents' exposure to the undeniable humanity of "aliens," of "bodies," of their "targets," are critical breaks in the normative foundation of their work. After all, agents' good guy role is premised on the existence of the criminal alien archetypes that motivate their work: drug and human smugglers, gang members, terrorists, sexual predators. When agents interact with immigrants they cannot easily recognize as one of these archetypes, they can experience insecurity about the *rightness* of their work, and this insecurity can give way to emotions like sympathy or even guilt and shame. These emotions are incongruous with agents' exclusionary role and with the logic of the immigration system, which is based on bureaucratic staples like distance, ignorance, and even obstinance, as well as the us/them boundaries that separate foreigners from citizens along legal, racial, and moral lines.

These moments of ambiguity and agents' emotional reactions are racialized and gendered on both sides of the bureaucratic encounter. The stories of moral ambiguity agents told me almost always feature women, children, or families. The Latina agents told mostly stories of children and of the care work they were expected to engage in or wanted to engage in given how sympathetic they felt for the children. Latinas' experiences serve as a reminder that the emotional lives of immigration bureaucrats are shaped not only by institutional arrangements but also by broader racial and gender schemas and expectations.[36] Agents seldom experience their interactions with men as morally dubious; Latinos are to immigration agents what Black men are to the local police, the symbolic assailant that embodies the threat they perceive protecting themselves and others against.[37]

Latina/o agents respond to these moments of ambiguity by denying their responsibility, or reframing immigration control as helping or at least not hurting immigrants. White agents are more free to take on the role of righteous punisher as they deny the victims of immigration control, a denial strategy made possible for them as the archetypes of White nationhood. While all agents' denial may emerge from the most basic human instinct to have a positive sense of self, denial is not just about coping. As agents reconcile the moral ambiguities of their work, they are repairing the normative system that underlies their compliance with their organizational mandates, allowing them to continue performing their job and protecting the status quo in the US immigration bureaucracy. In short, these denial strategies make bureaucratic indifference possible, especially in the face of global inequality and human suffering.[38]

In the next chapter we observe a phenomenon that is intimately related to denial and compliance with organizational mandates. But instead of learning how agents resolve moral ambiguities for themselves, in specific situations, we see how agents cultivate legitimacy for the entire immigration system. Agents' legitimation narratives are tied to their own sense of morality, but they are most powerful as examples of how frontline agents engage in statecraft on behalf of the US government.

5

Cultivating Legitimacy

IMMIGRATION AND CUSTOMS ENFORCEMENT officer Ximeno Cortez was more than irked by the media's portrayal of ICE. The "liberal" media was pushing the "heartless inhumane bastards" narrative, while on "the other side" agents appeared "too kind, too gentle." To some extent, this was par for the course in such a political environment, and Officer Cortez thought that all the criticism could be a good sign. "If both sides hate you equally, then you're doing your job." Still, bad press was bad for morale. Agents "get frustrated and fed up with hearing all these negative comments about themselves."

On top of the media, which was a proxy for different political segments of the American public, agents also had to answer to their families. "Whenever these negative things come out in the media . . . their family is going to call them up and say, 'Hey, I'm hearing that this is going on. What's going on down there?'" The family piece was particularly contentious for the Latina/o agents, who on top of all the regular politics also had to deal with the racial politics of their work. Officer Cortez knew this firsthand. "My ancestry is Mexican. So I've had family members tell me I'm a traitor and I've turned on my family and stuff like that. I've heard it all."

Officer Cortez tried to ignore all of this, especially the family piece. He did not have time to waste on people "too ignorant . . . to do their own research" about how immigration control works, or its importance. It would be like "arguing with a wall" trying to convince his critics of his perspective, so he just "let them go ahead and believe in their own little world. . . . They can stay where they're at, and I just continue doing what I'm doing."

Officer Cortez was convinced that taking the high road was the thing to do, but he also thought it was counterproductive. Officer Cortez believed that if agents or the agency could release details about the people they were deporting, they could effectively rebut media accounts that portrayed ICE officers as inhumane family separators. "We would love to plead our cases and say, 'Okay, well, if you want to say this, then we're going to go ahead and . . . rebut what you're saying and give the full details of the case.'" Agents would be in major trouble if they did that, though. They were bound by law to keep details of people's immigration cases confidential, to avoid releasing personally identifiable information. Agents were destined to be silent, tried in the court of public opinion without the courtesy of rebuttal.

Fortunately for Officer Cortez, there I was, a member of the public with whom he could share the "full story." He took the opportunity. "This is what kills me," Office Cortez explained; "you have the narrative of you're separating the father from the children, you hear this all the time." What Officer Cortez thought the public needed to know was that "these people that we're removing, a lot of them are the criminals." In the case of the deported father, for example, Officer Cortez thought it would be redeeming if people knew that "he might've been in prison the whole time, and he hasn't given any type of support whether it's emotional, financial, or anything." The public, through the welfare system, had been supporting the father's children and his wife. Officer Cortez continued that the public might like to know why he was in prison. "Oh, well, he beat the mother." Not such a great guy after all, even if "she sticks by his side" after everything he's done to her. But no matter those details, the family would "plead the case through the media trying to portray this person as an angel and [saying] that he's just here to support his kids and help his wife."

Officer Cortez thought the family members who reproached him for participating in the repression of his own people, other Mexicans, were also clueless. "They call us racists; I'm like, 'How?'" How could he be racist as a Hispanic himself? They just did not understand, he contended, that the country needed to have laws He understood his family thought those laws were "really inhumane," but that was yet another sign that they had not done their research. Compared to other countries, the United States was lax, even charitable. "If they would see Mexico's immigration laws . . . they would freak out." All of this was exasperating to Officer Cortez, but also moot. No one was looking outside "their narrative of what they want to push." It was the agents, rather than the "aliens," who ended up looking like the bad guys.

This chapter is about how agents cultivate legitimacy, both for themselves and for the state. By legitimacy I mean the moral authority to be in a position of power over others.[1] Immigration agents are invested in being seen as legitimate by various audiences that range in abstraction from "the public" to their immediate communities, friends, and family. Agents are not unique in this regard; all power holders, from elite political rulers to frontline bureaucrats, want and need legitimacy because without it their authority is on precarious ground.[2] The issue for agents is that they suffer from various legitimacy deficits, or threats to their moral authority.

The legitimacy deficits agents are grappling with range from the macro to the group and individual level. At the individual and group level, agents resent their reputational issues.[3] They do not like that the media portrays them as "inhumane bastards" as Officer Cortez put it, that are excluding people who are trying to improve their lives through migration. For agents, these media portrayals are not just abstract mischaracterizations. These representations threaten agents' sense of virtue and create fodder for people in their lives, everyone from friends and family to local community members, to reproach them for their work. These reputational issues shape the experiences of all agents in my study, regardless of their racial/ethnic background. For Latina/o agents, these legitimacy deficits are layered with their in-between position vis-à-vis the state and their coethnics; they are seen as not just family separators but also race traitors.[4]

At the macro level, the legitimacy deficit that agents are grappling with inheres in their employer—the US government. Sovereign countries have the legal right to control their borders and determine who enters and remains within their territory. From this perspective, immigration control is legitimate. Nevertheless, the state's moral authority to exclude foreigners is on precarious ground, especially when those foreigners are fleeing hardships brought on by economic globalization, political conflict, climate change, and other forms of displacement that are created and advanced by powerful countries like the United States.[5] For its part, the US government, via its bureaucratic ideologies and other forms of statecraft, is actively engaged in addressing this legitimacy deficit, primarily by attacking immigrants' moral character, through criminalization, and by framing undocumented migration as a threat to American prosperity.[6] Agents serve as ambassadors for the state's legitimation efforts, but they are also a critical audience, as they too must believe in their own moral authority as enforcers of the borders and boundaries that divide the globe.[7]

In agents' day-to-day lives, these multilayered legitimacy deficits manifest as moral taint, which is a stigma associated with work that is ethically dubious in its purpose, its consequences, or its methods. The concept of moral taint comes from sociologist Everett Hughes's pioneering work on "dirty work" occupations, or jobs that are shunned by the public or stigmatized for various reasons.[8]

Dirty work occupations may simultaneously be denounced and respected. Such is the case with immigration agents who have high status as federal law enforcers, but also face multiple sources of taint vis-à-vis the various public critiques of their work.[9] Like all workers who deal with occupational stigma, immigration agents want to construct a positive professional identity. In fact, dirty workers tend to identify strongly with their work group and cultivate ideologies to dispel the identity threats brought on by occupational stigma. Immigration agents are no exception.[10] Therefore, what we see in this chapter is agents grappling with various threats to their sense of virtue and deploying stigma-management strategies to restore their own sense of legitimacy. In doing so they discredit outsiders' critiques of them and their work, protecting the status quo in the US immigration system from the inside out.

To repair their moral taint agents *conceal* their work and *refute* what they see as misconceptions about themselves and their job. When at all possible, agents try to conceal what they do by not talking about their work in "polite company" or avoiding outright disclosures about their job. Sometimes this involves lying about what they do for a living, often flippantly (e.g., "I tell people I'm an EMT"), but mostly agents try to avoid discussions about immigration that would lead to disclosure.

When agents cannot conceal what they do, they confront their critics and try to *refute* what they believe are misconceptions about their work. The main misconception, from agents' perspective, is that undocumented migrants are law-abiding, family-oriented people who come to the United States for a better life—this is the image of the "good" migrant that makes agents look like callous dream crushers, as agents often put it. All agents, regardless of racial/ethnic background, conceal and refute, but only Latina/o agents emphasize their Americanness when repudiated for their work— evidence that their race/ethnicity creates multilayered legitimacy deficits for these agents. Rather than a static identity, Latina/o agents' *defensive nationalism* appears as a boundary-making effort to shift critics' attention away from the identity that is inconsistent with their job—their Latinx identity— and toward one that does align—their Americanness.[11]

The product of concealment, refutation, and defensive nationalism is a sense of legitimacy that protects the immigration system's status quo from the ground up. When agents repair their moral taint, they can exist in a social reality where they are virtuous envoys of the state's sensible approach to dealing with immigration lawbreaking, instead of bureaucrats engaged in the work of implementing a system of racial exclusion. Thus, agents' quest for legitimacy, whether it be on the level of individual, racial/ethnic group, or occupation, serves a critical stabilizing function within the US immigration bureaucracy. Legitimacy stifles the potential for internal and external critiques that could bring about change within the system because it allows agents to reject those critiques as misplaced, misguided, and just plain wrong. Legitimacy is the glue that maintains agreement among agents, assures their compliance with their mandates, and steadies the precarious ground on which the government rests its moral authority to exclude.

Conceal: Avoiding Disclosure of Immigration Work

Immigration and Customs Enforcement officer Hudson Simon was not a fan of the border town where he worked. A Black military veteran from the East Coast who had moved to Mountain Valley for the job, he felt like he was out of his element. He had been trying to transfer back home for years, but most of the immigration jobs were in the Southwest. He lamented not being younger; perhaps he would have been able to adapt to the area more easily if he had moved earlier in life. Now in his early forties and having lived in multiple parts of the world, he had seen too much to be content in a town where the locals got excited about the opening of a new discount store. It did not help that the community was not a big fan of his agency. "They don't like us. . . . We're like nobodies." Sure, the agency was "part of the economy," but there was a difference between being a valuable source of employment and being held in esteem. Immigration and Customs Enforcement passed as the former but lacked the latter.

The biggest issue was the community's perception that all immigration agents do is separate families. Officer Simon laughed: "For me, it's like embarrassing sometimes." Officer Simon rarely told people what he did for work. If someone asked, he would tell them he worked for the government. If they insisted on more information and he was in the mood to entertain, he might pull out his wallet and show them his card. He demonstrated, handing me his business card. "I'll say this is what I do. And I'll leave it at that . . . because it doesn't say anything about removing kids." I looked at the card, thinking that if the point was to downplay his work, the "Immigration and Customs Enforcement" headline was counterproductive. I started to make the point, "Well, yeah, but—," at which point he leaned in. He pointed at the words under the headline: "If you look on here, you know, [that's] what I really do." I read the words aloud: "Criminal Alien Program." "Exactly," he told me. "It's a little dignified."

Officer Hudson was one of many immigration agents who told me they rarely disclose what they do for work. It was not that agents were ashamed of their work per se, just that immigration was such a "touchy subject" that disclosing their affiliation was like asking for a fight. It was easier to tell people they worked anywhere else—in education, in dining, as a first responder, in construction, or in a nondescript government job—anything but immigration.

Police officers are known for being judicious about whom they share their work with, yet another way that immigration agents' outlooks mirror the profession. Police officers typically explain that this practice is about staying safe, and immigration agents shared that sense of danger, too. For instance, ICE officer Leon Camargo shared that one day while out for lunch he saw a person he had deported awhile back. The man stared daggers at him while Officer Camargo tried to eat his meal. When Office Camargo finally returned the man's stare, holding eye contact with his previous charge, the man told him, "I saw you already, motherfucker. I saw you." Unsettled, Officer Camargo left the restaurant immediately. This experience impressed on him the importance of not telling people where he worked. You could never be too cautious, he said, what with the myriad of people who disliked immigration agents.

For most agents, however, the issue of not telling people where they work was mostly about avoiding conflict. Immigration and Customs Enforcement officer Noah Webb, a Black man, told me, "It's kind of a taboo subject. So people avoid it. . . . It's just like the big elephant in the room." Immigration and Customs Enforcement officer Manolo Gil agreed that immigration was like "sex, politics, and religion, things you shouldn't talk about." For Officer Gil, there was no winning when you got into a conversation about immigration, even with people who were "on the same side." Sometimes you got "the guy that says you ought to arrest them all. Where am I going to go from that?" On the other end were people who told him, " 'You are a bad person, and you're basically modern-day Nazis.' Where am I gonna go with that?" He preferred to stay out of it: immigration was not a topic for polite conversation.

It was not, however, as if agents walked around cloaked in shame. They found parts of the job deeply satisfying. Immigration and Customs Enforcement officer Mark Dunst, a White man, told me that "when we actually go after someone who has a strong history of hurting someone, spousal abuse, that excites me. I'm not gonna lie." Officer Dunst thought that "immigration should just be another tool . . . that we use to get rid of these people," by which he meant people who commit criminal acts other than breaking immigration law. But Officer Dunst was not the one calling the shots. He was being paid handsomely to follow orders. He just wished people could see beyond the narrative, to see that he was just doing a job:

> What I do for a living does not dictate who I am. ICE pays me over a hundred thousand dollars a year to basically, in a nutshell, do what I'm told. And there's times I despise ICE, but there's other times I'm like, there's not another job in the world I can go make a hundred thousand dollars at right now. . . . With no school loans, with none of that crap, there's just nothing else out there. And it's just a job. I don't tell people what I do. . . . I don't take great amounts of pride at what we do.

Agents displayed a certain amount of self-consciousness in how they talked about their job, given what they perceived as a general dislike for the immigration system. This was not a paralyzing insecurity, as there was plenty to be proud of, especially when agents were able to arrest and remove "bad people." But that type of work—the *real police work* that involved them keeping the criminals away from the public—was not only hard to come by; it was also increasingly overshadowed by the reality that getting bad guys also involved separating families.

Concealing or at least trying to avoid disclosure of their work is one way that agents can avoid getting into uncomfortable conversations that remind them of their polemic work. However, sometimes engaging is the only option, either because people who know what they do for work bring it up, or because they feel compelled to defend themselves when they see what they believe are misconceptions about them.

Refute: Attacking Immigrants' Moral Character

When agents cannot avoid talking about their work in public, they become ardent defenders of it. The critiques that agents were most interested in debunking were those that framed undocumented migrants as law-abiding, family-oriented people who were coming to the United States for a better life. This was the narrative that most challenged agents' sense of legitimacy because it made them look like they were callous "dream crushers" instead of principled law enforcers. Family separation and the detention and deportation of women and children pose particularly strong challenges to the legitimacy of immigration control in countries like the United States because these state practices run counter to espoused social values about the importance of family.[12] It is not surprising, then, that agents' legitimation efforts involved chipping away at the image of migrants as family people whose only offense is breaking immigration law to improve their life.

Officer Luke Newman told me that the public got a "convoluted and diluted" version of immigration work. There was the narrative of ICE deporting a mother, for example. Officer Newman felt that the public's idea of a "mother" simply did not apply to this person. "This lady with five kids. . . . She's got drug convictions; she works as a prostitute. . . . The media [says], 'Oh well her children.' She hasn't lived with her children in five years. She lives on the street." Yes, Officer Newman conceded, some immigrants are mothers, but they aren't *good mothers*.

Immigration and Customs Enforcement officer Hal Bruekner engaged in a similar exercise of framing an immigrant father whom he had deported as a *bad father*. Officer Bruekner told me about an enforcement action in which "dad had come home from work, and we snatched him up. . . . He was in Mexico within two hours." To Officer Bruekner, this was a good day at work—a swift deportation of someone who deserved to be removed. But if "the media" gets a hold of that story, Officer Bruekner said, they would frame it as a family separation instead of the removal of a criminal alien. "They don't get into what dad did. Dad almost killed mom. . . . Dad beat one of the children unconscious. . . . Dad moves large amounts of meth amphetamine. Dad needs to go. I think that's the frustrating part."

Agents Newman and Bruekner told me these stories because they believed that they were redemptive. They assumed that if members of the public knew that these supposedly moral migrants were actually bad parents, then the court of public opinion would sway to their side. In presenting these narratives they expose the logic underlying the government's moral authority to separate families: the idea that the state is more fit to decide the fate of the immigrant family unit than the "criminal alien" parent.[13] In attempting to justify their work vis-à-vis the media, agents lay bare the racialized, classed, and gendered logics about the state's power to regulate the intimate sphere generally, and immigrant families specifically.

Agents believed that the media was largely responsible for the public's erroneous ideas about immigrants as worthy individuals and families. They thought that the media manipulated stories and put out images of sympathetic characters that made agents look bad. While agents' resentment was most often directed at "the media" writ large, it was clear that their indignation was reserved for outlets that were critical of the government's policies. Agents were not mad at outlets, like Fox, that told stories about immigration that aligned with their own views. When agents said they wanted media outlets to tell "the full story," they meant the full story from their perspective. This was true even when agents believed that all media were biased.

Border Patrol agent Ezra Aniston, for example, told me that all media outlets were after ratings because that is how they made profit. "Fox, CNN, ABC, CBS, NBC—they're all about making money." It followed, then, that the media was going to frame issues mostly to echo their viewers' preexisting political preferences. "The media is going to show you what they want to show you from whichever side of the aisle you sit. . . . It doesn't matter if you watch Fox and you're conservative or you watch CNN and you're liberal." At the same time, Agent Aniston thought it was the "liberal" outlets that were showing an incomplete picture about immigration. "You'll see a baby and a mom come across, and they're so poor, and they look at the cameras, and the cameras show how poor they are and how they need to come here."

> The cameras stop when you learn that she's the daughter of a drug kingpin and that's not her baby, it's the drug king pin's granddaughter, and underneath the car seat there's like fifteen pounds of heroin worth like two million dollars.

The moral of the story, according to Agent Aniston, was that the media was going to tell you what you wanted to hear. "Sometimes it's the truth, and sometimes it's half of it." Agents thought it was the truth when the media reflected their own views of the issue.

All this "negative media coverage" led agents to feel annoyed, misunderstood, or aggrieved, but none of them thought that things were going to change. The (liberal) media's (negative and incomplete) coverage of immigration issues was just the way things were. In fact, for many agents, the media's negativity was just another manifestation of the public's lack of support for law enforcement in general.

For ICE officer Ash Harding and many of his colleagues, all law enforcement agents were "under attack" by the public. The public's "attack on law enforcement" created a sense of solidarity, "a banding together in a much tighter ring, a total distrust of the public." This banding together is typical of police officers' sense of solidarity with each other and distrust of outsiders.[14] Furthermore, Agent Harding is articulating something we know about people who are part of "dirty work" occupations—they tend to have "relatively high occupational esteem" in large part because the act of defending their work produces pride in it.[15] Still, Officer Harding lamented that immigration agents had it worse than other officers.[16] Apologizing for his language, he put it this way: "We're a turd that can't be polished. We're the bastard stepchildren of law enforcement. . . . We're never going to be respected by the public."

The difference between other law enforcement officers and immigration agents, Officer Harding thought, was that there were many situations in which the public liked and needed cops. "A gangbanger's momma is getting raped, he wants a cop. . . . Victims of crimes love correctional officers who hold these people in prison. . . . The DEA . . . FBI is prestigious." Nobody was happy when immigration agents showed up. Well, Officer Harding corrected himself, maybe there were some exceptions. "There's nobody except for, unfortunately, racist xenophobes who are like, 'Ah, immigration, yeah.' . . . We don't relish that."

Officer Harding put the blame squarely on the public's ignorance about immigration. "Joe Public," the average citizen living somewhere in the interior of the country, away from the chaos of the border and without the benefit of an agent's knowledge, just did not understand.[17] In addition to being ignorant, Joe Public was also being misled by biased media outlets that fed him erroneous information about undocumented migrants. Between their ignorance and the media's distortion, the public ended up siding with migrants and thinking that it was agents who were in the wrong. Officer Harding thought this was particularly true of the Latina/o community, with whom immigration agents were exceptionally unpopular. "Of course, to much of the Hispanic public we're the bad guys." This was an issue that Latina/o agents dealt with intimately.

Like the rest of their colleagues, Latina/o agents also believe that there is an inverse relationship between migrants' morality and their own. They are invested in cultivating legitimacy by attacking immigrants' moral character, a reflection of their employer's bureaucratic ideologies.[18] However, the questions that prompt their legitimation efforts are layered—Latina/o agents are called to account not just for their work, but for their work in light of their racial/ethnic background. Often those who are repudiating Latina/o agents, whether family members or immigrants themselves, ask them whether they feel bad for immigrants or for their role in keeping them from entering the United States. Border Patrol agent Amalia Fonseca demonstrates how she responds when people say, "Don't you feel bad because you're Spanish?"

> No, I don't feel bad. I get paid to do this. I'm supposed to do this. Imagine if we would let our border wide open. . . . People assume that people coming from the border are coming here to work. It used to be that way, absolutely.

Many agents, especially Border Patrol agents, asserted that the criminality of immigrants had increased over time. They often told me, just as they told others who judged them for their work, that it used to be that their arrestees were labor migrants, trying to make it to the United States for a better life. In their telling, those labor migrants had been replaced by the cunning criminal alien. As Agent Fonseca puts it, "I met a lot of good people on the border or in the desert that come here and do want to work. But I've met far too many rapists, smugglers, drug traffickers, sex trafficking, murderers, you name it. And it's like no, I don't want those people here."

What agents are doing when they differentiate between labor migrants and criminal aliens is reproducing readily available social constructions of illegality to justify their work, but they are also identifying a hierarchy of targets for that work.[19] The criminal alien epitomizes the warrant for immigration enforcement, from the government's perspective. It is no surprise, then, that agents try to manifest this image of the criminal alien when legitimizing immigration control. One way they do this is by using their authority as people on the front lines of immigration control to argue that the criminality of immigrants has increased over time, an idea that has long been espoused by frontline agents. Josiah Heyman's study of immigration officers in the 1990s showed that agents "consistently asserted that migrants were better behaved in the past, no matter when that past was for the particular officer."[20]

What we know from the government's own immigration statistics, however, is that most people who attempt to cross the border without documentation do not have a criminal record. Between 2014 and 2016, during my fieldwork, 89 to 95 percent of deported people who did not have a criminal record (i.e., noncriminal removals) had been apprehended by CBP agents at or between ports of entry.[21] I was in the field during a period in which asylum seeking at the US-Mexico border dramatically increased. At the very moment that agents were telling me that the aspirant foreigner searching for a better life was invented by the media, or was an outdated view of migration, their agency was mishandling a major humanitarian crisis. Still, even if the claim that economic migrants were replaced by felons is not supported by the government's own statistics, organizational myths like this one need not be accurate to be powerful. Organizational myths serve as cognitive heuristics that guide workers' day-to-day practices, even when those practices are not empirically sound or efficient.[22]

Latino men have consistently served as the personification of the deeply racialized and gendered "criminal alien" construct. This has resulted in a disproportionate targeting of Latino men for arrests and deportation.[23] After deportation these men have no legal recourse for returning to the country they called home for years, even as they face significant obstacles incorporating into their birth countries.[24] Many of the Latino men deported from the United States will attempt to reenter the country without authorization in order to reunite with family or simply to return to the country where they have made a life.[25] When Border Patrol agents and ICE officers arrest these men again, their records reinforce agents' ideas that the criminality of immigrants has increased. Instead, what agents are witnessing is an ever-widening immigration dragnet,[26] and the product of their own deeply gendered and racialized practices.

The sex offender looms large in the archetypes that animate agents' work. Agents consistently gave examples of "rapists," "child molesters," and "sex traffickers" to convey just how bad the *bad guys* were. Agents brought up these examples because they animated the reliably reviled criminal alien archetype that they believed people on both sides of the aisle agree ought to be arrested, detained, and deported.[27] These racialized and gendered ideas about immigrant criminality are master narratives about Latinx people as a threat to the American way of life, where Latino men are a violent and sexual menace, and Latinas are a reproductive scourge.[28] That fact that Latina/o agents use them is not surprising, given that they are talking to me in the context of work where these archetypes dominate, but it is still notable as evidence of the power of institutions over social group memberships.

Immigration and Customs Enforcement officer Marta Vela used the image of Latinos as sexual predators to justify her work. Officer Vela was born in Mexico, a fact that members of her network sometimes used to reproach her about her job. Her sister was particularly critical, launching "very judgmental" reminders that she was an immigrant. Although Officer Vela sometimes wondered whether she should have chosen a different career, she held on to the wins. "When I'm able to deport . . . a child rapist, it's satisfaction." Those are the stories she shared with her family, stories she felt were redemptive. She said she reserved sympathy for labor migrants—just not the people who had engaged in criminal activity. "I feel bad for [those] that are just coming to work. . . . I don't feel bad for the people that we're actually removing because they committed a heinous crime."

Border Patrol agent Camila Sarto also got flack from her family for being in immigration control. She understood it to a certain extent; she thought that it was normal for people to resent the agencies that were keeping family members out. She tried not to engage, but every once in a while, she would go into storytelling mode. "I tell them a story of like . . . child molesters, and they look at me, like, no." This usually did the trick, Agent Sarto said. To dispel the ideas that her family had about good immigrants, she told them about bad immigrants. They sometimes responded incredulously, "So everybody that comes doesn't want to work in the fields?" She told them, "No . . . there's very bad people out there."

Defensive Nationalism:
Latina/o Assertions of Americanness

While all agents thought the media gave them a bad rap, Latina/o agents' reputational issues went beyond unfavorable media coverage. Latina/o agents' most salient source of stigma was their doing a job that was widely understood as anti-Latina/o. These critiques were so central to their experience that my seemingly innocuous question about whether they ever received feedback from their community, either positive or negative, consistently led back to the question of race for Latina/o agents. My conversation with Border Patrol agent Paco Linal is illustrative.

We met Agent Linal in chapter 1, as one of the agents who drifted into the Border Patrol when he needed a good job. I asked him if people in the local community ever gave him positive or negative feedback, perhaps when he was picking up lunch in his uniform. He told me that it was "mostly the snowbirds"—the White retirees from Canada, the Midwest, and the East Coast who travel to places like Mountain Valley and Desert City in search of warmer temperatures during the winter—who had positive things to say. These were the people who were most likely to say "thank you for your service" to agents in uniform.

Agent Linal was clear that the "Hispanic community" was less keen on his service. "Sometimes you get these comments like, 'Oh, you're chasing your own kind,' because I am Mexican American or Latino." The people who told him those kinds of things had "this view of like it's a race thing. . . . They think about, 'You guys are only going [to arrest people] because they're Mexicans.'" That was tough on him as a Latino because he felt strongly that the assessment was wrong; he did not come into the agency to "chase Mexicans," even though he understood why people thought that. He too was once on the outside looking in, and he recognized that things looked different from that vantage point. What Agent Linal thought people needed to know was that his work was not racial or personal—it was just a job.

Agents like Paco Linal have much in common with their non-Latina/o counterparts. They also believe the media misrepresents the issue of immigration and, in so doing, misrepresents them. However, for Latina/o agents, their profession's reputational issues are layered with intragroup sanctions. These sanctions are epitomized by such questions as "How does it feel to arrest your own people?" or the less explicit but equally incisive ones like "Aren't you Mexican?" Agents responded to these questions in various ways. Sometimes agents refused to engage; other times they engaged by emphasizing their humanness, as we saw in chapter 3; and here we see them turning to their Americanness in defense. Immigration and Customs Enforcement officer Andrea Lopez demonstrates this last approach.

Officer Lopez had been working in immigration enforcement for decades, and it was clear that she was proud of her job. The more I talked with her about that pride, though, the more it started to look like a defense mechanism to deal with "all the negativity" that came her way as a Latina in immigration control: "It's the most unfavorable position at times." Officer Lopez dreaded the moment when people asked her what she did for work. "Do I really have to answer that?" she joked. "What do you say?" I asked her.

> Depends. If it's at the nail place, "Oh, where do you work?" "Jack in the Box." None of your business. But if we go somewhere like workwise or, you know, amongst friends: "Well, I work for ICE." And I have to be very proud of where I work.

Officer Lopez thought she had to be proud of where she worked because the alternative was to give in to the shame that others tried to impose on her. "They look at me like, 'What is she doing here?' I'm like, 'Ugh.'" Instead of dropping her head, Officer Lopez raised her chin by reminding people she was American. "They're like, 'How can you do that job? It's all against our race'— I'm like, 'First of all, I was not born in Mexico. I never lived in Mexico.'" If her Mexicanness was the issue, then people needed to know she was born and raised in the United States.

At the same time, Officer Lopez expressed a certain amount of sympathy for people on the other side of her mission. She was even certain that if the tables were turned, she would also be trying to make it into the United States and stay, even without documentation. Still, that was not the reality she inhabited. "I'd probably do the same thing. . . . But I am not, and this is my job." It was nonsensical for people to shame her. It was the equivalent, she said, of not liking how expensive license plates are and taking it out on the DMV employee. "It's the same thing. . . . You can't be mad at the people taking the payment for DMV. . . . Don't hate on me. Just, look, it's a job, there is laws, somebody has to abide and enforce them." None of this felt good to Officer Lopez. That is why she had a rule against talking shop when she was out with friends. "I never talk work amongst my friends. Never. Never."

Many Latina/o agents resorted to emphasizing their Americanness when it came to defending how they, as Latinx people, could keep other Latinx people from their efforts to live in the United States. This emphasis on their Americanness exemplifies how citizenship boundaries cut across the Latinx population, restricting the level of empathy that citizens can feel for coethnic immigrants on the other side of the bureaucratic encounter.[29] Border Patrol agent Esteban Luar gives a poignant example of these intragroup boundaries.

Agent Luar explained that when people say to him, "Really, you're going to arrest your own family, your own people?" it just did not compute. Agent Luar had one Mexican immigrant parent and one Mexican American parent. He grew up close to a large border town but "hardly spent any time in Mexico." And his Spanish wasn't "the greatest," even though he could "get by." Agent Luar knew he was Mexican, but he felt "predominately from the US side."

To communicate how American he and his family were, he told me about something his children had said to him at a restaurant just a couple of days earlier. While waiting for their food, his son looked around and commented, "Wow, there's a lot of Mexicans here." Officer Luar thought that was hilarious. "I looked at them like, 'You know you guys are Mexican, right?' " His child responded, "Yeah, but we're American now." This was a matter of fact, Agent Luar thought, but also the sign of a certain "mentality" among some Latinx people. "Some of us have it [this mentality]. It's that no, those aren't my people. Yes, we're all Mexican, but they're a different kind of Mexican."

Agent Luar's perspective points to a much larger pattern of intragroup boundaries among Latinx people, along generational lines (e.g., between US- and immigrant-born Latinx) as well as along national origin, class, and other axes of difference within the community.[30] His words serve as a powerful reminder that a shared racial/ethnic background does not guarantee affinity between agents and migrants. As Agent Luar put it, "It's . . . that mentality. . . . You're not looking at someone as, 'Oh yeah, we're the same race, same nationality.' You're just like, 'That guy looks like he could be wet.' And it's just a job." The "how can you do this to your own people?" question was just not going to land with Agent Luar, because he did not think of immigrants as his people; he led with his American identity, despite being an earlier-generation Mexican American who grew up close to the border. As Jennifer G. Correa and James M. Thomas put it, Latina/o agents like Agent Luar "demonstrate an inability to see themselves within the Other despite sharing an ethnic-racial cultural background."[31]

Agent Luar is not alone among the broader Latinx population, but he is in the minority. Only about 14 percent of Hispanic/Latinx people in the United States say that they most often identify as American. The remainder identify either with their national origin or as Hispanic/Latina/o.[32] But even among his Latinx colleagues, Agent Luar's views are somewhat marginal. Few agents expressed his level of distance from immigrants or from their ethnoracial identity, even when they emphasized their Americanness. This bears repeating. Many Latina/o agents emphasized their American identity when they were repudiated for their job, but that did not mean that they only identified as American. Emphasizing their Americanness allowed these Latina/o agents to emphasize a part of their identity that was aligned with their work and downplay the one that was in conflict with it.

Border Patrol agent Guillermo Bobadilla offered a response that shows how turning to American-centered discourse allows Latina/o agents to cultivate legitimacy when they feel judged. Agent Bobadilla was born in California to Mexican immigrant parents who had taught him, both by example and through counsel, to always work hard, to stay humble, and to be a good person. He took their advice to heart and always tried to do the right thing at work and in his personal life. He was one of the agents who saw themselves deploying the caring control practices we learned about in chapter 3. All of this meant that Agent Bobadilla met people's criticism of his job with much chagrin and even some puzzlement. The worst part was when his own family looked at him with suspicion.

One time his aunt told him warily, "Ay Guillermo, portate bien con la gente." Or "Oh Guillermo, behave well with people." Agent Bobadilla felt judged and somewhat hurt. Her lamenting tone made him question whether his aunt thought he was one of the bad guys. He asked his mom, "Is she serious? . . . Is she really looking at me like I'm a bad guy or something? I really can't tell." These glimpses of judgment made Agent Bobadilla feel insecure about his job but also prompted a surge of conviction. He told me he does feel bad for "illegals," but that him quitting his job is not going to change things. He explained,

> I respect my country's laws. I'm proud of serving in the military and being an American. I consider myself an American before anything else. My

parents are from Mexico, but I was born and raised in [the United States], and this is a country that afforded me the opportunity. . . . My dad didn't make much money, and I was able to do all that, get a bachelor's.

Agent Bobadilla's patriotic discourse could suggest that he, like Agent Luar, does not see immigrants as part of his group.[33] The way he talked about Mexican immigrants later in the interview, however, suggests otherwise. "I know that there's some agents out there that hate Mexicans or they hate immigrants and want to keep these people out." To those agents he says, "How many Hispanic . . . transients do you see? You can call *my people* [emphasis added] whatever you want. A Mexican or Hispanic can come over here with no identity and make something of himself." Later in the interview, Agent Bobadilla told me he would not stand for his colleagues saying xenophobic or racist things about immigrants. For instance, a colleague once commented, "I think if you don't speak English, you should get out." Agent Bobadilla responded, "You know what, my grandmother is ninety-something years old. She does not know one word of English. And she's a US citizen. . . . What the fuck are you gonna do about it?"

While some Latina/o agents may favor an American over an ethnoracial identity, most do not. They do, however, consistently turn to their American identity as a defensive strategy to combat accusations that they are race traitors for working in immigration enforcement. The logic is that it makes sense that they, as Americans, would be enforcing immigration law even if they would be criticized for doing so as Latinos. Latina/o agents express defensive nationalism as a strategic turn to an identity that is more aligned with their job.[34]

Immigration and Customs Enforcement officer Lorenzo Delgado also turns to citizenship to deflect the criticism he gets for being a Latinx person in immigration enforcement. However, instead of emphasizing his own Americanness, he talks about how his immigrant mother obtained her citizenship. "When I first got hired, you know, 'How can you take our people back?' I'm like, 'Well, my mom, she worked hard, and she made it over, and she got her green card, and now she's a naturalized citizen.'" Latina/o agents who had immigrant parents or family had the option of using their family as an example of immigrants who did it "the right way." This was another way they distanced themselves from the aspect of their identity that people found most problematic. That is, if people thought it is wrong that they are in immigration enforcement because their own parents were immigrants, then the agents needed to show that their parents were good immigrants. Their family members were not the same as the undocumented immigrants—the criminals—they were charged with regulating.

Latina/o agents draw citizenship boundaries, emphasizing their own Americanness or otherwise differentiating themselves from coethnics on the other side of the bureaucratic encounter.[35] They deploy this boundary-making strategy when they are reproached for working for an institution that targets their own community. As members of the profession, they also rely on the broader legitimation strategy favored by state: criminalizing immigrants.

Immigration agents are invested in being seen as legitimate, as having the moral authority to arrest, detain, and deport immigrants who fall outside the law. This desire, to be seen as moral and to be seen as good, is shared by most social actors. Justifying our actions, defending the groups we are a part of, and validating our ways of being in the world are fundamental parts of social life.[36] This pull toward legitimation is particularly strong for members of morally dubious occupations and for people in power—immigration agents are both.[37]

When agents feel judged or rejected for their work, agents *conceal* their work and *refute* what they see as misconceptions about themselves and their job. Latina/o agents also engage in *defensive nationalism* where they emphasize their Americanness to distance themselves from the racialized moral taint of being a Latina/o in immigration control.

These efforts reveal an unspoken assumption: agents believe there is an inverse relationship between their and migrants' morality. If migrants are the good guys, then agents must be the bad guys, and that would be untenable as a matter of professional philosophy. This possibility also presents a threat to their own sense of virtue. Therefore, when it comes to legitimating their work, agents are very invested in the public seeing immigrants as undesirables who deserve to be deported or arrested at the border. Just as the broader American public erroneously stratifies the immigrant population into good and bad migrants—family people or criminals; good workers or job stealers; blameless youth or undeserving freeloaders—so too are agents invested in that most pervasive and specious political project.[38] Agents attack undocumented migrants' moral character because their sense of legitimacy depends on those migrants being seen as righteously excluded. Agents insist that undocumented migrants are the bad guys so that they may be seen as the good guys.

When confronted with the general occupational stigma of being an immigration agent, Latina/o agents cultivate legitimacy by resorting to concealment and refutation like the rest of their colleagues. However, *defensive nationalism* is how they respond when members of the public and even their families call them to account for participating in what is widely recognized as an anti-Latina/o racial project.[39] Agents' emphasis on their Americanness is best understood as a stigma-management strategy, rather than a static national identity. All social actors engage in boundary making to create a positive sense of self in response to stigmatized group memberships.[40] When someone calls a Latina/o agent a race traitor, or asks them how it feels to police their own, agents respond defensively by trying to shift critics' attention from the identity that is inconsistent with their job—their Latina/o identity—and toward one that does align—their Americanness.

In the battle for legitimacy there can only be one winner—if undocumented immigrants can be good, then immigration agents can be bad. Conveniently for agents, they have at their disposal both their employer's ideologies about immigrants as a threat to American prosperity, and their own frontline war stories about the cunning criminals they have arrested. In their eyes, agents have no shortage of ways to be redeemed.

While we know that members of stigmatized groups go to great efforts to construct a positive sense of self, we must not neglect the institutional origins and political functions of immigration agents' legitimation efforts. The US government, via its bureaucratic ideologies and other forms of statecraft, is actively engaged in addressing this legitimacy deficit, primarily by attacking immigrants' moral character, through criminalization, and by framing undocumented migration as a threat to American prosperity.[41] Agents are ambassadors for the state's legitimation efforts, but they are also a critical audience, as they too must believe in their own moral authority as enforcers of the borders and boundaries that divide the globe.[42] It would therefore be a mistake to understand immigration agents' legitimation strategies only as self-created and self-serving identity processes.

Agents' insistence that immigrants are criminals is not simply state propaganda either. When agents insist that immigrants used to be workers, but are now criminals, they are digging their heels into the state-created fiction of immigration to legitimize their work to themselves and others. Yes, they are serving as ambassadors for the state's view of migration as a crime and security issue, and in doing so, they are cultivating legitimacy for the state's misguided approach to migration control. But they are also yielding legitimacy benefits for themselves, a critical resource for them as frontline agents of social control.

Agents' legitimation narratives are not simply an expression of self-worth but are also normative mechanisms that protect and stabilize the status quo in the USBP and ICE. Any effort to create change in the US immigration system will have to contend with the legal and bureaucratic criminalization of immigrants and with the equally obstinate, but more veiled, normative mechanisms that legitimize and sustain its agents' indifference.

Conclusion

IMMIGRATION AND CUSTOMS ENFORCEMENT officer Jacinto Estrada joked that if Donald Trump won the presidency, he might have to deport himself. Chuckling dismissively, he told me, "That guy's a character. Three-quarters of the things he says he's gonna do, he can't . . . [but] people feed off of that. . . . It's a joke." Officer Estrada and I had been talking about the 2016 presidential election and what was then a tight race between Hillary Clinton and Donald Trump. Trump was the preferred candidate among immigration agents. The National Border Patrol Council and National Immigration and Customs Enforcement Council, the unions that represent immigration agents, had endorsed Trump. The endorsement had been unprecedented, but not entirely surprising. Trump had actively courted immigration agents, along with the broader restrictionist public, making a racist and xenophobic immigration agenda the centerpiece of his campaign.

Officer Estrada thought that Trump's goals for immigration enforcement were unrealistic, but that did not mean that he was a fan of Hillary Clinton or of then president Barack Obama. Through executive actions and bureaucratic memos, President Obama had compelled immigration agents to exercise prosecutorial discretion in favor of certain qualifying immigrants, and to do so at any point from the initial investigative phase, to arrest, detention, prosecution, and removal. President Obama's Priority Enforcement Program had narrowed the population of noncitizens that agents like Jacinto Estrada could target for deportation. These mandates were a source of much frustration to agents who felt they were handcuffed, prevented from enforcing the law.[1] Hillary Clinton represented more of the same, while Trump articulated ideas that resonated with frontline agents.

In our conversation Officer Estrada had issued an ominous warning, "Yeah, President Obama can paint it nice and pretty that 'Hey . . . we're gonna give you prosecutorial discretion.'... The next president can come back and say, 'You know what? This is no more prosecutorial discretion. You guys are coming in.'" That is exactly what happened when Trump got elected months later.

Even though immigration agents working during the Obama administration removed a historic number of people, earning him the "Deporter in Chief" moniker, the Trump years unleashed a less selective immigration bureaucracy onto the public. Trump had argued that Obama's selective mandates exempted classes of undocumented immigrants from deportation, a complete fabrication given the hundreds of thousands of people removed under Obama. Nevertheless, within the first one hundred days of his presidency Trump dismantled Obama's selective mandates, all but eliminating the few humanitarian protections his predecessor had tried to build into the immigration bureaucracy. Deportations went up by 30 percent in 2017, during Trump's first year in office.[2]

Perhaps the largest adjustment that Trump made at the agent level was to dramatically widen their discretionary power to arrest people based on immigration status, instead of the targeted enforcement priorities of the Obama administration. That is, where Obama delineated how agents would exercise discretion, under Trump discretion was highly individualized and constituted "countless low-visibility decisions" that were more reflective of agents' cultural preferences than had been the case under Obama.[3] This resulted in a more decentralized and opaque enforcement era, which made it more difficult to litigate and otherwise address the harms of immigration policies.[4]

Joe Biden's election represented another swing of the pendulum toward a more selective system in the country's interior, but he also continued some of Trump's border policies. During the last three months of the first Trump administration ICE officers had been conducting an average of sixty-eight hundred arrests per month; those rates decreased by more than 60 percent, to twenty-five hundred, by February 2021, President Biden's first full month in office.[5] However, the story was different at the US-Mexico border, where Biden continued the controversial Title 42, an emergency health measure that allowed the government to swiftly oust asylum seekers and undocumented migrants arrested by the Border Patrol.[6] In perhaps the starkest reversal of Biden's campaign to create a less cruel, more humane immigration system, in May 2023 his administration began implementing an ill-fated rule that barred people from requesting asylum unless they applied and were rejected in another country before making it to the United States. Biden also neglected to file a lawsuit to stop the building of up to twenty feet of border wall in Texas, even though he campaigned on the promise that he would not build one foot of border wall during his administration.[7]

The promises and proclamations of presidents can be captivating, as political theater and because they have very real consequences for what happens in immigration. Along with Congress's role in legislating immigration, presidents have a great deal of power to set immigration policy according to their own priorities and visions.[8] President Obama was particularly prolific in his use of executive power to direct enforcement resources toward "felons, not families," as he famously declared.[9] Trump and Biden followed suit in using executive power to pursue their own ideas. In simplest terms, what presidents are doing when they use executive orders is trying to compel the immigration officers who serve at their disposal to use their discretion in a way that aligns with the executive's vision. This does not always work, because agents have their own preferences and powers.

Throughout the dizzying pendulum swings of the Obama-Trump-Biden administrations, what has not changed is how immigration agents are trained and socialized to understand and carry out their work. Indeed, while political elites dominate public debate about immigration control, it is the frontline agents working behind the closed doors of nondescript government offices, inside inaccessible detention centers, and in remote desert areas who shape how migrants experience immigration control. This book has been a deep dive into those agents' worlds.

Bordering on Indifference: Immigration Agents Negotiating Race and Morality examines the "moral economy" of immigration control, the affective reactions and evaluative principles that are mobilized in relation to migrants and immigration and that undergird how states and their agents frame and regulate international migration.[10] Examining how frontline immigration agents— both Border Patrol agents and ICE deportation officers—understand and justify their role on the front lines of the highly coercive and racialized US immigration system reveals the normative structures that uphold the hegemony of immigration law from the ground up. Latina/o agents have been my main interlocutors in this analysis because they both represent the state and embody the state's archetypal "illegal aliens." This in-betweenness is revelatory because it forces Latina/o agents to contend with the moral and racialized character of their work much more consistently and explicitly than agents of other backgrounds. Non-Latinas/os are also key to my analysis because they too deal with the normative issues that inhere to their profession: issues about the moral legitimacy of their work, the racialized character of their outcomes, and the inhumanity of the system they represent. Comparing agents along racial/ethnic lines reveals which legitimacy issues are about immigration control as work and which emerge from the intersection of agents' race/ethnicity and their professional role.

My starting point was to show how Latinas/os have come to represent half of the Border Patrol and one-third of Immigration and Customs Enforcement nationwide. Limited opportunity structures along the US-Mexico border, coupled with a high concentration of jobs in immigration and other forms of social control, powerfully shape the kinds of jobs that Mexican and Mexican American youth in the region can aspire to and acquire. Once employed by the immigration state, all agents are thrust into a police socialization process that involves learning to see immigration through the lens of homeland security and crime. On the job, agents learn there is a gap between their professional mission and their bureaucratic function, a gap they close through a *manufactured ambiguity* that allows them to reconcile the social reality of their work, given the political fiction in which it is embedded. Manufactured ambiguity is particularly useful in the early days when Latina/o agents are dealing with rejection and, sometimes, remorse. Latinas/os incorporate race/ethnicity into the meaning they ascribe to interactions with coethnic migrants. Some see themselves as culturally competent and, therefore, more humane agents who engage in *caring control*, while others reject the idea that race/ethnicity should matter at work, adopting instead a *disinterested professionalism*. Regardless of their approach, all agents carry out their mandates with common vigor and dedication.

Morally dubious situations are unavoidable at the implementation stage of immigration control, and this is true for all agents, no matter their racial/ethnic background. Immigration agents have a variety of denial strategies that allow them to look away from human suffering and recalibrate incongruous emotions. Latina/o agents favor denial strategies that negate their responsibility for the harm done by immigration law or rebuff the idea that immigration law creates harm at all. In the end, all agents are invested in being seen as legitimate—in having a moral authority to exclude foreigners on behalf of the state, whether agents happen to share a racial/ethnic background with those foreigners or not. I end with an analysis of how agents resolve the reputational issues they contend with and argue that the resultant sense of legitimacy allows them to continue with an uncritical performance of their work.

My entry into the moral economy of US immigration control was in service of revealing the various structures—legal, bureaucratic, and normative—that produce indifference and undergird how agents understand and enact their professional role. Agents' worldviews reflect, despite their efforts to refract, threats to their moral authority, as well as the logics that allow them to face the contradictions of their work and go about doing it anyway.

Bordering on Indifference is thus a deep dive into the logics that normalize human suffering and create apathy toward that suffering among US immigration enforcement agents. Those logics are (re)produced at all levels of the bureaucracy, and agents deploy them strategically to reconcile their insecurities and to cultivate legitimacy for their organization. In this way, my analysis has shown how bureaucracies produce indifference and perpetuate exclusion through culture, law, and process.

Lessons Learned:
On Improving Policing through Workforce Diversity

Workforce diversity, which most often means recruiting groups that have been historically underrepresented in policing (e.g., Black and Latina/o people, but also women), is a major goal for many law enforcement organizations. The idea—often explicit, but sometimes implicit—is that a more diverse or representative police workforce will improve public relations, often by reducing police misconduct but also by creating more humane, less discriminatory policing procedures. That is the notion that runs through major reform projects, like the Department of Justice's "Advancing Diversity in Law Enforcement" task force, which makes the hiring of non-White police officers a key to the "cultural and systemic changes" that the public has long called for.[11] The issue with equating diversity with improved policing outcomes is that research has shown time and again that formal training, informal socialization, and the culture of the profession are often more powerful indicators of how police officers will treat the public than the officer's racial/ethnic background.[12] In other words, workforce diversity is not a panacea, especially not when we leave the structure of policing untouched.

In centering the experiences of Latina/o immigration agents, *Bordering on Indifference* joins those who have warned about equating racial representation with cultural and systemic change in policing. If reformists were going to choose a group of agents to create a more humane immigration system, it is Latina/o agents whom they might turn to for this purpose: Latina/o agents, especially those who grew up along the US-Mexico border, who have immigrant parents, who speak English and Spanish with similar ease, and who pursued immigration work for economic stability. Agents like many of the ones I interviewed would be the ones chosen in a project of reform through representation. Yet the picture that emerges from my analysis is inauspicious to this prospect. Latina/o agents' presence in the US Border Patrol and ICE does not disrupt these organizations' status quo; it legitimizes it. This is true for various reasons.

For one, Latina/o immigration agents are not reformers. Throughout my analysis, we see that they figure out ways to reconcile their insecurities about the work and do the job. This forces us to think more substantively about what having a "representative" workforce in policing means. Belonging to a certain racial/ethnic category is not enough; true representation is about being accountable to, and having the intention, influence, and status to make organizational change.[13] This is not what we see in the case of Latina/o immigration agents. Not only do they show a strong commitment to their mission as members of the highly solidary law enforcement profession, but they may also lack equal status in these agencies where they are members of the racial/ethnic group that represents their main targets.

In fact, most Latina/o immigration agents are concentrated on the low end of the command hierarchy with no clear path toward positions of power within the USBP and ICE.[14] Those who do move up are careerists who are being rewarded for performing the values that immigration enforcement agencies espouse. Latina/o immigration agents—whether on the front lines or in supervisory positions—are not reformers. We should be clear about this, lest the public confuses a "diverse" (i.e., Latina/o) immigration workforce with a more humane immigration system.

My argument—that Latina/o agents do not disrupt but, in fact, sustain the status quo in the USBP and ICE—does not mean that they are indistinguishable from their non-Latina/o counterparts. Compared to their colleagues of other racial/ethnic backgrounds, Latina/o agents were less ideological about their work, both in describing their motivations for entering the profession, and in how they talked about immigrants once on the job. They reported deploying culturally grounded wit and affability, through caring control, to lighten the custodial experience, but also as a strategy to gain compliance. Furthermore, when we looked at Latinas/os' denial strategies in times of moral ambiguity, we saw that they were more likely than Whites especially to explain rather than justify their work.[15] This suggests that Latina/o agents remain more self-conscious about the work than White agents and conceded, even if implicitly, that immigration control may be legal, but not necessarily morally correct. Finally, agents' legitimation strategies reveal that Latinas/os deal with layered legitimacy deficits, those that inhere to the profession but also those that are produced by the intersection of their race/ethnicity and professional role.

Yes, Latina/o agents are distinguishable from non-Latina/o agents throughout my analysis, but these are distinctions without a difference. Even if many of the Latinas/os I interviewed are somewhat self-conscious about their work, they are still implementing the same racialized policies their colleagues are. They are not dissenting or reforming the immigration system; they are sustaining it and even lending the system the legitimacy that comes from having a "racially representative" workforce.

The conclusion that Latina/o agents, regardless of their intentions or how they understand their work, do not disrupt the immigration system's status quo is predictable for those who understand immigration control as a form of legal and structural violence.[16] It will also be foreseeable for those who understand that policing is an inherently racialized and coercive form of state power.[17] However, it is important to remember that among large segments of the public, structural accounts of racism are rare to nonexistent. In the post–civil rights era, racism either is understood as a thing of the past, hidden under color-blind ideologies, or thought of as the disgrace of individual bad actors, instead of something that is embedded in laws, policies, and institutions.[18] This way of thinking about racism—as an individual problem of bad apples— thwarts the structural analyses necessary to understand why policing systems continue to churn out the same exclusionary outcomes, mostly independent of what their workforces look like.

Avoiding overly individualistic accounts of immigration and other forms of racialized social control is also important because on any given day one can find an assortment of news stories and reports about the excesses of individual immigration agents. Without the language to attribute these events to structural issues we allow organizations to deflect responsibility to individual bad actors, instead of the laws, policies, and cultures supported by these institutions.

I want to be clear that the Border Patrol and ICE are not somehow experts at collecting unethical people who are eager to abuse, exclude, and discriminate. In fact, the federal government need not select people with ill intentions to produce ill outcomes. What the federal government needs to do, and what it does, is recruit people and train them to believe that they are on the right side of the series of debates about law, race, and morality that come with their immigration control job. *Bordering on Indifference* shows how that process happens, centering the experiences of Latina/o agents for whom those normative issues are most salient and least avoidable.

Paths Forward: On the Perils of Creating More "Humane" Immigration Systems

My research has dramatically changed how I understand frontline immigration agents and the system they represent. I did not have this metaphor in mind then, but when I started this project I understood agents as representatives of a structure—something like a layered cake. That cake included vote-seeking politicians, a hardened legal edifice, and an obstinate bureaucratic ecosystem. I knew there was a generous dollop of structural racism folded into the mix, but I thought that I could slice the cake and examine one of those layers, the bureaucracy, and that this would help us understand how each layer upheld the whole. I also thought that understanding that layer could inform, even identify, what we could do to *change the immigration system for the better*.

I now think about that structure differently. The metaphor I have in mind now is not a layered cake but a marbled one. Politics, laws, and bureaucracy are not layers, but ingredients that are thoroughly mixed in with the normative staples of immigration debates throughout the globe: xenophobia, racism, gendered nationalism, resource hoarding, and citizenship myths, to name just a few of the muddled flavors. You can still slice a marbled cake, but there are no defined layers to inspect. It's all in there.

For a long time, I thought that what I had to do in this conclusion was to say whether after careful study, I thought we should smash the cake or somehow salvage it. A choice between abolition and reform. That kind of dichotomous thinking was unhelpful for writing, but also for the kind of political imagination that we need to develop in order to transform immigration and policing systems.[19] I also struggled with the reasonable expectation imposed on people who have spent years researching a *problem*—the idea that they may know how to fix it. The trouble is not that I am short on ideas on what could be done, but that I am skeptical about their viability in our current political environment. Still, because skepticism is not the same as defeatism, I spend the last few pages of this book discussing some paths forward given the lessons of my analysis.

The first point that I want readers to take is the most macro: it is our global organization of sovereign nation-states that manufactures the need for agencies like the US Border Patrol and ICE. In other words, it is borders themselves that beget coercion and exclusion. This is the reason that some combination of armed guards, technological and physical walls, and state-sanctioned violence are the staples of bordering around the world, not just at the territorial meeting points of two countries, but also within those countries. Any vision to *improve* or *dismantle* systems of immigration control always contends with the counterpressure exerted by the very idea of national sovereignty and the fact that country rights consistently eclipse human rights, especially as it relates to migration.

Coercion and exclusion are thus definitional components of immigration control. There is no such thing as a truly humane immigration system, no matter the proclamations of political elites who often tout their reform efforts in these terms. A humane immigration system would be one that centers human interests and life over national sovereignty, and that is not what we see anywhere in the world today. Yes, there are immigration systems—including that of the United States—where humanitarianism is part of the state's immigration discourse. But those words of sympathy, compassion, and benevolence amount to compassionate repression,[20] because they cannot do away with the inhumanity of shunning and forcibly removing people based on political constructions like "citizenship" and "illegality."

To boot, immigration control is always applied in racialized ways. In the United States it is Latinx people who bear the brunt of immigration control, but we find different racialized archetypes when we expand our outlook beyond the United States and behind states' color-blind narratives.[21] This is why many agree that the US immigration system is not broken, rather that it is working the way it is meant to—as a racialized system of exclusion and control.[22] When we stare this reality in the face, it becomes difficult to come up with something like a "solution" to the problem of inhumane systems of immigration control. In fact, there are many examples where efforts to insert humaneness into the US immigration control system end up growing the immigration bureaucracy without making substantive change to its core.

The most recent example is the Department of Homeland Security's newest position, the "Border Patrol Processing Coordinator" (BPPC). This is a position created by the government to address the humanitarian needs of asylum seekers at the US-Mexico border. The mission of BPPCs is to "support Border Patrol Agents with humanitarian care and intake processing of detainees and provide other clerical/administrative support to agents and other agency personnel."[23] Their duties include administrative processing, registering property, transporting migrants to medical facilities, and logging welfare checks, among other duties. The idea is to free up Border Patrol agents to do their enforcement job, while having a corpus of staff dedicated to do the care work that is an inevitable part of processing displaced people.

It remains to be seen what impact BPPCs will have on immigration processes at the US-Mexico border because the agency graduated its first class in January 2021 and they have not been studied as of this writing. My hope is that BPPCs both speed up the processing of asylum seekers and improve migrants' qualitative experiences with the bureaucracy, of course. What is clear already is that this position gives the government a formal mechanism to claim humanitarianism, while growing the bureaucracy without addressing one of the most fundamental issues in US asylum: the need to dramatically increase the number of immigration judges and asylum officers who can process these cases.[24]

What is more, even though BPPCs are not law enforcement agents, their seven-week training program is conducted by the Federal Law Enforcement Training Center, the same entity that trains USBP agents and ICE officers. Their curriculum includes many of the same elements that current immigration agents undergo: law, operations, physical techniques, first aid, firearms, and driving tactics. Importantly, the government requires that aspiring BPPCs be Spanish proficient at the time of application. This all but guarantees that Latinas/os will dominate these positions, a hunch I confirmed by watching online videos of these graduations.[25] The BPPC is one program in a longer list of examples that show how efforts to build humaneness into the US immigration system often grow the bureaucracy, without changing the system much if at all. The Alternatives to Detention (ATD) programs are another example.

These programs allow ICE to release migrants, instead of detaining them while their immigration case is being processed. From the perspective of ICE, ATD programs are compliance programs that create a mechanism for the government to surveil nondetained migrants so that they comply with their release conditions, and if they do not, they are easily identifiable for ICE to carry out its enforcement actions. Still, these ATD programs are often touted as evidence of humanitarianism in the US immigration system even though they do almost nothing to disrupt how the immigration system functions. Instead, Mirian Martinez-Aranda has shown that ankle monitors and other surveillance technology that is used in ATD programs actually extend the arm of the state into immigrant communities, fomenting fear and suspicion that can end up doubly isolating those already under state scrutiny. Andrea Gómez Cervantes, Cecilia Menjívar, and William G. Staples similarly show that programs that purport to keep immigrant families together through case management, but also family detention, also conceal "business as usual" enforcement tactics through gendered discourses of benevolence.[26]

The practices that I call "caring control," where agents say they engage in certain practices to improve the qualitative character of the custodial experiences for coethnic migrants, are another example of how humanitarianism cannot be taken at face value in the US immigration system. When Latina/o agents engage in caring control they come away from those interactions feeling good about themselves and perhaps even improving the qualitative character of the custodial experience for individual migrants. However, they are also using their racial/ethnic background to be more effective control agents, to yield compliance through cooperation instead of physical coercion. Of course, it is good to have respectful legal authorities, but ultimately caring control reproduces the status quo because Latina/o agents still do their work while allowing the government to co-opt their "humane practices" as part of the broader discourse of humanitarianism in immigration control.

I could go on like this, providing examples showing that the idea of a humane immigration system is oxymoronic. I do want to be clear that these efforts to improve material conditions for people caught up in the United States' border control, detention, and deportation system are critically important and must continue. But we must also be very honest that these harm-reduction strategies do not amount to the type of structural change that is necessary for more broadscale transformation that would have an impact not only on those migrants deemed most deserving but also on migrants writ large. At the risk of belaboring my cake metaphor, efforts to create a more humane immigration system are often the equivalent of redecorating the cake and growing it by doing so.

Transformative Potentialities:
Undo Crimmigration, Reduce Money, Change Culture

Despite the challenges, there are some transformative potentialities that could get us closer to something like substantive change. I draw the most optimism from the growing emphasis on "nonreformist reforms," or efforts to make fundamental and transformative changes in the US immigration system and other carceral institutions, while also addressing the immediate material needs of the people who are experiencing state violence. These nonreformist reforms are different from "reformist reforms," which aim to improve existing structures without questioning the legitimacy of the structures themselves.[27] The enduring danger of any type of reform, but particularly reformist reforms, is that the very solutions that purport to improve the system leave its core untouched. At worst, they can even end up growing and legitimizing the very system stakeholders are working to dismantle. Based on my research with immigration agents, I believe that the following three areas hold potential for widescale transformations of the US immigration system, while addressing harm reduction in a more immediate sense.

Uncouple Immigration and Criminal law

First, we need to uncouple immigration and criminal law. The criminalization of immigration, a process that began well before it reached its apex in the 1990s, is what created the conditions for the immigration bureaucracy to balloon to its current size, but it is also what shapes the qualitative character of its procedures. Legal scholars like Angelica Cházaro and César García Hernández and others have powerfully argued that immigration control, especially deportation and detention, should not be organized around the archetype of the criminal alien.[28] For one thing, the criminalization of immigrants does not have an empirical basis; noncitizens do not commit more crime than citizens,[29] but more fundamentally, organizing an immigration system around the idea of crime control reinforces ideas about "good" and "bad" migrants and makes those artificial boundaries the basis for deservingness in an array of immigration-related processes. Without disentangling immigration and criminal law, any changes we try to make to the current immigration system will be partial and inadequate.

Legal scholars and others have been writing about how we might undo the crimmigration system, identifying an array of solutions, including the decriminalization of border crossing, the creation of mechanisms that encourage compliance with immigration law, and solutions that scale back the enforcement bureaucracy, return judicial discretion to immigration judges, insert due process rights into deportation, and limit immigration agents' discretion. I encourage interested readers to engage with these writings.[30]

In addition to the uncoupling of criminal and immigration law, I am also invigorated by Antje Ellermann's argument for instituting a statute of limitations on deportation, based on the principle of legal certainty. Ellermann argues that when the state extends temporary stays of deportation, for example, the state is violating the principle of legal certainty because its intervention becomes unpredictable, and immigrants cannot make long-term plans for their lives in the United States. Ellermann is basically arguing that if the state cannot act within a reasonable amount of time, then it should cut its losses and let immigrants stay.[31]

Reduce the Money

In addition to uncoupling immigration and criminal law, we also must reduce the money that goes into immigration enforcement. Funding for immigration enforcement has grown exponentially over the past few decades and shows no sign of letting up. Together, CBP and ICE accounted for 27 percent of the DHS's $52.2 billion budget in 2022. That year, immigration enforcement received more money from the federal government than the Federal Bureau of Investigation, the Secret Service, and the Central Intelligence Agency combined.[32] The money itself is a product of bipartisan support for immigration enforcement, one of the few things Congress has been able to consistently agree on over the past few decades.

More money means that the government can hire more agents, but it also incentivizes profit-seeking corporations to get more creative about ways to make money off the incarceration and surveillance of immigrants. Corporations like the Geo Group and Core Civic can build more prisons for immigrants, private security companies can get government contracts to staff those prisons, and technology companies can create more tools to surveil immigrants not imprisoned, while construction companies can secure billions to build physical walls on the US-Mexico border.[33] There is profit to be made off of immigration enforcement, and that creates a self-perpetuating cycle where private companies are profiting off of the surveillance, incarceration, and deportation of immigrants and lobbying the government for more opportunities to do so. The US government would do well to shut off the money hose.

Change the Bureaucratic Culture

Any effort to create positive change, however defined, must contend with the cultural status quo in the US immigration system. Culture is notoriously hard to change because it is constantly being replenished and reinforced, through both informal mechanisms like agent-to-agent socialization, and formal mechanisms like training.

There are three things I believe we can do in the immediate sense, and these have to do with how we hire and train agents, as well as how we hold them accountable for their actions. For example, requiring that federal immigration agents have a college education is one area that holds promise. Not only would this decrease the pool of qualified applications, which itself may have a shrinking impact on the larger system, but it also substantively changes the qualitative character of the applicant pool. This is not a panacea, but there is evidence that among local police, those who have a college degree use less force and are more professional, which can lead to more democratic policing.[34]

Training is another key area that can produce cultural shifts in the US immigration bureaucracy. Right now, agents are taught in an excessively enforcement-oriented way that neglects the more administrative functions of their role. This is fundamentally tied to the militarization of policing, which is a broader issue in law enforcement. Still, agents' academies do not include education on migration as a social phenomenon, its underlying mechanisms, or empirically grounded teachings about agents' role in migration management. Agents leave the academy believing they can actually "solve the immigration issue" through border enforcement and deportation, which breeds resistance to inclusionary immigration measures and leaves them disappointed by the reality of their work.

Finally, there simply needs to be more accountability within CBP and ICE—something about which there is wide consensus.[35] We need robust accountability mechanisms that can provide oversight, both in the form of citizen commissions and in the form of government watchdogs that already exist. Empowering agencies like the Government Accountability Office, the Civil Rights and Civil Liberties Office, and the Office of the Inspector General with mechanisms to oversee and swiftly remove agents who engage in abuse or corruption, or otherwise break the law, is an urgent matter.

We also must address formal and informal mechanisms that silent dissent among agents. There could be more robust training on agents' duty to intervene when they witness deviant behavior by colleagues, as well as training on how to issue conscientious objections to policies that compel them to engage in unethical behavior. I talked to agents who were disturbed by certain mandates (e.g., family separation) but felt they did not have an outlet for voicing those concerns without sacrificing their job and their social status within the organization.[36] Along these same lines, increasing oversight over agents' labor unions is another area that could increase accountability. The National Border Patrol Council and National ICE Council leadership represent some of the most extreme views among immigration agents and have even been known to try to undercut inclusionary immigration measures.[37] These unions conceal much variation in viewpoints among immigration agents and serve to silent dissent.

I am aware that these objectives—uncoupling immigration from criminal law, reducing the money in enforcement, and changing the bureaucratic culture—are located on different parts of the spectrum of nonreformist to reformist reforms. Some, like changing the culture, are closer to the reformist reform end of the spectrum than, say, divestment and undoing the crimmigration system. This is an enduring tension in any effort to transform systems, a tension we need to be able to withstand if our efforts aim to both pursue broad visions of transformation and attend to the needs of people currently subject to the immigration state's extraordinary power.

Borders and Boundaries in a Globalized World

The political philosopher Seyla Benhabib argues that there is a "constitutive dilemma" at the heart of Western liberal democracies, like the United States.[38] This dilemma is the tension between two espoused principles in these countries: their claims to sovereign self-determination and their purported commitment to human rights. These two principles are in opposition to each other because sovereignty has an inherently exclusionary character that makes citizenship the basis of rights, while human rights principles compel inclusion based on personhood. This constitutive dilemma is evident in the stories that agents told me and shows no sign of letting up.

Migration, whether forced or voluntary, will not go away. It is the most natural of human instincts to move for life improvement, whether the need for improvement is created by negligent states or natural phenomena. Once migration flows are established, there are social, economic, and political mechanisms that sustain them, giving international migration a self-perpetuating character that is impossible to disrupt via enforcement mechanisms alone. Even so, states continue to harden their borders—the physical, virtual, and symbolic ones—because bordering is how sovereignty is signaled and maintained. Those escalated enforcement efforts seldom meet their stated goals, because they leave the mechanisms that generate and replenish migrations untouched, but they are often wildly successful in a performative sense.[39]

What is more, these performances have dire material consequences for migrants.

Even if countries cannot seal their borders or deport their way out of migration, undocumented or not, their laws can make it very difficult for people to live outside of their countries of origin. Immigration systems—especially those of dominant countries like the United States—have extraordinary power to alter life courses, to determine fates, to warp the very essence of existence for millions of people within and outside of the country's borders.

Given the inherent inequality of a bordered world and that the maintenance of sovereignty begets coercion, questions about the moral legitimacy of territorial borders will persist. Until the United States and other Western democracies reconcile the gap between liberal ideals and their punitive approach to migration, the moral authority of the state and its agents will rest on precarious ground, no matter what their workforce looks like.

ACKNOWLEDGMENTS

THIS BOOK WOULD NOT EXIST without an extraordinary group of people who have supported me from near and far, consciously and without knowing it, and over the course of many years. This book is as much their accomplishment as my own.

I want to thank the editors who have shaped this book in one way or another: Eric Crahan, Rachael Levay, Meagan Levinson, and Margy Thomas. Thank you, all, for believing in this project and for getting it to this point. Audra Wolfe deserves special mention for helping me find my book voice and pushing me to be bold and honest. Audra, I'll be forever grateful. Thank you, also, to Kathleen Kageff for copyediting and Jill Harris for ushering the book along the publication process.

While researching and writing this book I benefited from financial support from the Ford Foundation, Eugene Cota-Robles Fellowship, UCLA Institute of American Cultures, UC MEXUS, UC President's Postdoctoral Fellowship Program, Citizens and Scholars, and the Princeton University Press Book Proposal Development Grant.

I did most of the fieldwork for this book while a graduate student at UCLA, where I had an extraordinary dissertation committee consisting of Vilma Ortiz (chair), Ingrid Eagly, Rubén Hernández-León, and Roger Waldinger. I don't know how they remember it, but I don't think any of them flinched when I told them that I wanted to interview immigration agents for my dissertation, a goal that might've seemed far-fetched at the time. Thank you for your vote of confidence and for your enduring mentorship. I hope that you each recognize your influence on this work. Any shortcomings are my own and not due to a shortage of brilliant feedback from each of you.

Even as a faculty member, I still think of myself as one of "Vilma's students," which I suspect is how many of us who have had the privilege of her mentorship will continue to think of ourselves throughout our career. Being one of "Vilma's students" means that I am part of a phenomenal community of mostly mujeres who have long sustained me intellectually and through their friendship.

I know the community has grown, but when I was at UCLA it was the following mujeres who read the earliest versions of what would eventually become a dissertation and then this book: Karina Chavarria, Deisy Del Real, Laura Enriquez, Rocio Garcia, Celia Lacayo, Mirian Martinez-Aranda, Erica Morales, Laura Orrico, Cassandra Salgado, Ariana Valle, and Sylvia Zamora. Thank you for lending me your brilliance and confidence when I needed it most and for the enduring support and community.

Amada Armenta has seen this book through and through, and her lovely mother, Sra Alicia Armenta, was a huge source of support to me during fieldwork. Thank you both so much! Amada, the carrot isn't real, but we continue to chase it, and it's best to do it together.

At the University of California, Irvine, I have benefited from a wonderfully supportive department, full of people who have cheered me on and helped me settle into academic life. Nina Bandelj, Rachel Goldberg, Julia Lerch, David Meyer, Francesca Polletta, and Kristin Turney all have been guiding lights in their own way. Thank you to Peter Pantaleon for key reference-page assistance.

To Glenda Flores, Mirian Martinez-Aranda, and Rocio Rosales: you make work feel like play (sometimes), and I (always) feel incredibly lucky to have colleagues who are also my homies. Gracias for cheering me on, for helping me celebrate the small and big milestones, and for sharing your life with me and my little family. I am so grateful for each one of you.

To my respondents, thank you for talking with me. When any of you asked me what I was going to write in the dissertation (and eventually this book), I always answered truthfully that I would not know until I finished collecting and analyzing the data. Now that this book is in the world, I would venture to guess that many of you will not agree with its focus on race, morality, and indifference. My hope is not that you agree, but that you are open to understanding your work in these terms and take seriously the implications of doing so.

There are so many other people who have made this book possible in one way or another. Cristina Mora, thank you for the support during and after the Career Enhancement Fellowship and for the bubbles! Ariana Valle, thank you for the bubbles and also for reminding me to always celebrate! Anita Casavantes-Bradford, thank you for helping me get through the last leg, filling my tank when I most needed it. Anthony Ocampo, remember when we were writing buddies way back when? Let's do it again! Cynthia Feliciano, thank you for the many ways that you have supported me all these years. Geoff Ward, thank you for supporting me during the postdoc and especially for getting me through the job market. Val Jenness, thank you for the lunches, the coffees, and for never sugar-coating the advice. Carlos Vélez-Ibañez, thank you for the mentorship and for knowing that I was a sociologist before I did. Maartje van der Woude, thank you for all the laughs, collaboration, and friendship. Laura Orrico, thank you for the party motivation! Jennifer Cordero, SSMP! Kelly Ward and Edelina Burciaga, how we do what we do is a mystery, but I know we do it better when we can laugh about it, even if from afar.

Chema, Clau, Lolita, Martica, Roji, and Vero—thank you for being my core. We have joked for years that no one knows what I do, but now look, here is proof that I do work! Las amo. To the Berrelleza family and especially my big sis, Lily, thank you for always being there for the fun and not-so-fun parts.

My sister Diana, you're the only one who understands what it was like to be raised by the force of nature that was Juana Vega and the only one who truly understands what it has been like to lose her. Thank you for always being there, for reminding me not to take myself too seriously, and for being proud of me even if you don't tell me enough, ha! To Damara, my first baby: I'm so proud of the woman you've become. Your fearlessness and perseverance are truly inspiring, and I will forever be in awe of you.

To Penelope and Lucas, my unruly muses: You really are my inspiration and my absolute joy. You have sustained me all these years, even if you didn't know that was what you were doing when you bounced into my office for a hug or to stand behind me trying to make out the words I was typing. You've grown alongside this book, and I hope that has encouraged you to pursue your own passions. I absolutely adore you and am what I am because of and for you.

Joey, your nurturing spirit and easy smile have carried me through many challenges, and I know that I am at my best when I can see myself through your eyes. Thank you for making me celebrate the good times and for holding me up when life has pushed me around. I literally could not have done this without you.

I dedicate this book to my mother, Juana Vega. It is from her that I learned not to take no for an answer and to get right back up after a fall. We had the honor of being a multigenerational household for many years, and after a long day of work I could always count on my mom to ask me about this book in her gentle way. "Como te fue, hija? Pudiste aventajar?" She is no longer with us, but I feel compelled to answer her here: Si que pude aventajar, ma. Aquí está el libro.

Methodological Appendix

IMMIGRATION AGENTS are a hard-to-reach population, but not because they are marginalized. Instead, they are difficult to study because they have the gate-keeping resources of the Department of Homeland Security at their disposal, and because they are members of an insular occupational group that is skeptical of outsiders. In this methodological appendix, I outline how I gained access to immigration agents, as well as some of the power dynamics and ethical questions inherent to interviewing these famously indisposed bureaucrats.

Gaining Access to Immigration Agents

I gained access to US immigration agents by making an unannounced visit to the Border Patrol sector headquarters in "Desert City," Arizona, in July 2014. By the time I walked into this government office, I had already tried all the conventional ways of getting access to a social group, including using my networks, sending emails, making phone calls, and so on. None of that had worked, so I decided to "just show up."

It is worth stating the obvious before moving further: the fact that "showing up" occurred to me as a possibility is evidence of my citizenship privilege. I am a US-born citizen, and I did not feel structurally vulnerable to immigration agents. I did not have close family members who were structurally vulnerable to the immigration state either. I discuss other aspects of my positionality below, but it is important to acknowledge my citizenship privilege at the outset.

The day I walked into the Border Patrol sector headquarters, I found a very standard waiting room with large pictures of heads of state, including then president Barack Obama. To my immediate left was a large, thick glass partition with a busy-looking, middle-aged White woman sitting behind it. I approached the glass and tried to strike a casual tone as I leaned into the small opening at the bottom of the glass and said, "I'm a graduate student, and I want to talk to Border Patrol agents about their job. Is there someone who can help me?" She seemed confused and maybe a little bit annoyed. "What did you say?" I tried again. "I'm a graduate student, and I want to talk to Border Patrol agents about their job. Is there someone who I can talk to about that?" Looking slightly less confused, she got on the phone. I looked around, pretending not to strain to hear what she was saying. Seconds later she told me, "Someone is on their way."

That someone was Agent Frank Garrison, a senior Border Patrol agent who was on temporary assignment with the Public Affairs Office at the time. A White man in his early forties, he was imposing at over six feet tall and with a build that could be described as previously athletic, leaning toward portly. He had a round face that gave him a youthful, friendly aspect, but he had the look of someone who had been sent to investigate a bizarre request. I answered his "How can I help you?" with the same statement I had used with the receptionist, but realizing that this could be my only shot, I tried to fit in all the information that I thought was relevant. "I'm from the area, and I'm getting my PhD in sociology at UCLA. I want to write about people who are on the front lines of immigration enforcement. I think we know a lot about immigration from the perspective of politicians and media, but we don't really know a lot about agents enforcing the law, and that is what my study is about." Much to my surprise, he seemed receptive and asked what kind of questions I wanted to ask agents. I answered that it was "questions about their experiences and perspectives." He asked if I had a copy of the questions, and I answered that I could email the questions to him within the hour.

As he pulled out his card, I tried to prolong the interaction. "Look," I said, sounding a little too abrupt, "I know this isn't a good time for the agency, especially because of what is going on at the border right now, but I'm not a reporter. I'm a graduate student doing research for a dissertation, and I really want to understand how agents think about their job."

For reference, this was the end of July 2014, when thousands of Central American asylum seekers, including unaccompanied children, were arriving at the US-Mexico border. This "crisis" as it was referred to, turned out to be one of many subsequent "crises" that the Border Patrol and the broader US immigration bureaucracy has mismanaged. This was a particularly bad time to study immigration agents, not only because there was a huge amount of media attention on them, but also because many of them were being deployed to various parts of the Southwest where the influx was higher than in Arizona.

There were also reports that the government had issued a gag order. I knew all of this was working against me.

My acknowledgment of this context seemed to resonate with Agent Garrison, who handed me his card, saying, "Yes, this is a pretty bad time, but I'll see what I can do. Email me the questions." I emailed Agent Garrison my interview protocol and all the relevant information about the study within hours. His short response contrasted starkly with my detailed message, but it seemed like progress: "Thank you for the request. I will forward this information to my chain of command and get back with you when I hear from them. Have a great day." I now know that the chain of command included the sector's top brass; everyone from supervisors in the Public Affairs Office to various assistant chiefs saw and approved my request. They did not recommend any changes to the interview protocol. I was back at the sector headquarters in early September, interviewing Border Patrol agents.

My access to the Border Patrol in Arizona facilitated subsequent access to the agency in California and, eventually, to ICE. Having interviewed thirty-seven agents and conducted participant observation in a Border Patrol Citizens Academy in Arizona buttressed my efforts to interview agents in California. An Arizona agent connected me with their counterpart in a California sector I call "Mountain Valley." I spent months in Mountain Valley, participating in a weeks-long Border Patrol Citizens Academy and interviewing twenty-three agents there.

I had been trying to get access to ICE on and off, almost the entire time I was in the field with the Border Patrol. I had gotten very close when, the same summer that I walked into the Border Patrol sector headquarters, I met with an ICE officer in Arizona, who had agreed to help me recruit his colleagues for my study. Before we could begin, he required that I submit an official study request through the Department of Homeland Security's Office of Academic Engagement in Washington, DC. I sent the exact email and documents, approved by UCLA's Institutional Review Board (IRB), that I had sent to the Border Patrol. I received a confirmation from them within twenty-four hours of sending the request. This was August 2014, almost the same time as things were progressing with the Border Patrol. I was encouraged, elated even, until weeks turned into a month and a half, and I heard nothing. I emailed a follow-up in September, with no response. I emailed again in October, with no response. During this time I had also called and left messages. Then, in November 2014, I received a vague but ominous phone call from my contact in DC telling me that while my request was being processed, "legal is very busy with some things coming down the pipe so I can't give you a time frame for approval." I unsuccessfully tried to pin down a more precise update but eventually accepted that these efforts were not yielding the access I sought.

I had all but lost hope of studying ICE and was making contingency plans to interview Border Patrol agents working on the border with Canada to see how their experiences differ from those patrolling the US-Mexico border. But before officially moving on I decided to try ICE one more time. In February 2016, I again emailed a public affairs officer with ICE, and I then received a response. Their message was short: "Hi Irene, For this type of interview, please contact [Name, Position]." The message also provided me the direct email and phone number of someone I call Officer Travis Boise. I emailed him the exact message I had used before, this time adding that I had already conducted sixty Border Patrol interviews in Arizona and California. He called me unexpectedly one weekday.

After we exchanged requisite pleasantries, Officer Boise got to the point. "Why do you want to do this study?" I could answer in my sleep because I had been talking to Border Patrol agents for months. "I want to understand how immigration agents think about their job. We hear a lot about immigration enforcement from the perspective of politicians and the media, but not from the people on the front lines." He asked what I would do with the study. I told him that I would write my dissertation, and eventually a book. He asked whether I could produce a student ID and my transcript. Yes. I also volunteered that the study had been approved by my university's IRB and that I could share the approval, along with the interview protocol and other study documents. He said he'd take a copy of those items. Then he asked if I was undocumented.

I was momentarily taken aback, but not completely surprised. I knew he was gauging my biases. "I was born in California." "Is your family undocumented?" A simple "No" did not satisfy him, judging by the expectant silence on the other side of the line. "My mom is a naturalized citizen, and my dad died when I was seven." That stopped the questions, but he wanted proof. He asked me to send my passport and driver's license along with my student documents. He said he could not make any promises—a statement reminiscent of what Agent Garrison had said to me years earlier. With that, we thanked each other and said good-bye. The call was over almost as suddenly as it had begun, and the interviews started three weeks later. I went on to interview a total of thirty agents working in two distinct regions within Southern California. Officer Boise also arranged for me to see two immigration detention centers, and

I spent time—mostly waiting for scheduled or prospective interviewees—in two distinct field offices in the region.

Access Lessons

The approach I used with the Border Patrol resonates with what police researchers call strategic ambush access.[1] This is the practice of showing up without an appointment, to try to gain an audience with police officers. The idea is that with organizations that are weary of outsiders, showing up in person is more effective than relying on advance appointments or waiting for bureaucrats to answer formal communication requests, including emails and phone calls. This absolutely resonates with my experience. By the time I showed up at the Border Patrol sector headquarters, I had already tried conventional research access approaches. I had emailed, called, and tried to get my contacts to put me in contact with people inside the bureaucracy. None of that had worked, but showing up did because ignoring a person is harder than overlooking an email or phone call.

Strategic ambush access is unlikely to work for all people and all policing organizations, and I specifically do not think that it would have worked for ICE. My unannounced visit was fruitful in large part because the Border Patrol has a formal public-facing component, their Public Affairs Office. When I walked into the sector headquarters there was a whole office of people whose role is to interact with the public—the receptionist knew whom to call. In contrast, when I was in the field, there was one person charged with ICE's public affairs for an area of responsibility that spanned almost all Southern California, and their office location was not public. One precondition for strategic ambush access to work may then be that the agency must have a public-facing mechanism that can be visited in person. The fact that most local law enforcement agencies have public information officers and similar mechanisms is good news for researchers looking to try this approach. Of course, it is important to sample out of the public affairs network, which I did.

It is one thing to show up and talk to someone; it is something else to secure the formal approvals needed to study a closed-off bureaucracy. The first is a matter of finding the place and enduring the awkwardness; the second is a matter of gaining what Rachel Ellis calls institutional legitimacy.[2] Institutional legitimacy is the buy-in afforded to researchers when organizational gatekeepers assess proposed research as appropriate and worthy within the context of institutional priorities, norms, and values. Writing within the context of prison ethnography, Ellis reminds us that not all "hard-to-reach" populations are elusive for the same reasons. Some are difficult to reach because of various forms of structural precarity, while others have gatekeeping resources to keep researchers at bay. Such is the case for immigration agents; they are hard to reach because they work for the Department of Homeland Security, a powerful government bureaucracy that can keep observers out under the guise of security concerns. Thus, my gaining access to agents was a matter of being legible to gatekeepers like Agent Garrison and Officer Boise, both White men in positions of power who could open the door to an outsider.

I believe that a combination of factors resulted in my being read as a low-risk person to talk to by immigration agents. As a woman and as a student, I was likely seen as less threatening than male researchers or researchers with more formal titles. As a Mexican American from a border region, I was likely seen as familiar, perhaps even friendly to immigration agents' cause. I was also a relatively anonymous doctoral student without any published work on the US immigration bureaucracy. If my respondents searched for me online, they likely found a student profile on the UCLA Sociology Program webpage and a developing curriculum vitae. I did not have active social media accounts at the time. I cannot know exactly how agents read me, but my best guess is that I was read as unthreatening.

That Officer Boise asked if I was undocumented and required proof of citizenship epitomizes the kind of discretion that gatekeepers have when evaluating researchers. I cannot think of a formal reason why my citizenship status or my family's immigration status was part of the conversation, but I can think of many informal reasons that ICE would want this information.[3] As I said before, Officer Boise was gauging my biases. He was using citizenship status as a proxy for my politics around immigration. I suppose he could have just asked me what I thought about the current president or his policies directly, but that would have been too obvious. He opted for a more roundabout approach.

Then there is the issue of race/ethnicity. My assumption is that Officer Boise saw my Spanish surname, perhaps saw my picture after a couple of online searches, and then thought to ask if I or my family was undocumented. I cannot know this for sure, but I highly doubt that this question would have come up in a conversation with someone of European ancestry. Would he have approved my study if I had lacked documentation that proved my citizenship? I think it is unlikely. To boot, this would have been completely within his discretion, and I would have had to move on. My experience shows how precarious and arbitrary the process of gaining access to the US immigration bureaucracy can be.

Another factor that facilitated my access is that I inadvertently articulated the research in a way that appealed to organizational gatekeepers. When I was deciding how to describe my study to potential participants I had settled on the following sentence and delivered some version of it throughout my fieldwork: "We hear a lot about immigration enforcement from the perspective of politicians and the media, but not from the people on the front lines." This sentence ticked all the boxes for a graduate student looking for a pithy description of the tortuous web of words that is the nascent dissertation. It was short, devoid of academic jargon, clear enough that people would nod in understanding, but broad enough that the study had room to evolve in the field. It also articulated the literature gap I was attempting to fill. I was very proud of it as a feat of academic translation. But what I did not fully understand was that I had stumbled upon a line that achieved a prerequisite of gaining access to penal institutions: it articulated the study in a way that was consistent with how immigration agents see their world.[4]

My description of the study appealed to a sense of aggrievement that pervades the culture of immigration enforcement. Mirroring the broader policing profession, immigration agents often feel underappreciated by the public, misrepresented by the media, used by politicians, and unsupported by bureaucratic leaders, who they perceive as engaged in political pandering. When I described my study as centered on agents' experiences and perspectives—standard focuses of sociology of work studies—I inadvertently tapped into something that agents think is missing in the broader immigration debate: their viewpoints. When I said, "We know a lot about immigration from the perspective of politicians and the media," I was naming primary actors in the symbolic struggle over immigration in the United States, and from the perspective of agents, those actors know a lot less about the issue than they did. What I thought was a pithy description of my dissertation was interpreted by agents as an opportunity to *tell their story*. This fundamentally shaped not just my access, but also how agents related to me, and the kinds of narratives that I ultimately recorded.

On Accounts and Power Dynamics in Interviewing Agents

Immigration agents' job is at best a source of mild controversy in their everyday lives, and at worst a source of stigma. This is not to say that they are not proud of what they do or that they think they are doing something wrong. Not at all. Immigration agents see themselves as the "good guys" engaged in a morally righteous battle against a variety of threats, ranging from terrorists, to criminals, to moochers, to clueless politicians. However, they are also deeply aware of how *others* (namely, progressives) see them: as racists, Nazis, heartless family separators, corrupt government officials, mindless cogs in a machine, political footballs, and so on.[5] There I was, with a recorder, interviewing them about their job—a sensitive topic. It does not take an advanced methodologist to think of the issue of social desirability, or the tendency of interviewees to present themselves in a favorable light.

Agents are also organizational elites, people who hold positions of power within an institution. Their status as organizational elites presents a distinct set of conditions to navigate as a researcher: elites may act as a spokesperson for their organization in interviews, they may take control of the interview, and the researcher is a status subordinate to interviewee.[6] In short, the power dynamics of studying elites are different from those when we study marginalized populations; in these interactions, staying in control of the interview is a central task.[7] Do these challenges mean that we discard the interview as a methodological tool in elite and other studies? Absolutely not. Given elites' gatekeeping resources, interviews are often the best and sometimes only viable method to study these power holders. Researchers studying elites have a different set of challenges and corresponding tools to negotiate their interactions.

For instance, the rapport-building strategy of leveling status and power differentials between interviewer and interviewee requires more nuance. I alternated a learner and expert stance in my fieldwork. I was a status subordinate in all my interviews because I was an outsider to the organization, and agents had the power to rescind access at any point. But there were important subtleties in these dynamics based on agents' position in the bureaucracy. When I interviewed high-ranking officials, I leaned into my expertise on immigration policy and my knowledge of the history of immigration and enforcement in the region. This allowed me to stay in control of the interview since one risk of interviewing elites is that they will exert rhetorical dominance over their interviewee, leaving the former flailing to get in a word.[8] This was less of a risk when I was sitting across from frontline agents who did not try to control the interview and only seldom tried to evade questions. In fact, in some instances I sensed they were intimidated by my credentials as a PhD student, judging by their demeanor or by their qualification of their statements. I emphasized my learner stance in these interactions, reminding agents that I was interested in their views and that there were no right or wrong answers.

Another principle of interviewing is that we should not challenge our respondents and that we call attention to their logical inconsistencies at our own peril. In this approach, interviewers are often submissive and always empathetic, active listeners who create a conversation-like atmosphere that enhances and maintains rapport.[9] Their scrutiny comes only at the analysis and writing phase. This principle also requires qualification when studying elites. If researchers adopt a purely submissive stance, then elites are very likely to take control of the interview with company lines that may be as easily gleaned from marketing materials. The submissive approach also allows elites to avoid sensitive issues.[10] Kathleen Blee, a social movements scholar who studied the KKK, reminds us that challenging our respondents and focusing our analysis on events and causal reasoning is how we stay in control and avoid giving a platform to elites engaged in exclusionary activities.[11]

Instead of adopting a submissive stance, I adopted an approach that allowed for interviewee-led dialogue, as well as some confrontational questions.[12] While admittedly risky and somewhat awkward, this strategy can be analytically fruitful. For instance, like most people, immigration agents do not want to be seen as racists. Yet, they know that this is how many people see them. At a certain point in the interview, after I felt rapport was established or when there was a natural segue into the question, I would ask agents to weigh in on the question of race. I would directly ask, "When people say you [immigration agents] are racists, how do you respond to that?" This type of question achieved two feats. First, it put distance between me and the question—it framed the premise that they were racists as a matter of public talk, instead of my own perspective. Second, it prompted the interviewee to issue a defensive response. That defensive response, with careful follow-up prompts, could be eased into a conversation on race where I would suggest alternatives to their interpretations, or offer counterpoints for them to weigh in on. These interactions were delicate and did not always go as planned, especially with high-ranking officials who were much more experienced at evading questions and asserting themselves than the frontline agents.

For the most part, though, the strategy worked, and I was able to engage agents on race beyond the sound bite that they might have given me had I not challenged them. What is more, I did this without losing the interview or sacrificing subsequent recruitments. Confrontational questions and even criticisms are useful and even necessary in elite interviews because it forces interviewees out of the spokesperson role, pushes them to "spell out their thinking and acting in rather precise ways,"[13] and lays bare their causal reasoning.[14]

Regardless of our strategies, the issue of an elite approaching the interview as a spokesperson for their organization will remain a formidable issue. There will always be a risk that an interview will yield organizational doctrines. In fact, all interviewees—regardless of their location in the societal power structure—tend to engage in display work during interviews. This is the basis for a major critique of the method: that people can be unreliable narrators of past events, motivations, and future goals so that we cannot take what they say at face value. Sociologists Colin Jerolmack and Shamus Khan refer to this as "the attitudinal fallacy" or the mistake of conceptualizing talk as predictive or indicative of social action.[15]

Discussions about the validity of interviews remind us that the onus is on researchers to ensure their inferences and arguments are within the method's scope conditions. This is true for all methods. Interviews can yield accounts that are good indicators of how people define themselves and seek to be seen by others, and of the categories of thought they apply to future and past situations.[16] They are also good expressions of respondents' emotional lives, their visceral reactions, and their metafeelings, or how they feel about how they feel.[17] They may not always mirror behavior or predict social action.

I embrace the fact that my interviews with agents captured "accounts" or statements that we, as social actors, issue to one another to explain behavior that is perceived to be "unanticipated" or "untoward."[18] I analyze agents' accounts, looking for unspoken assumptions, logics, ideologies, and normative mechanisms that are difficult to articulate or unpopular to voice. My analysis turns on three questions: (1) What is assumed and left unspoken in this statement? (2) What is this statement doing for the agent as an individual? (3) What is this statement doing for the agent as a member of an organization? These questions allowed me to uncover the tacit principles that guided agents' causal reasoning and ultimately their normative worlds.

An example of my analytical approach may be helpful here. When Border Patrol agents discussed their use-of-force decisions, a sensitive topic, they would often mention immigrants' moral character, always in a negative light. They often said things like, "the media makes them out to be angels, but what they don't tell you is that that guy had a rap sheet longer than this table." If you were to ask an immigration agent whether a person's criminal record matters to their use-of-force decisions, they would tell you no. Use-of-force decisions are supposed to happen within context, given the "totality of circumstances" in a particular situation at a particular moment in time. This is the official line of the Border Patrol; this is what you will see stated by CBP and what agents will tell you if you ask how they make use-of-force decisions.[19]

However, the fact that agents bring up immigrants' moral character in their justifications means that they consider this a relevant detail. They assume that offering that detail—that the person who got shot had a criminal record—is redeeming. The unspoken premise may be that use of force against criminals is more acceptable than use of force against people without a criminal record. From this, we might infer that agents' judgments about immigrants' moral character matter to how they behave toward them. If an analyst took agents' talk uncritically, they might have reported that agents make use-of-force decisions based on the totality of the circumstances, independent of their own individual judgments about immigrants. By paying close attention not just to what respondents are saying, but to what is implied in their statements, we can uncover causal reasoning and unspoken principles that undergird behaviors.

Empathizing with the Unsympathetic

I have discussed the methodological issues at stake in this study, as well as the strategies I used to negotiate them. I now turn to a final question, which is often the elephant in the room when I present my work: How does one build rapport and empathize with people they are ideologically opposed to? Does a study of immigration agents, people who carry out one of the most racialized and exclusionary bodies of law in the United States, somehow empower and legitimize them? No one has ever asked me these questions directly, but more than one person has implied them, a reminder that a certain amount of stigma accrues to researchers who study unsympathetic respondents.[20] Our conflation of empathy and sympathy is one important reason for this.

At its core empathy is about vicarious understanding, trying to see the world from another's vantage point. That is why empathy is central to qualitative research. What else are we doing if not trying to present and interpret another's vantage point? Sympathy is about feeling sorrow for another person's troubles and hardships. These are different constructs that are mistakenly used interchangeably. We often assume that if a qualitative researcher has made inroads with a particular social group, then they must be at least somewhat sympathetic to them or even have positive feelings toward them.[21] We find it hard to believe that empathy can coexist with negative feelings about our respondents, or at least find it taboo to discuss negative feelings toward our respondents.[22] We present ourselves as sympathetic observers, even implying that our research was cathartic for our respondents and sometimes even emancipatory.[23] We confuse empathy and sympathy, leaning into the latter.

It is helpful to focus on my own discipline to make this point. Sociologists are interested in social inequalities of various sorts. We are interested in understanding how inequalities come to be, how they are perpetuated, and yes, how we might disrupt them. Many of us do research because we have a deep-rooted commitment to changing and improving society, dismantling power structures that marginalize and exclude. It follows that most of our research focuses on the marginalized and excluded, people to whom we are sympathetic. Research on immigration enforcement is an example. Much of this work focuses on immigrants themselves, carefully and compassionately documenting the myriad of ways that immigration control devastates communities. This work is critical because it demonstrates just how inhumane, racialized, and destructive immigration law is. It also shows that working-class immigrants of color and their descendants bear the brunt of the system's deleterious consequences.

But what about the system itself? What about the ecology of politicians, local and federal bureaucrats, and other authorities who produce these outcomes? Should they not be subject to a researcher's critical gaze? Should we not seek to understand how they see their role in reproducing citizenship and race-based inequalities? If we truly believe that our work has the potential to make change, and I think it does, then we need to take a more holistic view of the social problems we aim to remedy. A sociology of exclusion is not complete without a sociology of power. We need to do what Laura Nader described as "studying up," subjecting power holders to the same scrutiny we subject minoritized populations to.[24]

A counterargument may be that we study people we are sympathetic to because we want to give voice to the voiceless, empower the powerless, humanize the dehumanized. That resonates with me. But as Mario Small reminds us, "there is nothing inherently liberating" in researching or writing about the poor—it is what we do with our research that matters most.[25] This is not to say that research on the marginalized is inconsequential, quite the opposite. If it were not for the scholars (and advocates) who focus on inequalities and their dire impacts on various communities, those inequalities would continue unabated and unexamined, and the policies to remedy them would be nonexistent or much less effective. At the same time, I think it is only fair that scholars acknowledge that, often, we get much more out of our research than the people we study.[26] Giving voice to the voiceless, the narrative that we sometimes adopt uncritically, could use more of the skepticism that we academics pride ourselves on. The research itself is not liberation for the marginalized; that depends on what we do with the research, and that is where many of us fall short.

I concede that studying people we disagree with is difficult. There is the risk of colleagues questioning our convictions, of respondents assuming we agree with them, and worst of all, of our research being understood as support for the causes we aim to change. Then there is the emotional labor and cognitive dissonance required to achieve empathy where there is no sympathy. But those are not reasons to foreclose on studies of power. We simply need to be more intentional about developing research principles to study those we disagree with.

One place to start is to think critically about how we present our research to our respondents. When agents asked me what I was going to say in my dissertation and subsequent book (an effort to position me on the immigration debate), my response was always the same: I would not know until I had finished collecting and analyzing my data. This was true. I take seriously the charge to remain nimble as qualitative fieldwork refines our research questions, hones our interests, shapes the data we can collect, and demarcates the arguments we can make. But it was also true that I could have answered this question differently. I certainly had opinions, but I was taught to suspend those opinions to seek understanding. I always told agents that I was interested in an accurate portrayal of their perspectives and experiences, independent of mine.

Had my qualitative methods training included more guidance on how to relate to respondents we disagree with, I may have presented in a different way. In her study of racist activists Kathleen Blee positioned herself as a "distant—but not neutral observer" making clear that she disagreed with her respondents' cause.[27] I have wondered how taking an explicitly critical stance would have impacted my data collection. There is no way of knowing for sure, but my working assumption is that it would have thwarted my access and not changed my data much. That is because I'm not sure that the neutral persona I tried to cultivate was ever accepted.

My sense is that agents viewed me with some combination of skepticism, suspicion, and perhaps even contempt because they (rightly) assumed that my politics were unlike theirs. I viewed them with a combination of intellectual fascination, disapproval, and confusion, especially when it came to the most morally dubious aspects of their work. Perhaps they were curious about me precisely because of these dynamics. I would never presume that they saw me as an insider, nor did I seek to become one. I shared characteristics that made me very similar to most of my sample, Latina/o agents. Being Mexican American from the border meant that we were familiar to each other, culturally and in terms of language and the experience of growing up in immigrant communities and families. But moments of mutual recognition are not enough to achieve insider status, and certainly not with an insular occupational group.

Admitting this might seem like a faux pas to researchers—a red flag that betrays that I did not achieve the holy grail of insider status. How could my fieldwork possibly yield "good" data when my respondents were suspicious of me? How can my disapproval of their work coexist with my empathy as a researcher? The reality is that all that does coexist when we think about what empathy truly is—it is not sympathy. Empathy is complexity. It is understanding, not agreement. I do understand how immigration agents do their work, and I hope that reading this book will yield understanding for others— understanding, independent of agreement.

I firmly believe that we do a disservice to ourselves and to other researchers when we paint a veneer of generalized trust and cooperation between researchers and respondents. To report only the ways that we were accepted, and not awkward moments of mutual rejection, is misleading. To do so is to ignore the emotional toll that our respondents pay in telling us their stories and the emotional toll that we pay in acting as though we do not have opinions about them, or worst yet, as though we agree with them wholeheartedly. The reality is that if we are going to do "good" qualitative research, we must be reflexive about all the parts of the research. That is how we can better evaluate our influence over the highly interactive data collection process and ultimately ensure that our arguments emerge from the data. We need to tell each other what we accomplished, not what we think qualitative research ought to accomplish, or what we wish we had accomplished.

Where does that leave my interviews with immigration agents? I know I captured organizational doctrines, face-saving performances, and ideologies that may bear little resemblance to how agents behaved when outsiders were not around. But I also know that I uncovered unspoken behavioral logics, contradictory beliefs, and unseated memories whose visceral emotionality were disorienting to me and the agent recalling them. I sat across from agents whose sheer normality was instructive. I learned that the caricature of the heavy-footed, red-faced, callous agent is misleading because it makes agents seem like they are a particular type of person. It makes us believe that only a particular type of person can separate children from their families, shoot pepper balls at asylum seekers, and incarcerate people seeking a better life. It turns out that immigration agents are normal people, and that is precisely the point.

NOTES

Introduction

1. I use "Latina/o" to refer to my respondents, and sometimes "Hispanic" when my respondents referred to themselves in this way. I use the gender-neutral "Latinx" to refer to broader community.

2. Throughout the book I will refer to the collection of US immigration policy implementation agencies and their employees as "the immigration state."

3. Fassin (2009, 1237); see also Fassin (2005); Chauvin and Garcés-Mascareñas (2020).

4. Herzfeld (1991, 1).

5. It is critical to understand that US immigration control, especially along the US-Mexico border, is a wrought, contemporary manifestation of the United States' settler colonialist ventures, which alternate between racial conquest and exclusion of Mexicans specifically, but Latinx people more broadly. Scholars have written exceptional books on this topic, and I encourage interested readers toward those sources for a more thorough examination of this historical context: Gómez (2018); Lytle Hernández (2017); Molina (2014).

6. For more on how state categories are created and normalized, see Bourdieu (1994); Menjívar (2023); Monk (2022); J. Scott (2020).

7. On "bureaucracies of displacement," see Menjívar (2023); on immigration bureaucrats working in distinct parts of the world, but cohering around rationalities related to indifference, see, for example, Aliverti (2021); Barak (2023); Barker (2017); Borrelli (2018); Bosworth (2014); Fuglerud (2004); Graham (2002); Griffiths (2024); Hall (2013); Heyman (2000); Tuckett (2018).

8. See De Genova (2013) on the spectacle of immigration enforcement, where he argues that immigration enforcement agencies create scenes to render illegality an objective fact. See Ward (2015) for racialized social control as slow violence where victimization is hidden and dispersed. See Lee (2019) for an elaboration of family separation through immigration enforcement as "slow death." On cruelty in immigration control see Aradau and Canzutti (2022); Beltrán (2020); US Commission on Civil Rights (2019); Souris (2024).

9. Arendt (1963).

10. Bosworth, Parmar, and Vázquez (2018); FitzGerald and Cook-Martín (2014).

11. Molina (2014); Ngai (2014).

12. De Genova (2004).

13. Gómez (2018); Lytle Hernández (2010); Lytle Hernández (2017).

14. Chavez (2020).

15. Andreas (2022); de León (2015); Dunn (1996); Nevins (2010); Slack, Martínez, and Whiteford (2018).

16. Asad and Clair (2018); R. Flores and Schachter (2018); Menjívar (2021).

17. Baker (2021); US Immigration and Customs Enforcement (2020).

18. Andrews (2023); Golash-Boza and Hondagneu-Sotelo (2013).

19. Abrego (2014); Asad (2023); Castañeda (2020); Dreby (2015); García (2019); Golash-Boza (2019); Enriquez (2015); J. Lopez (2021); Prieto (2018); Zamora (2022).

20. Golash-Boza and Hondagneu-Sotelo (2013); see also Aranda and Vaquera (2015); Armenta (2017b); Armenta and Vega (2017); Chacón and Coutin (2018); and Provine and Doty (2011), who similarly identify US immigration enforcement as a racial project.

21. Golash-Boza (2009); Massey (2012).

22. Lytle Hernández (2010, 234).

23. Johnson (2020).

24. Office of Personnel Management (2020).

25. Murdza and Ewing (2021).

26. Heyman (2002); Correa and Thomas (2015); Prieto (2015); Finch (2022).

27. De León (2015); for border deaths, see also Eschbach, Hagan, Rodriguez, Hernández-León, and Bailey (1999); D. Martínez, Reineke, Rubio-Goldsmith, and Parks (2014).

28. See Massey, Pren, and Durand (2016) on the backfiring of border enforcement; and Slack, Martínez, and Whiteford (2018) on violence in border crossings. See Ryo (2013) on how migrants balance the threat of enforcement and the morality of immigration law in their decision to make undocumented crossings.

29. See, for example, the US Equal Employment Opportunity Commission's (2016) report "Advancing Diversity in Law Enforcement," which is premised on the idea that increasing the diversity of law enforcement agencies will increase trust in the police. I do not take issue with efforts to diversify police forces—quite the contrary—I firmly believe it is an important goal. However, efforts to increase numerical diversity and "representation" are not the same as making structural and cultural change in law enforcement and should not be treated as such.

30. G. Flores (2017); Bristol and Martin-Fernandez (2016).

31. Nowacki, Schafer, and Hibdon (2021); Weitzer (2014; 2017).

32. Skrentny (2013, 3002) calls this assumption "racial realism" and argues that it deeply shapes how American employers think about race and organizational diversity in the post–civil rights era.

33. Ward and Hanink (2016) argue that demographic proportionality is often used as a proxy for representation in the criminal justice field, when in fact representation requires that legal authorities be aware of and accountable to the preferences of those subject to their power, as well as in positions of power themselves. See also Ward (2006).

34. Ray (2019); Ray, Herd, and Moynihan (2023); Wingfield and Chavez (2020).

35. Watkins-Hayes (2009, 235).

36. I define morality as a contested space where different actors mobilize evaluative codes that specify right and wrong. Morality has to do with norms and values, but also with political ideology and power. For more on morality, see Turner and Stets (2006); Stets and Carter (2011).

37. Elcioglu (2020).

38. R. Flores and Azar (2023).

39. Rodríguez and Paredes (2014).

40. Lytle Hernández (2017).

41. Andreas (2022); on how US immigration policy has maintained and shaped Mexico-US undocumented migration, see also Durand and Massey (2019); and Massey, Pren, and Durand (2016).

42. Hughes (1951, 319); C. Rivera (2014); Vega (2018).

43. Prieto (2015); see also Vega (2012) for racial sanctions against restrictionist Mexican Americans.

44. See Vega (2019) for the importance of studying immigration agents' culture and where I discuss distinct approaches to this concept in sociology. Moral economy and occupational or professional culture are related concepts. I will use "moral economy" to refer to the larger normative realm of immigration control and will use "culture" when discussing more meso-level professional or organizational commonsense principles. In chapter 2 I discuss culture most directly in relation to the policing profession. For more on culture, see DiMaggio (1997); Swidler (1986); Vaisey (2009).

45. Fassin (2009).

46. Menjívar (2023); see also Menjívar and Abrego (2012) for immigration control as legal violence.

47. Ellermann (2009, 3); see also Weissinger (2017) for an analysis of immigration enforcement agents as social control agents.

48. Lytle Hernández (2010); Golash-Boza (2015).

49. Lipsky (2010).

50. Calavita (2010); Ellermann (2009); Macias-Rojas (2016); Magaña (2003); Weissinger (2017).

51. Armenta (2012); Barak (2023); Gilboy (1991); Heyman (1995); Asad (2019); Shiff (2021).

52. Kang (2016).

53. See Ewick and Silbey (1998) for classic conceptualization of law in everyday life; and Gould and Barclay (2012) for a review of gap studies.

54. For other examples of this approach, see Jackall (2009); Liebling (2011); Maynard-Moody and Musheno (2003); Oberfield (2014); Presser (2013); Watkins-Hayes (2009); Zacka (2017).

55. Zacka (2017, 14).

56. Cohen (2013); Herzfeld (1991); Presser (2013).

57. Wilson (1989), based on Weber's (1978) idea of bureaucracy as rational-legal authority.

58. On mollifying moral instincts, see Balfour, Adams, and Nickels (2019); Jackall (2009); Zacka (2017); Herzfeld (1991).

59. Herbert (1996); see also Heyman (2000).

60. Bosworth, Franko, and Pickering (2018).

61. Achermann (2021); Aliverti (2021); Barker (2017); Borrelli and Lindberg (2018); Bosworth (2013); Campos-Delgado and Côté-Boucher (2022); Hall (2013); Loyd and Mountz (2018); Tuckett (2018); van der Woude and van der Leun (2017); Wettergren (2010).

62. My emphasis in this brief legal/historical account is on contemporary developments, namely from the 1970s and onward. It is important to note, however, that racialization and criminalization have always been central to US immigration control lawmaking and

enforcement. For more comprehensive histories of racialization and criminalization in US immigration control, see excellent accounts in Chacón (2013); FitzGerald and Cook-Martín (2014); Goodman (2020); Lytle Hernández (2010); Kanstroom (2007); Ngai (2014).

63. Stumpf (2006); Franko (2019); See also Koulish and van der Woude (2020).

64. Bigo (2002).

65. Chacón (2009); Dowling and Inda (2013).

66. Abrego, Coleman, Martínez, Menjívar, and Slack (2017); Ewing, Martínez, and Rumbaut (2015).

67. See, e.g., Stumpf (2006); see also Stumpf (2023).

68. Elites have long used Americans' fear of crime to push various political and economic agendas forward, in the process creating a highly punitive society and retributive criminal justice system that has created a repressive context for African Americans and Latinx people. See Garland (2001); Kennedy (1999); Massey (2020); Simon (2007).

69. Massey (2020, 18).

70. The Page Act of March 3, 1875, prohibited the immigration of people who had been convicted of a crime in their own country, other than political offenses. See Chacón (2013); for more on the criminalization of illegal entry through the Immigration Act of 1924, see Ngai (2003); for more on the racialized character of so-called illegal entry restrictions in the 1920s and beyond, see Lytle Hernández (2010); Lytle Hernández (2017).

71. For transcript of President Ronald Reagan's speech, see Reagan (1986).

72. Chishti, Meissner, and Bergeron (2011); De Genova (2014).

73. Chishti and Kamasaki (2014).

74. Dunn (1996).

75. See text of law in Immigration Reform and Control Act (1986).

76. This provision gave rise to the Institutional Removal Program (IRP) and the Alien Criminal Apprehension Program; see Armenta (2017); Inda (2013).

77. Morawetz (2000, 1939); Tosh (2019).

78. For transcript of President Bill Clinton's speech, see Clinton (1996).

79. Kanstroom (2007, 226).

80. Chacón (2013, 85).

81. White House (2002).

82. The DHS assumed responsibility for twenty-two stand-alone agencies as diverse as the Federal Emergency Management Agency, the Secret Service, and the Coast Guard, to name a few. The federal immigration bureaucracy has gone through various evolutions since its creation in the late 1800s. The INS and its predecessors had been at the helm of US immigration law since the turn of the twentieth century, when the federal government consolidated power over immigration.

83. I will use the terms "deportation" and "removal" interchangeably throughout the book. Removal is the legal term for what is colloquially known as deportation, meaning the formal expulsion of a noncitizen. This was not always the case. Prior to the passage of the IIRIRA, there were deportations (the removal of noncitizens from the United States) and exclusions (the denying of entry into the country). The IIRIRA collapsed these two processes and called them "removals." There is also a related term, "returns," that refers to removals that do not involve a formal court order and that impact citizens of adjacent countries, namely Mexicans and Canadians.

84. American Immigration Council (2021); Department of Homeland Security (2022).

85. Meissner, Kerwin, Chishti, and Bergeron (2013).

86. Rumbaut (2016).

87. Longazel (2013a); Longazel (2013b); Tosh (2019).

88. C. Rivera (2014); see also Vega and van der Woude (2023).

89. R. Ellis (2021).

90. Nader (1972).

91. Providing a more precise demographic profile of my research sites may inadvertently disclose them. The research site-related statistics I cite here and in the rest of the manuscript come from the U.S. Census and its related publications, as well as the Bureau of Labor Statistics.

92. US Immigration and Customs Enforcement (2014); US Immigration and Customs Enforcement (2015); US Immigration and Customs Enforcement (2016).

93. Whether I proxied a skeptical or friendly audience was based mostly on the assumptions that agents projected since I tried to always present myself as a neutral.

94. See Herbert (1996) and Herbert (2006) for more on this approach.

95. M. Scott and Lyman (1968, 46).

96. Goffman (1963).

97. Orbuch (1997, 461).

1. Taking the Job

1. Castañeda Pérez (2022); Chávez (2016).

2. Monforti and McGlynn (2021). The documentary *At the Ready* (directed by Maisie Crow, 2021, Gravitas Ventures, Cleveland, OH) powerfully demonstrates how linkages between educational institutions and employment programs, as well as broader social and economic forces, shape Mexican American border youth's interest in policing.

3. Guerra (2015); see also García Hernández (2009).

4. E. Flores, Medeiros, and Pachon (2007).

5. This statistic comes from the Bureau of Labor Statistics. Providing a more precise citation would disclose my research sites. The important point is that both Mountain Valley and Desert City were among the metropolitan statistical areas with the highest concentration of protective service occupations in the country. Most of the jobs in this category require a high-school diploma or equivalent for entry. .

6. Eason (2019).

7. García Hernández (2023, 126).

8. Border Patrol jobs have a default assignment to the US-Mexico border. Assignments to northern or coastal border sectors are considered competitive transfers, which means that they are hard to come by.

9. Heyman (2002).

10. Flores-González (2002).

11. This is a conservative estimate of my respondents' starting salaries. Immigration agents' salaries are based on the federal government's "Law Enforcement Officer" salary tables, which calculate salaries based on grades (1–15) and steps (1–10) within those grades. Most of my

respondents started their jobs at entry-level pay rates, which correspond to grades 5, 7, 9 (denoted as GL5, GL7, and GL9). On top of those base rates there is a "locality pay area," which is meant to counter or reduce the gap between federal and private-sector jobs in the same region. The rates that I report are based on the "Rest of the United States" locality rate, which is the area that applies to federal employees who work in a city that does not fall within another locality pay area. However, some of my respondents started their careers in other, higher-paying localities. The nearest highest-paying locality, which I will not identify by name because it would identify my research sites, had starting annual rates of $42,000 to $48,000. See Office of Personnel Management (2014) for the 2014 salary tables for law enforcement officers.

12. When I was in the field, AUO came under scrutiny as agents were using it to pad their paychecks without proper justification. The Border Patrol Agent Pay Reform Act of 2014 (effective January 10, 2016) replaced AUO as of May 2015. As of this writing, Border Patrol agents elect "a preferred tour of duty," which corresponds to the number of hours worked in a week, as well as an overtime pay supplement. Those who elect to work five ten-hour days per week received 25 percent overtime pay. Those who elect to work five nine-hour workdays each week get a 12.5 percent overtime supplement. See Department of Homeland Security (2016).

13. When we take CBP as a whole, which includes officers who work at ports of entry, the agencies' size differential is even more staggering. More than five times as many officers are employed by CBP than by ICE. See American Immigration Council (2021).

14. Alex (1976); Bayley and Mendelsohn (1969); Harris (1973); Westley (1970).

15. White, Cooper, Saunders, Raganella (2010).

16. Several of the ICE officers I interviewed started as CBP agents and eventually transferred to ICE, but none of the Border Patrol agents were former ICE officers. This suggests that ICE is considered a promotion or at least of higher status that the USBP.

17. Getrich (2013).

18. Heyman (2009, 370).

19. Castañeda Pérez (2022).

20. Latinas/os had varied evaluations of immigration agents before they were agents themselves. Having positive perceptions of immigration agents is not a necessary condition for going into immigration control, just as having negative perceptions of immigration agents does not prevent people from pursuing this work.

21. The gendered aspect of law enforcement aspirations is evident in my findings. It was the male agents who told me they grew up aspiring to work in law enforcement. The women who I interviewed were more likely to drift into the profession or come in through the military-to-policing pipeline, which is itself also gendered.

22. Wyllie (2018).

23. US Customs and Border Protection (n.d. [d]).

24. US Immigration and Customs Enforcement (2014).

25. Dávila and Mora (2000).

26. McGlynn and Monforti (2010).

27. Garza (2015, 246).

28. Monforti and McGlynn (2021).

29. Huerta (2015); Martinez and Huerta (2020).

30. Pérez (2015).

31. Barroso (2019).

32. Mariscal (2005).

33. Weichselbaum and Schwartzapfel (2017).

34. I interviewed twice as many Border Patrol agents as ICE officers, so most of the veterans in this sample are Border Patrol agents. However, veterans make up a higher percentage of the ICE sample.

35. Bloom, Orr, Bell, Cave, Doolittle, Lin, and Bos (1997, 550).

36. Plascencia, Waterston, and Pérez (2015, 158).

37. Prieto (2015).

38. Heyman (2002, 487).

39. Cortez (2021).

40. Ward (2006).

41. Oberfield (2014).

42. Kaufman (2006, 162).

43. Desmond (2007, 30).

44. There are interesting questions about selection that are beyond the scope of the research design of this study. I asked active agents about what attracted them to the position; future research could study what repels similar others from this job. We might also study Latina/o and other immigration agents before and after their training to better document selection and socialization effects. Having said that, I will say that while studying selection is very important, it can sometimes overly emphasize individual dispositions. This dispositional focus can distract from deep analysis of the opportunity structures in which working-class youth are making career decisions, as well as the normative structures they function within once on the job.

45. Gutierrez (1995); Vila (2005); see also Vega (2014); Vega and Ortiz (2018).

46. Beltrán (2020).

47. Political conservativism has been growing among Latinx people, and the concentration of Latinx people in law enforcement professions may be one factor moving the political gauge toward the right. See Beltrán (2023).

48. Desmond (2011, 65) defines organizational common sense as "the set of unquestioned assumptions beneath organizational behavior and dialogue, tacitly agreed on by members of that organization, that buttresses organizational orthodoxy and ensures consensus between members of the organization."

2. Becoming an Agent

1. Bittner (1970); Skolnick (1966); Van Maanen (1973).

2. Ellermann (2009); Weissinger (2017); Vega (2019).

3. Knowles and Heeran (2019, 749); see also Koh (2020).

4. See Herbert (1996) for a discussion of the highly moralistic character of policing and how the good guy / bad guy dichotomy lends police officers an internal sense of validity.

5. "Just illegal" is a term that agents use to refer to undocumented immigrants who do not have a criminal record; they distinguish them from criminal aliens. Throughout this chapter I will use the terms "criminality" and "illegality" to distinguish between these two categories.

"Criminality" refers to the fact of a person's having committed some criminal offense, while "illegality" is the condition of lacking the state's permission to be in the country. Both are state-created categories.

6. Arata (2023).

7. US Customs and Border Protection (n.d. [a]); US Immigration and Customs Enforcement (n.d. [a]).

8. Federal Law Enforcement Training Centers (2019).

9. Lalonde (2019, 593); see also Chappell and Lanza-Kaduce (2010); Conti and Doreian (2014); Conti and Nolan (2005); Rahr and Rice (2015).

10. The fact that the training in policing principles is not aligned with the day-to-day work is not just true about the United States. See Lalonde (2019) for similar findings in Canada; and see Aliverti (2020) for similar findings in the UK; see also Borrelli (2021) and Loftus (2015).

11. Descriptions of the Border Patrol and ICE academies are accurate as of this writing. Both academies have gone through changes in their organization and location over time; to accommodate larger recruitments, for example, the government reduced the basic training curriculum in the early 2000s and created mechanisms to move agents through the training more swiftly, by, for example, allowing agents with a certain level of fluency to test out of Spanish. See Manjarrez (2021).

12. US Customs and Border Protection (n.d. [b]).

13. US Customs and Border Protection (n.d. [c]), emphasis added.

14. US Immigration and Customs Enforcement (n.d. [b]).

15. US Immigration and Customs Enforcement (2018).

16. Oberfield (2020).

17. Harris (1973); Hopper (1977); Van Maanen (1975).

18. Conti (2009).

19. Hodgson (2001, 528).

20. Doreian and Conti (2017, 83).

21. Bittner (1970); Skolnick (1966); Van Maanen (1973); Waddington (1999); Westley (1970).

22. Skolnick (1966).

23. See Loftus (2010) for recurring themes in police culture. Loftus argues that the cultural tenets of the profession are stable because the basic tensions of policing have not changed. Skolnick (1966) identified these tensions as: the potential for danger in police work, the authority they are endowed with as the coercive arm of the state, and the pressure to be efficient.

24. Rowe and Rowe (2021); Fassin (2017).

25. US Immigration and Customs Enforcement (2014); US Immigration and Customs Enforcement (2015); US Immigration and Customs Enforcement (2016).

26. US Customs and Border Protection (2015). The CBP's "National Standards on Transport, Escort, Detention, and Search" policy states that "detainees should generally not be held for longer than 72 hours in CBP hold rooms or holding facilities. Every effort must be made to hold detainees for the least amount of time . . . as operationally feasible."

27. Nakamura (2014).

28. Kalhan (2010); Ryo and Peacock (2018).

29. "Family residential centers" is how Immigration and Customs Enforcement refers to its detention centers that house family units. For more on how ankle bracelets and other

technology extends the arm of the immigration state into immigrant communities, see Martinez-Aranda (2022).

30. Rabin (2013).

31. Patler (2018).

32. Asad (2019); Farrell-Bryan (2022); Ryo (2019).

33. Ellermann (2006).

34. On prosecutorial discretion, see Cox and Rodriguez (2020); Motomura (2014); and Wadhia (2019).

35. Immigration and Customs Enforcement ERO assignments are variable. Some officers are managing the nondetained docket, which includes people who are in the Alternative to Detentions program or were released on bond while their cases are in progress. Other officers are managing the detained docket, which includes people who are detained in one of the multiple immigration detentions centers that ICE runs. Still others are working on the Fugitive Operations team, which is charged with finding and deporting people who have failed to leave the United States after a final order of removal or have failed to report to ICE upon receipt of a notice.

36. These are the terms used by my interviewees. Immigration and Customs Enforcement defines an "immigration fugitive" as someone who has failed to leave the country after a final order of removal or who has not reported to ICE after being ordered to. See US Immigration and Customs Enforcement (n.d. [c]).

37. In the field office that I studied, there were three Fugitive Operations teams for a region with almost 3.5 million inhabitants. The supervisor for one of those teams told me he had five deportation officers and one clerk who assisted the officers with administrative tasks. It is important to remember that I conducted ICE interviews at the end of the Obama administration, when the selective enforcement mandates had curbed much of the enforcement that these teams were able to do. Fugitive Operations arrests increased under Trump.

38. TRAC Immigration (2017).

39. Armenta (2017).

40. Vega (2022).

41. Border Patrol agents' assignments are variable, in that they might be patrolling a border city or a highway, "sitting on an X" (which refers to a stationary surveillance position), overseeing the "scope truck" (an autonomous surveillance tower mounted on a truck), or working a checkpoint or the processing unit. The language in quotation marks in this paragraph was used by many of my interviewees.

42. Muster is a briefing meeting led by supervisors where agents are informed of the prior shift's activity (i.e., how many people came through, where they came through, whether there is evidence that a group entered, but has not been found, etc.) and are given their assignments.

43. See Muñiz (2022) for technological advances in border policing.

44. It is hard to say this with certainty since the government does not release statistics that tell us how most people are located when crossing the border. My sense, however, is that technology plays a bigger role than agents let on—yet more evidence of how invested they are in the organizational myths and fictions around their work.

45. In leapfrogging, the agent who has identified the sign asks another agent who is stationed in the direction where the sign is headed to see if they can identify it in their area. If they can, then the original agent can drive over to that location quickly, having "leapfrogged" an entire

area of land. They continue doing this until they either lose the sign and start over or find the people they are tracking.

46. Riley (2022).

47. Agents used the pronoun "he" when giving me examples of troublemakers, a reminder that men are the immigration state's archetypal target; see Golash-Boza and Hondagneu-Sotelo (2013). The other language in quotation marks in this paragraph was used by many of my interviewees.

48. Jones (2014).

49. Martínez (2016).

50. Vega (2018, 2552).

51. Maynard-Moody and Musheno (2003); Oberfield (2014).

52. J. Scott (2020).

53. Branch (2021, 992).

54. Hall (2013).

55. Light and Miller (2018).

56. War stories are a key mechanism in the reproduction of police culture; through these stories police officers convey lessons to new members, each other, and outsiders to their profession. Kurtz and Upton (2017).

57. Shapira (2013).

58. Longazel (2013a); Longazel (2013b); Tosh (2019).

59. Andreas (2022); Nevins (2010).

60. De Genova (2004); Rodríguez and Paredes (2014); Shapira (2013).

61. Chacón (2014); Menjívar (2006).

62. Ellermann (2006).

63. See Lipsky (2010) for more on how street-level bureaucrats balance discretionary power and their autonomy against the constraints of bureaucratic and legal rules.

64. Menjívar (2023); Monk (2022).

65. Chishti, Pierce, and Bolter (2017).

66. TRAC Immigration (2016).

67. Goodman (2020); Kanstroom (2007).

68. US Immigration and Customs Enforcement (2014); US Immigration and Customs Enforcement (2015); US Immigration and Customs Enforcement (2016).

69. See Borrelli (2018); Vega (2018).

3. Between Caring Control and Disinterested Professionalism

1. Martínez, Slack, and Heyman (2013, 4).

2. Translated from Spanish:

"Oh, y usted es Mexicano?" And I go, "Pues mis papas." He goes, "Eres traidor?" And I go, "Que prefieres, que te agarre yo y te de algo de comer, que te de agua, o que te agarre un gabacho y te parta en la madre?" He goes no, "No, mejor usted Oficial."

3. Lipsky (2010), Maynard-Moody and Musheno (2003); see also Heyman (2009).

4. Heyman (1995).

5. The expectation of Latinx solidarity against restrictionist immigration policies and politics is rooted in racialization, not in an inevitable sense of commonality or primordial cultural bond

among Latinos. See Mora (2014); Rodríguez-Muñiz (2021); Zepeda-Millán (2017). For how Latinx immigration agents are called race traitors, see García Hernández (2009); Heyman (2002); Prieto (2015).

6. The analogous case is Black officers policing and "locking up our own" (Forman 2017). Black officers who were desegregating the profession believed that their presence would help police agencies "operate in a more professional and humane way"; they saw themselves as their profession's "moral conscience" (Bolton and Feagin 2004, xi). Most African Americans wanted to see integrated police teams and were explicit about wanting more diversity on the police force (Weitzer 2000). Yet, once African Americans were on the job, many other African Americans saw them as traitors who were selling out their communities (Bayley and Mendelson 1969).

7. Donato, Wagner, and Patterson (2008).

8. There is a great deal of phenotypic variation among Mexicans and other Latinx people. This phenotypic variation exists alongside very obstinate social constructions of Mexicans as short, brown, and indigenous. For more on racial constructions of Mexicanness, see Gómez Cervantes (2021); Zamora (2022).

9. Bosworth and Slade (2014).

10. Gallardo (2020, 458).

11. Todak, Huff, and James (2018).

12. Gau, Paoline, and Roman (2021).

13. Gau and Paoline (2017).

14. Raganella and White (2004).

15. Schuck (2021); Todak, Huff, and James (2018); White, Cooper, Saunders and Raganella (2010).

16. The use-of-force continuum specifies what level of force an officer can use according to the level of resistance they are met with.

17. Dau, Vandeviver, Dewinter, Witlox, and Beken (2023).

18. Sierra-Arévalo (2021).

19. Portillo (2012).

20. Castañeda Pérez (n.d.).

21. Watkins-Hayes (2011).

22. See Huo and Tyler (2000) for racialized expectations of minority police officers in general. For example, Gilad and Dahan (2021) argue that Black police officers empathize with the critiques that Black people have of police but are tokenized in their work and thus cannot risk their authority by being seen to show preferential treatment. Todak, Huff, and James (2018) show that Black citizens then issue critiques of Black police officers because they perceive them to be harsher than Whites.

23. Watkins-Hayes (2011); Portillo (2012).

24. Humphrey (2022, 742); see also Wingfield (2010); Wingfield (2021).

25. I also do not create typologies, because distinct orientations can coexist within one agent's work approach, and this may be particularly true for Latinas/os and other minoritized police officers. For example, Clifton, Torres, and Hawdon (2021) found that Hispanic/Latino/a officers tend to support a hybrid style of policing that combines a warrior and guardian mentality and that they are more likely to use such a style than White officers.

26. In Vega (2018) I treat caring control as a legitimation narrative, recognizing that agents have an incentive to frame themselves as humane; see Phillips, Hagan, and Rodriguez (2006) for evidence of migrants experiencing violence at the hands of immigration agents.

27. Armenta and Vega (n.d.).

28. Castañeda (2020, 139).

29. Heyman (2002, 480).

30. Huo and Tyler (2000). For instance, Emily Ryo (2017) found that detainees' perceptions of procedural justice—that is, being treated humanely and with respect—are positively associated with their felt obligation to follow immigration law.

31. Ray (2019).

32. Wingfield and Alston (2014, 274); see also Wingfield and Chavez (2020).

33. Murakawa (2017); see also Rios, Prieto, and Ibarra (2020) talk about the "legitimacy policing continuum," where officers may deploy a courteous approach to policing, what they term "mano suave," that does not disrupt policing's punitive logics or practices.

34. Tyler (2017).

35. Prieto (2015, 503).

4. Denying Responsibility

1. I follow Maynard-Moody and Musheno (2003) in using bureaucrats' stories to show how they resolve tensions during moments when the law is not in agreement with their moral judgments. The stories that immigration agents and other bureaucrats tell are ripe for analysis because they vividly illustrate how people "reference both rules and morality to defend their decisions, reveal internalized as well as interactive conflicts, and document shifting positions over time" (25). The stories that I present in this chapter communicate agents' uncertainty or insecurity, including instances of their "feeling bad," or about which they use words like "empathy," "sympathy," "shame," etc.

2. For key scholarship that has used emotion as an analytical tool to uncover the normative underpinnings of immigration work, see Bosworth (2019); Graham (2002); Hall (2012); K. Rivera and Tracy (2014).

3. Verifying the authenticity of agents' emotional displays is beyond the scope of most social scientific methods of discovery and certainly beyond the scope of my interviews. My own impression is that the agents I quote in this chapter *seemed genuine* in their lack of comfort when they were telling me stories that did not cohere with their visions of themselves as good people. They stirred in their seat, they sucked in their breath, the tone of their voice changed, some laughed awkwardly, and some took long pauses. Agents also seemed genuine when they told me stories that cohered with their sense of conviction about the rightness of their job. It is easier to believe that agents are being authentic when they are being strident regulators, instead of ambivalent bureaucrats, because the former coheres better with their public persona.

4. See Turner and Stets (2006) for more on moral emotions.

5. Cohen (2013).

6. Rodríguez and Paredes (2014).

7. In elaborating a sociology of denial, Stanley Cohen (2013) drew on Matza and Sykes (1957) neutralization theory, which focused on how juveniles who had committed delinquent

acts justified these actions. Thus, the forms of denial in Cohen's work are very much aligned with Matza and Sykes's neutralization techniques, which are denial of responsibility, denial of injury, denial of the victim, condemnation of the condemners, and appeal to higher loyalties.

8. Wilson (1989).

9. Balfour, Adams, and Nickels (2019).

10. Lipsky (2010).

11. Jackall (2009); Zacka (2017).

12. For more on the implementation of immigration control as a coercive and morally ambiguous state practice, see Ellermann (2009), who conceptualized immigration control, deportation specifically, as coercive social regulation (i.e., state action to regulate individual behavior in highly intrusive ways and often through the use of force).

13. See Lee (2019) for family separation as "slow death," a form of harm that is pernicious and more difficult to recognize than spectacular forms of state violence.

14. Hochschild (1979).

15. Martin (1999).

16. Borrelli, Lindberg, and Wyss (2022); Hall (2013); Shiff (2021).

17. Gómez Cervantes, Menjívar, and Staples (2017); Bosworth and Slade (2014).

18. My fieldwork predates the so-called zero tolerance policy of the first Trump administration, which separated children from their parents as a deterrence strategy.

19. Wingfield (2021).

20. Small (2015).

21. This woman had been deported, so she did not really "leave" her children.

22. The list Officer Lardin is talking about is an agent-generated list of people that the government considers "immigration fugitives." Immigration and Customs Enforcement defines an immigration fugitive as "an alien who has failed to leave the United States based upon a final order of removal, deportation or exclusion, or who has failed to report to ICE after receiving notice to do so." See US Immigration and Customs Enforcement (n.d. [c]).

23. Lipsky (2010).

24. M. Scott and Lyman (1968).

25. Department of Homeland Security (2016) defines derivative citizenship as "citizenship conveyed to children through the naturalization of parents or, under certain circumstances, to foreign-born children adopted by U.S. citizen parents, provided certain conditions are met."

26. Pallister-Wilkins (2015); Prieto (2015); Ugelvik (2016); Vega (2018).

27. Armenta (2012).

28. Turner and Stets (2006).

29. Rodríguez and Paredes (2014).

30. Massey (2007).

31. Bosworth and Slade (2014).

32. Borrelli (2018); McGoey (2012); Souter (2011); Stel (2016).

33. This is an example of what Aliverti (2023) calls the magic of immigration control, the largely concealed arbitrariness and myth that undergird the implementation of immigration law.

34. Stets and Carter (2011).

35. Farrell-Bryan and Peacock (2022)

36. Wingfield (2021).

37. J. Bell (2017).

38. Herzfeld (1991).

5. Cultivating Legitimacy

1. I will use the following terms interchangeably to refer to the threats to agents' moral authority to exclude migrants: "legitimacy deficits," "stigma," and "taint." I rely on "taint" when discussing immigration enforcement as dirty work. Some readers may note that these terms have distinct histories (those interested can read these intellectual genealogies in the suggested references below), but as it relates to agents' work, they all refer to a sense of being depreciated by various publics. On stigma, see Goffman (1963) and, more recently, Lamont (2018). Readers interested in legitimacy may turn to C. Johnson, Dowd, and Ridgeway (2006) for a review of the study of legitimacy in sociology. For work on taint and dirty work, see Hughes (1951) and Ashforth and Kreiner (1999).

2. Beetham (2013); Bottoms and Tankebe (2012).

3. In a survey of Border Patrol agents' job satisfaction, Rojek, Manjarrez, Wolfe, and Rojek (2017) found that agents who reported that the agency had "negative publicity" were less likely to report a strong sense of self-legitimacy.

4. Prieto (2015).

5. See, for example, Abrego (2018) on how Central American forced migration is a product of various forms of intervention in the region. See also Benhabib (2004) on the political philosophy of states' legal and moral obligations to outsiders.

6. Andreas (2022).

7. Some of the quotes and other content included in this chapter originally appeared in Vega (2018).

8. Hughes (1951) is credited with coining the term "dirty work" and identifying three sources of taint or stigma: physical, social, and moral. Hughes filled in these distinct sources of stigma with descriptors like work that is "physically disgusting . . . a symbol of degradation . . . [or] counter to the more heroic of our moral conceptions" (319). Ashforth and Kreiner (1999) build on Hughes's work by providing more specific definitions of these distinct types of taint. They argue that physically tainted jobs are those that involve literally dealing with physical manifestations of "dirt"—cleaning up refuse, discarding human or animal waste, etc. Socially tainted occupations put workers (e.g., psychiatric nurses and prison guards) in contact with societal outcasts, but such workers may also be celebrated for doing a necessary job. Morally tainted occupations are those considered "sinful" (e.g., prostitution) or ethically dubious (e.g., being a pawnbroker). See Ashforth and Kreiner (1999, 414–15).

9. K. Rivera and Tracy (2014).

10. For more on legitimation on the front lines of immigration work, see, for example, Aliverti (2020, 2023); Bosworth (2014, 2019); Campos-Delgado and Côté-Boucher (2022); K. Rivera and Tracy (2014); Ugelvik (2016); Vega (2018); Wittock, Cleton, Vandevoordt, and Verschraegen (2023).

11. See Vega (2014) for a discussion of boundary-making strategies among Mexican Americans who are repudiated for being race traitors.

12. Bosworth (2013); Stumpf (2023).

13. See Stumpf (2020) for an excellent discussion of how the logic of *parens patriae*, the state as a parent, intersects with crimmigration frameworks in justifying family separation.

14. Loftus (2010).

15. Ashforth and Kreiner (1999, 413); see also Dick (2005).

16. Aliverti (2021) also found that immigration officers in the UK felt that they were less appreciated than police officers.

17. Part of what Officer Harding is alluding to when he mentioned "Joe Public" in the country's interior is something that has long been true: border residents are more likely than those living in nonborder states to identity immigration as the "most important issue" facing the country. However, this has been changing. With amplified media coverage of immigration, especially since the early 2000s, immigration has become a salient issue throughout the country (Dunaway, Branton, and Abrajano 2010).

18. Rodríguez and Paredes (2014).

19. See R. Flores and Schachter (2018) for dichotomies that pervade social construction of illegality, and Shapira (2013) on how Minutemen, the militia groups that patrol the border, also construct a hierarchy of "enemies" in gendered and racialized imagery.

20. Heyman (2000, 641).

21. US Immigration and Customs Enforcement (2014); US Immigration and Customs Enforcement (2015); US Immigration and Customs Enforcement (2016).

22. See Meyer and Rowan (1977) on organizational myths; Vega (2022) for how organizational myths guide immigration agents' use of force at the US-Mexico border.

23. Golash-Boza and Hondagneu-Sotelo (2013).

24. Andrews (2023); Hagan and Wassink (2020).

25. Cardoso, Hamilton, Rodríguez, Eschbach, and Hagan (2016).

26. Asad (2020); Canizales (2023); Golash-Boza (2015).

27. Cházaro (2016); Kevin Johnson (2009); Keyes (2013).

28. Chavez (2020).

29. Heyman (2002).

30. Jiménez (2010); Ochoa (2004).

31. Correa and Thomas (2015, 246).

32. A 2019 survey by the Pew Research Center found that 14 percent of Hispanic/Latino people most often describe themselves as American, while 47 percent most often described themselves by country of origin, and 39 percent used the terms *Latino/a* or *Hispanic*. See M. Lopez, Krogstad, and Passel (2023).

33. We can understand Agent Bobadilla and Agent Luar as Latinx agents who are standing on opposite ends of a continuum of affinity toward coethnic immigrants. Agent Luar does not see immigrants as his people, while Agent Bobadilla does. We can easily imagine a scenario where instead of challenging a colleague who makes a xenophobic remark, like Agent Bobadilla did, Agent Luar might agree with the comment about speaking English in America or getting out. However, these distinctions are lost if we take Agent Bobadilla's patriotic discourse as evidence of a static identity, instead of a boundary-making strategy in response to stigma.

34. See also Vega (2014).

35. See Heyman (2002) for similar findings.

36. Boltanski and Thévenot (2006).

37. Thumala, Goold, and Loader (2011).

38. Chauvin and Garcés-Mascareñas (2014); Elcioglu (2020); Keyes (2011).

39. In chapter 3 we saw how, in interactions with migrants who begrudge them for excluding *their own*, agents adopt distinct modes of professionalism, sometimes underscoring their humanness through caring control and other times leaning into bureaucratic neutrality through disinterested professionalism.

40. Goffman (1963); Lamont (2018); Wimmer (2008).

41. Andreas (2022).

42. Vega (2018).

Conclusion

1. President Obama announced several executive actions to refine immigration agents' priorities. See White House (2014a). See also Coutin, Chacón, and Lee (2024).

2. Bialik (2018).

3. Rabin (2019, 142).

4. Rabin (2019).

5. Chishti and Bolter (2021).

6. Chishti and Bush-Joseph (2023).

7. Sprunt (2020).

8. Cox and Rodriguez (2020); Kanstroom (2007).

9. White House (2014b).

10. Fassin (2005).

11. US Equal Employment Opportunity Commission (2016).

12. Weitzer (2017).

13. Ward and Kupchik (2009); Ward and Hanink (2016).

14. Even though Latinos/Hispanics are 9.4 percent of the total federal workforce, they are only 4.7 percent of the Senior Executive Services. Office of Personnel Management (2020).

15. Explanations are accounts where the person admits the action they committed is bad or wrong, but they deny their responsibility, while justifications are the opposite. See M. Scott and Lyman (1968).

16. See Menjívar and Abrego (2012) for an elaboration of distinct forms of legal and symbolic violence in immigration control.

17. See M. Bell (2017) on the importance of a structural account of police reform; and Ellermann (2009) for a conceptualization of immigration control as coercive social regulation.

18. Bonilla-Silva (1997) for the New Racism; Murakawa (2019) for the idea of racial innocence as a dominant epistemology in American public policy, as well as in social science research on the carceral state; and Vega and van der Woude (2023) for color-blind ideologies in border control.

19. I found myself in a position to vent my frustrations to Anita Casavantes-Bradford, a historian of Latino/Latin American history and migration. Anita listened intently and responded brilliantly. She reminded me of the perils of Western dualism, which had led to my dichotomous thinking about whether we could reform *or* ought to abolish the immigration system. Anita also reminded me that I could reject the terms of the debate and that the biggest risk is not that I have nothing viable to suggest, but that I will not suggest anything at all.

20. Fassin (2005).

21. Vega and Van der Woude (2023).

22. Armenta and Vega (2017); Golash-Boza and Hondagneu-Sotelo (2013); Massey (2012).

23. See the "Border Patrol Processing Coordinator" page on the US Customs and Border Protection website, https://careers.cbp.gov/s/career-paths/usbp/bppc, accessed September 4, 2024.

24. See the discussion on revamping asylum at the US-Mexico border on the Migration Policy website, https://www.migrationpolicy.org/news/revamping-asylum-us-mexico-border, accessed September 4, 2024.

25. See CBP's Office of Training and Development YouTube video, "BPPC 08 Graduation," https://www.youtube.com/watch?v=0eHUgoPeARU, accessed September 4, 2024.

26. Gómez Cervantes, Menjívar, and Staples 2017, 269; see also Martinez-Aranda (2022).

27. Akbar (2022, 2497). Nonreformist and reformist reforms are not necessarily discrete categories and are more aptly thought of as occurring on a spectrum. Advocates and scholars are developing a set of evaluative criteria to identify the differences. See Cheer (2020); and the 2022 "Reforms" page of the Detention Watch Network website, https://www.detentionwatch network.org/sites/default/files/Abolitionist%20Steps%20vs%20Reformist%20Reforms _DWN_2022.pdf.

28. Cházaro (2016); García Hernández (2024).

29. Light and Miller (2018).

30. García Hernández (2018); Eagly (2020); Koh (2021); Lee (2011); Markowitz (2019); McLeod (2012).

31. Ellermann (2014).

32. Department of Homeland Security (2022).

33. Luan (2018).

34. See the March 2021 "Mandate for Higher Education for California Police Officers" page of the California Matters website, https://calmatters.org/justice/2021/03/mandate-higher -education-for-california-police-officers/.

35. Martínez, Cantor, Ewing (2014).

36. The union is a major silencer of agent dissent, and there are instrumental reasons to support the union, like law enforcement insurance. More oversight over the union and the power that it holds over agents is an urgent area for study and for intervention.

37. See discussion of the Department of Homeland Security labor agreement with ICE workers on the Immigration Policy Tracking website, https://immpolicytracking.org/policies /dhs-signs-labor-agreement-afge-national-ce-council-118-ceding-unprecedented-policy-power -union/#/tab-policy-documents, accessed September 4, 2024.

38. Benhabib (2004, 2).

39. Andreas (2022).

Methodological Appendix

1. Sowatey and Tankebe (2018).

2. R. Ellis (2021).

3. A colleague suggested that this question may have been part of their formal background check, that Officer Boise had to make sure that he wasn't putting his agents in close contact with people who were undocumented. I disagree. First, Officer Boise knew that I had already been

vetted by the Border Patrol, meaning that this "background check" was already done. Second, researchers do not go through the same background check as agents; my understanding is that they checked to see if I was in their criminal database, and they only needed my driver's license for that. Third, this question was asked in the context of what was, essentially, a grilling: a fast-paced set of questions he asked me to determine whether to move forward with my application. He was gauging my biases.

4. Gibson-Light and Seim (2020).

5. These are just some of the terms agents used to describe how others view them.

6. Delaney (2007).

7. Odendahl and Shaw (2002).

8. Delaney (2007).

9. Adler and Adler (2002).

10. Ostrander (1993).

11. Blee (1998).

12. On challenging respondents during research interviews, see Kvale (2006); Thuesen (2011); Vitus (2008).

13. Ostrander (1993, 24).

14. Blee (1998).

15. Jerolmack and Khan (2014).

16. Lamont and Swidler (2014).

17. Pugh (2013).

18. M. Scott and Lyman (1968, 46).

19. US Customs and Border Protection (2021).

20. Blee (2002); C. Ellis (1995).

21. Blee (1998).

22. Kleinman and Copp (1993).

23. Small (2015).

24. Nader (1972).

25. Small (2015, 353).

26. A less charitable interpretation of our penchant for studying the marginalized is that it is simply easier for us to do, in terms of both access and emotional labor.

27. Blee (1998, 387).

REFERENCES

Abrego, Leisy J. 2014. *Sacrificing Families: Navigating Laws, Labor, and Love across Borders*. Stanford, CA: Stanford University Press.

———. 2018. "Central American Refugees Reveal the Crisis of the State." In *The Oxford Handbook of Migration Crises*, edited by C. Menjívar, M. Ruiz, and I. Ness, 213–28. Oxford: Oxford University Press.

Abrego, Leisy, Mat Coleman, Daniel E Martínez, Cecilia Menjívar, and Jeremy Slack. 2017. "Making Immigrants into Criminals: Legal Processes of Criminalization in the Post-IIRIRA Era." *Journal on Migration and Human Security* 5 (3): 694–715.

Achermann, Christin. 2021. "Shaping Migration at the Border: The Entangled Rationalities of Border Control Practices." *Comparative Migration Studies* 9 (1): 1–17.

Adler, Patricia, and Peter Adler. 2002. "The Reluctant Respondent." In *Handbook of Interview Research*, edited by J. F. Gubrium and J. A. Holstein, 515–35. Thousand Oaks, CA: Sage.

Akbar, Anna A. 2022. "Non-reformist Reforms and Struggles over Life, Death, and Democracy." *Yale Law Journal* 132:2497–577.

Alex, Nicholas. 1976. *New York Cops Talk Back: A Study of a Beleaguered Minority*. New York: Wiley.

Aliverti, Ana, 2020. "Patrolling the 'Thin Blue Line' in a World in Motion: An Exploration of the Crime-Migration Nexus in UK Policing." *Theoretical Criminology* 24 (1): 8–27.

———. 2021. *Policing the Borders Within* Oxford: Oxford University Press.

———. 2023. "Manufacturing Obedience: Coercion and Authority in Border Controls." *Punishment and Society* 25 (2): 343–62.

American Immigration Council. 2021. "The Cost of Immigration Enforcement and Border Security." https://www.americanimmigrationcouncil.org/sites/default/files/research/the _cost_of_immigration_enforcement_and_border_security.pdf.

Andreas, Peter. 2022. *Border Games: The Politics of Policing the US-Mexico Divide*. Ithaca, NY: Cornell University Press.

Andrews, Abigail. 2023. *Banished Men: How Migrants Endure the Violence of Deportation*. Berkeley: University of California Press.

Aradau, C., and L. Canzutti. 2022. "Asylum, Borders, and the Politics of Violence: From Suspicion to Cruelty." *Global Studies Quarterly* 2 (2): ksab041.

Aranda, Elizabeth, and Elizabeth Vaquera. 2015. "Racism, the Immigration Enforcement Regime, and the Implications for Racial Inequality in the Lives of Undocumented Young Adults." *Sociology of Race and Ethnicity* 1:88–104.

Arata, Joe. 2023. "Episode 1: Careers at ICE 101." US Department of Homeland Security. https://www.ice.gov/podcasts/careers-ice/episode-1-careers-ice-101.

Arendt, Hannah. 1963. *Eichmann in Jerusalem: A Report on the Banality of Evil*. New York: Penguin.

Armenta, Amada. 2012. "From Sheriff's Deputies to Immigration Officers: Screening Immigrant Status in a Tennessee Jail." *Law and Policy* 34 (2): 191–210.

———. 2017. *Protect, Serve, and Deport: The Rise of Policing as Immigration Enforcement*. Berkeley: University of California Press.

———. 2017b. "Racializing Crimmigration: Structural Racism, Colorblindness, and the Institutional Production of Immigrant Criminality." *Sociology of Race and Ethnicity* 3 (1): 82–95.

Armenta, A., and Irene I. Vega. 2017. "Latinos and the Crimmigration System." In *Race, Ethnicity and Law*, ed. Mathieu Deflem, 221–36. Bingley, UK: Emerald.

———. n.d. "Narrating Mutual Recognition: Border Crossing Accounts from Migrants and Agents at the U.S.-Mexico Border." Unpublished manuscript.

Asad, Asad L. 2019. "Deportation Decisions: Judicial Decision-Making in an American Immigration Court." *American Behavioral Scientist* 63 (9): 1221–49.

———. 2020. "Latinos' Deportation Fears by Citizenship and Legal Status, 2007 to 2018." *Proceedings of the National Academy of Sciences* 117 (16): 8836–44.

———. 2023. *Engage and Evade: How Latino Immigrant Families Manage Surveillance in Everyday Life*. Princeton, NJ: Princeton University Press.

Asad, Asad L., and Matthew Clair. 2018. "Racialized Legal Status as a Social Determinant of Health." *Social Science and Medicine* 199:19–28.

Ashforth, Blake E., and Glen E. Kreiner. 1999. " 'How Can You Do It?': Dirty Work and the Challenge of Constructing a Positive Identity." *Academy of Management Review* 24:413–34.

Baker, Bryan. 2021. "Estimates of the Unauthorized Immigrant Population Residing in the United States: January 2015–January 2018." https://ohss.dhs.gov/sites/default/files/2023-12/unauthorized_immigrant_population_estimates_2015_-_2018.pdf.

Balfour, Danny L., Guy B. Adams, and Ashley E. Nickels. 2019. *Unmasking Administrative Evil*. New York: Routledge.

Barak, Maya Pagni. 2023. *The Slow Violence of Immigration Court: Procedural Justice on Trial*. New York: New York University Press.

Barker, Vanessa. 2017. "Nordic Vagabonds: The Roma and the Logic of Benevolent Violence in the Swedish Welfare State." *European Journal of Criminology* 14 (1): 120–39.

Barroso, Amanda. 2019. "The Changing Profile of the U.S. Military: Smaller in Size, More Diverse, More Women in Leadership." Pew Research Center. https://www.pewresearch.org/short-reads/2019/09/10/the-changing-profile-of-the-u-s-military/.

Bayley, David H., and Harold Mendelsohn. 1969. *Minorities and the Police: Confrontation in America*. New York: Free Press.

Beetham, David. 2013. *The Legitimation of Power*. London: Bloomsbury.

Bell, Jeannine. 2017. *The Symbolic Assailant Revisited*. Indiana Legal Studies Research Paper 371. https://dx.doi.org/10.2139/ssrn.2955845.

Bell, Monica C. 2017. "Police Reform and the Dismantling of Legal Estrangement." *Yale Law Journal* 126 (7): 2054–150.

Beltrán, Cristina. 2020. *Cruelty as Citizenship: How Migrant Suffering Sustains White Democracy.* Minneapolis: University of Minnesota Press.

———. 2023. "America's Increasingly Diverse Security State Is Changing Communities." *New York Times*, February 25. https://www.nytimes.com/2023/02/25/opinion/police-prisons-people-of-color.html.

Benhabib, Seyla. 2004. *The Rights of Others: Aliens, Residents, and Citizens.* Cambridge: Cambridge University Press.

Bialik, Kristen. 2018. "ICE Arrests Went Up in 2017, with Biggest Increases in Florida, Northern Texas, Oklahoma." Pew Research Center. https://www.pewresearch.org/short-reads/2018/02/08/ice-arrests-went-up-in-2017-with-biggest-increases-in-florida-northern-texas-oklahoma/.

Bigo, D. 2002. "Security and Immigration: Toward a Critique of the Governmentality of Unease." *Alternatives* 27 (1 supp.): 63–92.

Bittner, Egon. 1970. *The Functions of the Police in Modern Society: A Review of Background Factors, Current Practices, and Possible Role Models.* Washington, DC: US Government Printing Office.

Blee, Kathleen M. 1998. "White-Knuckle Research: Emotional Dynamics in Fieldwork with Racist Activists." *Qualitative Sociology* 21 (4): 381–99.

———. 2002. *Inside Organized Racism: Women in the Hate Movement.* Berkeley: University of California Press.

Bloom, Howard S., Larry L. Orr, Stephen H. Bell, George Cave, Fred Doolittle, Winston Lin, and Johannes M. Bos. 1997. "The Benefits and Costs of JTPA Title II-A Programs: Key Findings from the National Job Training Partnership Act Study." *Journal of Human Resources* 32 (3): 549–76.

Boltanski, Luc, and Laurent Thévenot. 2006. *On Justification: Economies of Worth.* Princeton, NJ: Princeton University Press.

Bolton, Kenneth, and Joe Feagin. 2004. *Black in Blue: African-American Police Officers and Racism.* New York: Routledge.

Bonilla-Silva, Eduardo. 1997. "Rethinking Racism: Toward a Structural Interpretation." *American Sociological Review* 62 (3): 465–80.

Borrelli, Lisa M. 2018. "Using Ignorance as (Un)Conscious Bureaucratic Strategy: Street-Level Practices and Structural Influences in the Field of Migration Enforcement." *Qualitative Studies* 5 (2): 95–109.

———. 2021. "The Border Inside—Organizational Socialization of Street-level Bureaucrats in the European Migration Regime." *Journal of Borderlands Studies* 36 (4): 579–98.

Borrelli, Lisa Marie, and Annika Lindberg. 2018. "The Creativity of Coping: Alternative Tales of Moral Dilemmas among Migration Control Officers." *International Journal of Migration and Border Studies* 4 (3): 163–78.

Borrelli, Lisa M., Annika Lindberg, and Anna Wyss. 2022. "States of Suspicion: How Institutionalised Disbelief Shapes Migration Control Regimes." *Geopolitics* 27 (4): 1025–41.

Bosworth, Mary. 2013. "Can Immigration Detention Centres Be Legitimate? Understanding Confinement in a Global World." In *The Borders of Punishment: Migration, Citizenship, and Social Exclusion*, edited by Katja Franko Aas and Mary Bosworth, 149–65. Oxford: Oxford University Press.

———. 2014. *Inside Immigration Detention*. Oxford: Oxford University Press.

———. 2019. "Affect and Authority in Immigration Detention." *Punishment and Society* 21 (5): 542–59.

Bosworth, Mary, and Gavin Slade. 2014. "In Search of Recognition: Gender and Staff-Detainee Relations in a British Immigration Removal Center." *Punishment and Society* 16 (2): 169–86.

Bosworth, Mary, Alpa Parmar, and Yolanda Vázquez, eds. 2018. *Race, Criminal Justice, and Migration Control: Enforcing the Boundaries of Belonging*. Oxford: Oxford University Press.

Bosworth, Mary, Katja Franko, and Sharon Pickering. 2018. "Punishment, Globalization and Migration Control: 'Get Them the Hell out of Here.'" *Punishment & Society* 20(10): 34–53.

Bottoms, Anthony, and Justice Tankebe. 2012. "Beyond Procedural Justice: A Dialogic Approach to Legitimacy in Criminal Justice." *Journal of Criminal Law and Criminology* 102:119.

Bourdieu, Pierre. 1994. "Rethinking the State: Genesis and Structure of the Bureaucratic Field." Translated by Loïc Wacquant and Samar Farage. *Sociological Theory* 12 (1): 1–18.

Branch, Michael. 2021. "The Nature of the Beast: The Precariousness of Police Work." *Policing and Society* 31 (8): 982–96.

Bristol, Travis J., and Javier Martin-Fernandez. 2019. "The Added Value of Latinx and Black Teachers for Latinx and Black Students: Implications for Policy." *Policy Insights from the Behavioral and Brain Sciences* 6 (2): 147–53.

Calavita, Kitty. 2010. *Inside the State: The Bracero Program, Immigration, and the INS*. New Orleans: Quid Pro Books.

Campos-Delgado, Amalia, and Karine Côté-Boucher. 2022. "Tactics of Empathy: The Intimate Geopolitics of Mexican Migrant Detention." *Geopolitics* 29 (2): 471–94.

Canizales, Stephanie L. 2023. "Caught in the Dragnet: How Punitive Immigration Laws Harm Immigrant Community Helpers." *Contexts* 22 (1): 38–43.

Cardoso, Jodi Berger, Erin Randle Hamilton, Nestor Rodríguez, Karl Eschbach, and Jacqueline Hagan. 2016. "Deporting Fathers: Involuntary Transnational Families and Intent to Remigrate and Salvadoran Deportees." *International Migration Review* 50 (1): 197–230.

Castañeda, Heide. 2020. *Borders of Belonging: Struggle and Solidarity in Mixed-Status Immigrant Families*. Stanford, CA: Stanford University Press.

Castañeda Pérez, Estefania. 2022. "Transborder (In)Securities: Transborder Commuters' Perceptions of US Customs and Border Protection Policing at the Mexico-US Border." *Politics, Groups, and Identities* 10 (1): 1–20.

———. n.d. "The Silence of Transborder Suffering: Emotions, Obedience, and Embodiment." Unpublished manuscript.

Chacón, Jennifer M. 2009. "Managing Migration through Crime." *Columbia Law Review Sidebar* 109:142.

———. 2013. "The Security Myth: Punishing Immigrants in the Name of National Security." In *Governing Immigration through Crime*, edited by Julie A. Dowling and Jonathan X. Inda, 77–94. Stanford, CA: Stanford University Press.

———. 2014. "Producing Liminal Legality." *Denver University Law Review* 92:709.

Chacón, Jennifer M., and Susan Bibler Coutin. 2018. "Racialization through Enforcement." In *Race, Criminal Justice, and Migration Control: Enforcing the Boundaries of Belonging*, edited by Mary Bosworth, Alpa Parmar, and Yolanda Vázquez, 159–75. Oxford: Oxford University Press.

Chappell, A. T., and L. Lanza-Kaduce. 2010. "Police Academy Socialization: Understanding the Lessons Learned in a Paramilitary-Bureaucratic Organization." *Journal of Contemporary Ethnography* 39 (2): 187–214.

Chauvin, Sebastien, and Blanca Garcés-Mascareñas. 2014. "Becoming Less Illegal: Deservingness Frames and Undocumented Migrant Incorporation." *Sociology Compass* 8 (4): 422–32.

———. 2020. "Contradictions in the Moral Economy of Migrant Irregularity." In *Migrants with Irregular Status in Europe: Evolving Conceptual and Policy Challenges*, edited by Anna Triandafyllidou and Sarah Spencer, 33–49.

Chavez, Leo. 2020. *The Latino Threat: Constructing Immigrants, Citizens, and the Nation*. Stanford, CA: Stanford University Press.

Chávez, Sergio. 2016. *Border Lives: Fronterizos, Transnational Migrants, and Commuters in Tijuana*. Oxford: Oxford University Press.

Cházaro, Angelica. 2016. "Challenging the 'Criminal Alien' Paradigm." *UCLA Law Review* 63:594.

Cheer, Siu-Ming. 2020. "Abolitionist Reforms and the Immigrants' Rights Movement." In "Discourse," special issue, *Law Meets World* 68:68–79.

Chishti, Muzaffar, and Jessica Bolter. 2021. "Border Challenges Dominate, but Biden's First 100 Days Mark Notable Under-the-Radar Immigration Accomplishments." https://www .migrationpolicy.org/print/17058.

Chishti, Muzaffar, and Kathleen Bush-Joseph. 2023. "U.S. Border Asylum Policy Enters New Territory Post–Title 42." https://www.migrationpolicy.org/article/border-after-title-42.

Chishti, Muzaffar, and Charles Kamasaki. 2014. *IRCA in Retrospect: Guideposts for Today's Immigration Reform*. Washington, DC: Migration Policy Institute.

Chishti, Muzaffar, Doris Meissner, and Claire Bergeron. 2011. "At Its 25th Anniversary, IRCA's Legacy Lives On." https://www.migrationpolicy.org/article/its-25th-anniversary-ircas -legacy-lives.

Chishti, Muzaffar, Sarah Pierce, and Jessica Bolter. 2017. "The Obama Record on Deportations: Deporter in Chief or Not." Migration Policy Institute. https://www.migrationpolicy.org /article/obama-record-deportations-deporter-chief-or-not.

Clifton, Stacey, Jose Torres, and James Hawdon. 2021. "Examining Guardian and Warrior Orientations across Racial and Ethnic Lines." *Journal of Police and Criminal Psychology* 36:436–49.

Clinton, William. 1996. "Statement by the President on 'Antiterrorism and Effective Death Penalty Act of 1996.'" April 24. https://clintonwhitehouse6.archives.gov/1996/04/1996-04-24 -president-statement-on-antiterrorism-bill-signing.html.

Cohen, Stanley. 2013. *States of Denial: Knowing about Atrocities and Suffering*. New York: John Wiley and Sons.

Conti, Norman. 2009. "A Visigoth System: Shame, Honor, and Police Socialization." *Journal of Contemporary Ethnography* 38 (3): 409–32.

Conti, Norman, and Patrick Doreian. 2014. "From Here on Out, We're All Blue: Interaction Order, Social Infrastructure, and Race in Police Socialization." *Police Quarterly* 17 (4): 414–47.

Conti, Norman, and James J. Nolan III. 2005. "Policing the Platonic Cave: Ethics and Efficacy in Police Training." *Policing and Society* 15 (2): 166–86.

Correa, Jennifer G., and James M. Thomas. 2015. "The Rebirth of the US-Mexico Border: Latina/o Enforcement Agents and the Changing Politics of Racial Power." *Sociology of Race and Ethnicity* 1 (2): 239–54.

Cortez, David. 2021. "Latinxs in La Migra: Why They Join and Why It Matters." *Political Research Quarterly* 74 (3): 688–702.

Coutin, Susan, Jennifer Chacón, and Stephen Lee. 2024. *Legal Phantoms: Executive Action and the Haunting Failures of Immigration Law.* Stanford, CA: Stanford University Press.

Cox, Adam, and Cristina Rodriguez. 2020. *The President and Immigration Law.* Oxford: Oxford University Press.

Dau, Philipp M., Christophe Vandeviver, Maite Dewinter, Frank Witlox, and Tom Vander Beken. 2023. "Policing Directions: A Systematic Review on the Effectiveness of Police Presence." *European Journal on Criminal Policy and Research* 29 (2): 191–225.

Dávila, Alberto, and Marie T. Mora. 2000. "English Skills, Earnings, and the Occupational Sorting of Mexican Americans along the US-Mexico Border." *International Migration Review* 34 (1): 133–57.

De Genova, Nicholas. 2004. "The Legal Production of Mexican/Migrant Illegality." *Latino Studies* 2:160–85.

———. "Spectacles of Migrant 'Illegality': The Scene of Exclusion, The Obscene of Inclusion." *Ethnic and Racial Studies* 36(7): 1180–1198.

———. 2014. "Immigration Reform and the Production of Migrant Illegality." In *Constructing Immigrant "Illegality": Critiques, Experiences and Responses,* edited by C. Menjívar and D. Kanstroom, 63–83. Cambridge: Cambridge University Press, 37–62.

Delaney, Kevin J. 2007. "Methodological Dilemmas and Opportunities in Interviewing Organizational Elites." *Sociology Compass* 1 (1): 208–21.

De León, Jason. 2015. *The Land of Open Graves: Living and Dying on the Migrant Trail.* Berkeley: University of California Press.

Department of Homeland Security. 2016. "Border Patrol Agent Pay Reform: Fiscal Year 2016 Report to Congress." https://www.dhs.gov/sites/default/files/publications/CBPpercent20 -percent20Borderpercent20Patrolpercent20Agentpercent20Paypercent20Reform.pdf.

———. 2022. "Budget-in-Brief: Fiscal Year 2022." https://www.dhs.gov/sites/default/files /publications/dhs_bib_-_web_version_-_final_508.pdf.

Desmond, M. 2007. *On the Fireline: Living and Dying with Wildland Firefighters.* Chicago: University of Chicago Press.

———. 2011. "Making Firefighters Deployable." *Qualitative Sociology* 34:59–77.

Dick, Penny. 2005. "Dirty Work Designations: How Police Officers Account for Their Use of Coercive Force." *Human Relations* 58 (11): 1363–90.

DiMaggio, Paul. 1997. "Culture and Cognition." *American Review of Sociology* 23:263–87.

Donato, Katharine M., Brandon Wagner, and Evelyn Patterson. 2008. "The Cat and Mouse Game at the Mexico-US Border: Gendered Patterns and Recent Shifts." *International Migration Review* 42 (2): 330–59.

Doreian, Patrick, and Norman Conti. 2017. "Creating the Thin Blue Line: Social Network Evolution within a Police Academy." *Social Networks* 50:83–97.

Dowling, Julie, and Jonathan X. Inda, eds. 2013. *Governing Immigration through Crime: A Reader.* Stanford, CA: Stanford University Press.

Dreby, Joanna. 2015. *Everyday Illegal: When Policies Undermine Immigrant Families*. Berkeley: University of California Press.

Dunaway, Johanna, Regina P. Branton, and Marisa A. Abrajano. 2010. "Agenda Setting, Public Opinion, and the Issue of Immigration Reform." *Social Science Quarterly* 91 (2): 359–78.

Dunn, Timothy. 1996. *The Militarization of the U.S.-Mexico Border, 1978–1992: Low Intensity Conflict Doctrine Comes Home*. Austin: CMAS Books / University of Texas Press.

Durand, Jorge, and Douglas Massey. 2019. "Evolution of the Mexico-US Migration System: Insights from the Mexican Migration Project." *Annals of the American Academy of Political and Social Science* 684 (1): 21–42.

Eagly, Ingrid V. 2020. "The Movement to Decriminalize Border Crossing." *Boston College Law Review* 61 (6): 1967–2030.

Eason, John. 2019. *Big House on the Prairie: Rise of the Rural Ghetto and Prison Proliferation*. Chicago: University of Chicago Press.

Elcioglu, E. F. 2020. *Divided by the Wall: Progressive and Conservative Immigration Politics at the US-Mexico Border*. Berkeley: University of California Press.

Ellermann, Antje. 2006. "Street-Level Democracy: How Immigration Bureaucrats Manage Public Opposition." *West European Politics* 29 (2): 293–309.

———. 2009. *States against Migrants: Deportation in Germany and the United States*. Cambridge: Cambridge University Press.

———. 2014. "The Rule of Law and the Right to Stay: The Moral Claims of Undocumented Migrants." *Politics and Society* 42 (3): 293–308.

Ellis, Carolyn. 1995. "Emotional and Ethical Quagmires in Returning to the Field." *Journal of Contemporary Ethnography* 24 (1): 68–98.

Ellis, Rachel. 2021. "What Do We Mean by a 'Hard-to-Reach' Population? Legitimacy versus Precarity as Barriers to Access." *Sociological Methods and Research* 52 (3): 1556–86.

Enriquez, Laura E. 2015. "Multigenerational Punishment: Shared Experiences of Undocumented Immigration Status within Mixed-Status Families." *Journal of Marriage and Family* 77 (4): 939–53.

Eschbach, Karl, Jacqueline Hagan, Néstor Rodriguez, Rubén Hernández-León, and Stanley Bailey. 1999. "Death at the Border." *International Migration Review* 33 (2): 430–54.

Ewick, Patricia, and Susan Silbey. 1998. *The Common Place of Law: Stories from Everyday Life*. Chicago: University of Chicago Press.

Ewing, W. A., D. Martínez, and R. G. Rumbaut. 2015. *The Criminalization of Immigration in the United States*. Special report. Washington, DC: American Immigration Council.

Farrell-Bryan, Dylan. 2022. "Relief or Removal: State Logics of Deservingness and Masculinity for Immigrant Men in Removal Proceedings." *Law and Society Review* 56 (2): 167–87.

Farrell-Bryan, Dylan, and Ian Peacock. 2022. "Who Gets Deported? Immigrant Removal Rates by National Origin and Period, 1998 to 2021." *Socius* 8:1–3.

Fassin, Didier. 2005. "Compassion and Repression: The Moral Economy of Immigration Policies in France." *Cultural Anthropology* 20 (3): 362–87.

———. 2009. "Moral Economies Revisited." *Annales: Histoire, sciences sociales* 64 (6): 1237–66.

———. 2017. "Boredom: Accounting for the Ordinary in the Work of Policing (France)." In *Writing the World of Policing: The Difference Ethnography Makes*, edited by Didier Fassin, 269–92. Chicago: University of Chicago Press.

Federal Law Enforcement Training Centers. 2019. "Budget Overview." US Department of Homeland Security. https://www.dhs.gov/sites/default/files/publications/Federal%20Law%20Enforcement%20Training%20Centers.pdf.

Finch, Jessie K. 2022. *Legal Professionals Negotiating the Borders of Identity: Operation Streamline and Competing Identity Management*. New York: Taylor and Francis.

FitzGerald, David S., and David Cook-Martín. 2014. *Culling the Masses: The Democratic Origins of Racist Immigration Policy in the Americas*. Cambridge, MA: Harvard University Press.

Flores, Edward, Jillian Medeiros, and Harry Pachon. 2007. *Equal Employment Opportunity or Enclave Employment in Federal Agencies?* Los Angeles: Tomas Rivera Policy Institute.

Flores, Glenda M. 2017. *Latina Teachers: Creating Careers and Guiding Culture*. New York: New York University Press.

Flores, René D., and Ariel Azar. 2023. "Who Are the 'Immigrants'? How Whites' Diverse Perceptions of Immigrants Shape Their Attitudes." *Social Forces* 101 (4): 2117–46.

Flores, René D., and Ariela Schachter. 2018. "Who Are the 'Illegals'? The Social Construction of Illegality in the United States." *American Sociological Review* 83 (5): 839–68.

Flores-González, N. 2002. *School Kids / Street Kids: Identity Development in Latino Students*. New York: Teachers College Press.

Forman, J., Jr. 2017. *Locking Up Our Own: Crime and Punishment in Black America*. Farrar, Straus and Giroux.

Franko, Katja. 2019. *The Crimmigrant Other: Migration and Penal Power*. Abingdon: Routledge.

Fuglerud, Oivind. 2004. "Constructing Exclusion. The Micro-Sociology of an Immigration Department." *Social Anthropology* 12 (1): 25–40.

Gallardo, Roberto. 2020. "To Help 'La Gente': Examining Helping People as a Motivation for Becoming an Officer in the Los Angeles Police Department among Male Mexican American Officers." *Criminal Justice Review* 45 (4): 452–63.

García, Angela S. 2019. *Legal Passing: Navigating Undocumented Life and Local Immigration Law*. Berkeley: University of California Press.

García Hernández, César C. 2009. "La Migra in the Mirror: Immigration Enforcement and Racial Profiling on the Texas Border." *Notre Dame Journal of Law, Ethics and Public Policy* 23 (6): 167–96.

———. 2018. "Deconstructing Crimmigration." *UC Davis Law Review* 52:197.

———. 2023. *Migrating to Prison: America's Obsession with Locking Up Immigrants*. New York: New Press.

———. 2024. *Welcome the Wretched: In Defense of the "Criminal Alien."* New York: New Press.

Garland, David. 2001. *The Culture of Control: Crime and Social Order in Contemporary Society*. Oxford: Oxford University Press.

Garza, Irene. 2015. "Advertising Patriotism: The 'Yo Soy El Army' Campaign and the Politics of Visibility for Latina/o Youth." *Latino Studies* 13 (2): 245–68.

Gau, Jacinta M., and Eugene Paoline III. 2017. "Officer Race, Role Orientations, and Cynicism toward Citizens." *Justice Quarterly* 34 (7): 1246–71.

Gau, Jacinta M., Eugene Paoline III, and Krystle Roman. 2021. "Hispanic and Latinx Police Officers' Perceptions of the Working Environment." *Crime and Delinquency* 69 (9): 1576–89.

Getrich, Christina M. 2013. "'Too Bad I'm Not an Obvious Citizen': The Effects of Racialized US Immigration Enforcement Practices on Second-Generation Mexican Youth." *Latino Studies* 11:462–82.

Gibson-Light, Michael, and Josh Seim. 2020. "Punishing Fieldwork: Penal Domination and Prison Ethnography." *Journal of Contemporary Ethnography* 49 (5): 666–90.

Gilad, Sharon, and Momi Dahan. 2021. "Representative Bureaucracy and Impartial Policing." *Public Administration* 99 (1): 137–55.

Gilboy, Janet A. 1991. "Deciding Who Gets In: Decisionmaking by Immigration Inspectors." *Law and Society Review* 25 (3): 571–99.

Goffman, Erving. 1963. *Stigma: Notes on the Management of Spoiled Identity*. New York: Simon and Schuster.

Golash-Boza, Tanya. 2009. "The Immigration Industrial Complex: Why We Enforce Immigration Policies Destined to Fail." *Sociology Compass* 3 (2): 295–309.

———. 2015. *Deported: Immigrant Policing, Disposable Labor and Global Capitalism*. New York: New York University Press.

———. 2019. "Punishment beyond the Deportee: The Collateral Consequences of Deportation." *American Behavioral Scientist* 63 (9): 1331–49.

Golash-Boza, Tanya, and Pierrette Hondagneu-Sotelo. 2013. "Latino Immigrant Men and the Deportation Crisis: A Gendered Racial Removal Program." *Latino Studies* 11:271–92.

Gómez, Laura E. 2018. *Manifest Destinies: The Making of the Mexican American Race*. New York: New York University Press.

Gómez Cervantes, Andrea. 2021. "'Looking Mexican': Indigenous and Non-indigenous Latina/o Immigrants and the Racialization of Illegality in the Midwest." *Social Problems* 68 (1): 100–117.

Gómez Cervantes, Andrea, Cecilia Menjívar, and William G. Staples. 2017. "Humane Immigration Enforcement and Latina Immigrants in the Detention Complex." *Feminist Criminology* 12:269.

Goodman, Adam. 2020. *The Deportation Machine: America's Long History of Expelling Immigrants*. Princeton, NJ: Princeton University Press.

Gould, Jon B., and Scott Barclay. 2012. "Mind the Gap: The Place of Gap Studies in Sociolegal Scholarship." *Annual Review of Law and Social Science* 8:323–35.

Graham, Mark. 2002. "Emotional Bureaucracies: Emotions, Civil Servants, and Immigrants in the Swedish Welfare State." *Ethos* 30 (2): 199–226.

Griffiths, Melanie. 2024. "The Emotional Governance of Immigration Controls." *Identities* 31 (1): 82–103.

Guerra, Santiago. 2015. "La Chota y Los Mafiosos: Mexican American Casualties of the Border Drug War." *Latino Studies* 13:227–44.

Gutierrez, David G. 1995. *Walls and Mirrors: Mexican Americans, Mexican Immigrants and the Politics of Ethnicity*. Berkeley: University of California Press.

Hagan, Jacqueline M., and Joshua T. Wassink. 2020. "Return Migration around the World: An Integrated Agenda for Future Research." *Annual Review of Sociology* 46:533–52.

Hall, Alexandra. 2013. "'These People Could Be Anyone': Fear, Contempt (and Empathy) in a British Immigration Removal Centre." In *Emotions and Human Mobility: Ethnographies of Movement*, edited by Maruška Svašek 17–34. New York: Routledge.

Harris, Richard. 1973. *The Police Academy: An Inside View*. New York: John Wiley and Sons.

Herbert, Steve. 1996. "Morality in Law Enforcement: Chasing 'Bad Guys' with the Los Angeles Police Department." *Law and Society Review* 30 (4): 799–818.

———. 2006. "Tangled Up in Blue: Conflicting Paths to Police Legitimacy." *Theoretical Criminology* 10 (4): 481–504.

Herzfeld, Michael. 1991. *The Social Production of Indifference: Exploring the Symbolic Roots of Western Bureaucracy*. New York: Berg.

Heyman, Josiah. 1995. "Putting Power in the Anthropology of Bureaucracy: The Immigration and Naturalization Service at the Mexico–United States Border." *Current Anthropology* 36 (2): 261–87.

———. 2000. "Respect for Outsiders? Respect for the Law? The Moral Evaluation of High Scale Issues by U.S. Immigration Officers." *Journal of the Royal Anthropological Institute* 6 (4): 635–52.

———. 2002. "U.S. Immigration Officers of Mexican Ancestry as Mexican Americans, Citizens, and Immigration Police." *Current Anthropology* 43 (3): 479–507.

———. 2009. "Trust, Privilege, and Discretion in the Governance of the US Borderlands with Mexico." *Canadian Journal of Law and Society* 24 (3): 367–90.

Hochschild, Arlie Russell. 1979. "Emotion Work, Feeling Rules, and Social Structure." *American Journal of Sociology* 85 (3): 551–75.

Hodgson, James F. 2001. "Police Violence in Canada and the USA: Analysis and Management." *Policing: An International Journal* 24 (4): 520–51.

Hopper, Marianne. 1977. "Becoming a Policeman: Socialization of Cadets in a Police Academy." *Urban Life* 6 (2): 149–70.

Huerta, Adrian H. 2015. "I Didn't Want My Life to Be Like That: Gangs, College, or the Military for Latino Male High School Students." *Journal of Latino / Latin American Studies* 7 (2): 119–32.

Hughes, Everett. 1951. *Work and the Self*. New York: Routledge.

Humphrey, Nicole M. 2002. "Racialized Emotional Labor: An Unseen Burden in the Public Sector." *Administration and Society* 54 (4): 741–58.

Huo, Yuen J., and Tom R. Tyler. 2000. *How Different Ethnic Groups React to Legal Authority*. Sacramento: Public Policy Institute of California.

Immigration Reform and Control Act of 1986. https://www.justice.gov/sites/default/files/eoir/legacy/2009/03/04/IRCA.pdf.

Inda, Jonathan X. 2013. "Subject to Deportation: IRCA, 'Criminal Aliens,' and the Policing of Immigration." *Migration Studies* 1 (3): 292–310.

Jackall, Robert. 2009. *Moral Mazes: The World of Corporate Lawyers*. Oxford: Oxford University Press.

Jerolmack, Colin, and Shamus Khan. 2014. "Talk Is Cheap: Ethnography and the Attitudinal Fallacy." *Sociological Methods and Research* 43 (2): 178–209.

Jiménez, Tomas R. 2010. *Replenished Ethnicity: Mexican Americans, Immigration, and Identity*. Berkeley: University of California Press.

Johnson, Catherine, Timothy Dowd, and Cecilia Ridgeway. 2006. "Legitimacy as a Social Process." *Annual Review of Sociology* 32:53–78.

Johnson, Kevin R. 2009. "Ten Guiding Principles for Truly Comprehensive Immigration Reform: A Blueprint." *Wayne Law Review* 55:1599.

Johnson, Kit. 2020. "Women of Color in Immigration Enforcement." *Nevada Law Journal* 21:997.

Jones, Reece. 2014. "Border Wars: Narratives and Images of the US-Mexico Border on TV." *ACME: An International E-Journal for Critical Geographies* 13 (3): 530–50.

Kalhan, Anil. 2010. "Rethinking Immigration Detention." *Columbia Law Review Sidebar* 110:42–58.

Kang, Deborah. 2016. *The INS on the Line: Making Immigration Law on the US-Mexico Border, 1917–1954*. Oxford: Oxford University Press.

Kanstroom, Daniel. 2007. *Deportation Nation: Outsiders in American History*. Cambridge, MA: Harvard University Press.

Kaufman, Herbert. 2010. *The Forest Ranger: A Study in Administrative Behavior*. New York: Routledge.

Kennedy, Joseph E. 1999. "Monstrous Offenders and the Search for Solidarity through Modern Punishment." *Hastings Law Journal* 51 829.

Keyes, Elizabeth. 2011. "Beyond Saints and Sinners: Discretion and the Need for New Narratives in the US Immigration System." *Georgetown Immigration Law Journal* 26:207.

———. 2013. "Defining American: The DREAM Act, Immigration Reform and Citizenship." *Nevada Law Journal* 14:101.

Kleinman, Sherryl, and Martha A. Copp. 1993. *Emotions and Fieldwork*. Newbury Park, CA: Sage.

Knowles, Robert, and Geoffrey Heeren. 2019. "Zealous Administration: The Deportation Bureaucracy." *Rutgers University Law Review* 72:749.

Koh, Jennifer L. 2020. "Executive Defiance and the Deportation State." *Yale Law Journal* 130 (4): 948–97.

———. 2021. "Downsizing the Deportation State." *Harvard Law and Policy Review* 16 (1): 85–114.

Koulish, Robert, and Maartje van der Woude, eds. 2020. *Crimmigrant Nations: Resurgent Nationalism and the Closing of Borders*. New York: Fordham University Press.

Kurtz, D. L., and L. Upton. 2017. "War Stories and Occupying Soldiers: A Narrative Approach to Understanding Police Culture and Community Conflict." *Critical Criminology* 25: 539–58.

Kvale, Steinar. 2006. "Dominance through Interviews and Dialogues." *Qualitative Inquiry* 12:480–500.

Lalonde, P. C. 2019. "Border Officer Training in Canada: Identifying Organisational Governance Technologies." *Policing and Society* 29 (5): 579–98.

Lamont, Michèle. 2018. "Addressing Recognition Gaps: Destigmatization and the Reduction of Inequality." *American Sociological Review* 83 (3): 419–44.

Lamont, Michèle, and Ann Swidler. 2014. "Methodological Pluralism and the Possibilities and Limits of Interviewing." *Qualitative Sociology* 37:153–71.

Lee, Stephen. 2011. "Monitoring Immigration Enforcement." *Arizona Law Review* 53: 1089–1136.

———. 2019. "Family Separation as Slow Death." *Columbia Law Review* 119(8): 2319–2384.

Liebling, Alison. 2011. "Moral Performance, Inhuman and Degrading Treatment and Prison Pain." *Punishment and Society* 13 (5): 530–50.

Light, Michael, and Ty Miller. 2018. "Does Undocumented Migration Increase Violent Crime?" *Criminology* 56 (2): 370–401.

Lipsky, Michael. 2010. *Street-Level Bureaucracy: Dilemmas of the Individual in Public Service.* New York: Russell Sage Foundation.

Loftus, Bethan. 2010. "Police Occupational Culture: Classic Themes, Altered Times." *Policing and Society* 20 (1): 1–20.

———. 2015. "Border Regimes and the Sociology of Policing." *Policing and Society* 25 (1): 115–25.

Longazel, Jaime G. 2013a. "Moral Panic as Racial Degradation Ceremony: Racial Stratification and the Local-Level Backlash against Latino/a Immigrants." *Punishment and Society* 15 (1): 96–119.

———. 2013b. "Subordinating Myth: Latino/a Immigration, Crime, and Exclusion." *Sociology Compass* 7 (2): 87–96.

Lopez, Jane L. 2021. *Unauthorized Love: Mixed-Citizenship Couples Negotiating Intimacy, Immigration, and the State.* Stanford, CA: Stanford University Press.

Lopez, Mark H., Jens M. Krogstad, and Jeffrey S. Passel. 2023. "Who Is Hispanic." Pew Research Center. https://www.pewresearch.org/short-reads/2023/09/05/who-is-hispanic/.

Loyd, Jenna M., and Alison Mountz. 2018. *Boats, Borders, and Bases: Race, the Cold War, and the Rise of Migration Detention in the United States.* Berkeley: University of California Press.

Luan, Livia. 2018. "Profiting from Enforcement: The Role of Private Prisons in U.S. Immigration Detention." Migration Policy Institute. May 2. https://www.migrationpolicy.org/article/profiting-enforcement-role-private-prisons-us-immigration-detention.

Lytle Hernández, Kelly. 2010. *Migra! A History of the U.S. Border Patrol.* Berkeley: University of California Press.

———. 2017. *City of Inmates: Conquest, Rebellion, and the Rise of Human Caging in Los Angeles, 1771–1965.* Chapel Hill: University of North Carolina Press.

Macias-Rojas, Patrisia. 2016. *From Deportation to Prison: The Politics of Immigration Enforcement in Post–Civil Rights America.* New York: New York University Press.

Magaña, Lisa. 2003. *Straddling the Border: Immigration Policy and the INS.* Austin: University of Texas Press.

Manjarrez, Victor M., Jr. 2021. "Change in the Organization Socialization of a Basic Law Enforcement Academy: How Supervisors Cope." *Police Practice and Research* 22 (1): 777–92.

Mariscal, Jorge. 2005. "Homeland Security, Militarism, and the Future of Latinos and Latinas in the United States." *Radical History Review* 93:39–52.

Markowitz, Peter L. 2019. "Abolish ICE . . . and Then What?" *Yale Law Journal Forum* 129:130–48.

Martin, Susan Ehrlich. 1999. "Police Force or Police Service? Gender and Emotional Labor." *Annals of the American Academy of Political and Social Science* 561 (1): 111–26.

Martínez, Daniel E. 2016. "Coyote Use in an Era of Heightened Border Enforcement: New Evidence from the Arizona-Sonora Border." *Journal of Ethnic and Migration Studies* 42 (1): 103–19.

Martínez, Daniel E., Guillermo Cantor, and Walter Ewing. 2014. *No Action Taken: Lack of CBP Accountability in Responding to Complaints of Abuse.* Washington, DC: American Immigration Council Immigration Policy Center.

Martínez, Daniel E., Robin C. Reineke, Raquel Rubio-Goldsmith, and Bruce O. Parks. 2014. "Structural Violence and Migrant Deaths in Southern Arizona: Data from the Pima County

Office of the Medical Examiner, 1990–2013." *Journal on Migration and Human Security* 2 (4): 257–86.

Martínez, Daniel E., Jeremy Slack, and Josiah Heyman. 2013. "Bordering on Criminal: The Routine Abuse of Migrants in the Removal System (Part 1: Migrant Mistreatment while in US Custody)." Special report. Washington, DC: American Immigration Council.

Martinez, Eligio, Jr., and Adrian H. Huerta. 2020. "Deferred Enrollment: Chicano/Latino Males, Social Mobility and Military Enlistment." *Education and Urban Society* 52 (1): 117–42.

Martinez-Aranda, Mirian G. 2022. "Extended Punishment: Criminalising Immigrants through Surveillance Technology." *Journal of Ethnic and Migration Studies* 48 (1): 74–91.

Massey, Douglas S. 2007. *Categorically Unequal: The American Stratification System*. New York: Russell Sage Foundation.

———. 2012. *The New Latino Underclass: Immigration Enforcement as a Race-Making Institution*. Working paper. Stanford, CA: Stanford Center on Poverty and Inequality.

———. 2020. "Creating the Exclusionist Society: From the War on Poverty to the War on Immigrants." *Ethnic and Racial Studies* 43 (1): 18–37.

Massey, Douglas, Karen Pren, and Jorge Durand. 2016. "Why Border Enforcement Backfired." *American Journal of Sociology* 121 (5): 1557–600.

Matza, David, and Gresham Sykes. 1957. "Techniques of Neutralization: A Theory of Delinquency." *American Sociological Review* 22 (6): 664–70.

Maynard-Moody, Steven, and Michael Musheno. 2003. *Cops, Teachers, Counselors: Stories from the Front Lines of Public Service*. Ann Arbor: University of Michigan Press.

McGlynn, Adam, and Jessica L. Monforti. 2010. "The Poverty Draft? Exploring the Role of Socioeconomic Status in US Military Recruitment of Hispanic Students." Paper presented at American Political Science Association Annual Meeting, 2010. https://ssrn.com/abstract =1643790.

McGoey, Linsey. 2012. "The Logic of Strategic Ignorance." *British Journal of Sociology* 63 (3): 553–76.

McLeod, Allegra M. 2012. "The US Criminal-Immigration Convergence and Its Possible Undoing." *American Criminal Law Review* 49 (1): 105–78.

Meissner, Doris, M., Donald M. Kerwin, Muzaffar Chishti, and Clair Bergeron. 2013. *Immigration Enforcement in the United States: The Rise of a Formidable Machinery*. Washington, DC: Migration Policy Institute.

Menjívar, Cecilia. 2006. "Liminal Legality: Salvadoran and Guatemalan Immigrants' Lives in the United States." *American Journal of Sociology* 111 (4): 999–1037.

———. 2021. "The Racialization of 'Illegality.'" *Daedalus: The Journal of the American Academy of Arts and Sciences* 150 (2): 91–105.

———. 2023. "State Categories, Bureaucracies of Displacement, and Possibilities from the Margins." *American Sociological Review* 88 (1): 1–23.

Menjívar, Cecilia, and Leisy Abrego. 2012. "Legal Violence: Immigration Law and the Lives of Central American Immigrants." *American Journal of Sociology* 117 (5): 1380–492.

Meyer, John W., and Brian Rowan. 1977. "Institutionalized Organizations: Formal Structure as Myth and Ceremony." *American Journal of Sociology* 83 (2): 340–63.

Molina, Natalia. 2014. *How Race Is Made in America: Immigration, Citizenship, and the Historical Power of Racial Scripts*. Berkeley: University of California Press.

Monforti, Jessica, and Adam McGlynn. 2021. *Proving Patriotismo: Latino Military Recruitment, Service, and Belonging in the US.* New York: Rowman and Littlefield.

Monk, Ellis P., Jr. 2022. "Inequality without Groups: Contemporary Theories of Categories, Intersectional Typicality, and the Disaggregation of Difference." *Sociological Theory* 40 (1): 3–27.

Mora, G. Cristina. 2014. *Making Hispanics: How Activists, Bureaucrats, and Media Constructed a New American.* Chicago: University of Chicago Press.

Morawetz, Nancy. 2000. "Understanding the Impact of the 1996 Deportation Laws and the Limited Scope of Proposed Reforms." *Harvard Law Review* 113 (8): 1936–62.

Motomura, Hiroshi. 2014. *Immigration outside the Law.* Oxford: Oxford University Press.

Muñiz, Ana. 2022. *Borderland Circuitry: Immigration Surveillance in the United States and Beyond.* Berkeley: University of California Press.

Murakawa, Naomi. 2017. "Weaponized Empathy: Emotion and the Limits of Racial Reconciliation in Policing." In *Racial Reconciliation and the Healing of a Nation,* edited by Charles J. Ogletree Jr. and Austin Sarat, 89–112. New York: New York University Press.

———. 2019. "Racial Innocence: Law, Social Science, and the Unknowing of Racism in the US Carceral State." *Annual Review of Law and Social Science* 1:473–93.

Murdza, Katy, and Walter Ewing. 2021. "The Legacy of Racism within the U.S. Border Patrol." American Immigration Council. https://www.americanimmigrationcouncil.org/sites /default/files/research/the_legacy_of_racism_within_the_u.s._border_patrol.pdf.

Nader, Laura. 1972. "Up the Anthropologist: Perspectives Gained from Studying Up." In *Reinventing Anthropology,* edited by Dell Hymes, 284–311. New York: Pantheon Books.

Nakamura, David. 2014. "Border Agents Decry 'Diaper Changing, Burrito Wrapping' with Influx of Children." *Washington Post,* June 20. https://www.washingtonpost.com/politics /border-agents-decry-diaper-changing-burrito-wrapping-with-influx-of-children/2014/06 /20/1a6b6714-f579-11e3-8aa9-dad2ec039789_story.html.

Nevins, Joseph. 2010. *Operation Gatekeeper and Beyond: The War on "Illegals" and the Remaking of the US-Mexico Boundary.* New York: Routledge.

Ngai, Mae M. 2003. "The Strange Career of the Illegal Alien: Immigration Restriction and Deportation Policy in the United States, 1921–1965." *Law and History Review* 21 (1): 69–108.

———. 2014. *Impossible Subjects: Illegal Aliens and the Making of Modern America.* Princeton, NJ: Princeton University Press.

Nowacki, Jeffrey, Joseph A. Schafer, and Julie Hibdon. 2021. "Workforce Diversity in Police Hiring: The Influence of Organizational Characteristics." *Justice Evaluation Journal* 4 (1): 48–67.

Oberfield, Zachary W. 2014. *Becoming Bureaucrats: Socialization at the Front Lines of Government Service.* Philadelphia: University of Pennsylvania Press.

———. 2020. "Discretion from a Sociological Perspective." In *Discretion and the Quest for Controlled Freedom,* edited by Tony Evans and Peter Hupe, 177–91. Cham: Springer Nature.

Ochoa, Gilda L. 2004. *Becoming Neighbors in a Mexican American Community: Power, Conflict, and Solidarity.* Austin: University of Texas Press.

Odendahl, Teresa, and Aileen M. Shaw. 2002. "Interviewing Elites." In *Handbook of Interview Research: Context and Method,* edited by Jaber F. Gubrium and James A. Holstein, 299–316. Thousand Oaks, CA: Sage.

Office of Personnel Management. 2014. "Salary Tables 2014—RUS (LEO)." https://www.opm
.gov/policy-data-oversight/pay-leave/salaries-wages/salary-tables/pdf/2014/RUS%20
(LEO).pdf.

———. 2020. "Federal Equal Opportunity Recruitment Program (FEORP) Report." https://
www.opm.gov/policy-data-oversight/diversity-equity-inclusion-and-accessibility/reports
/feorp2020.pdf.

Orbuch, Terri L. 1997. "People's Accounts Count: The Sociology of Accounts." *American
Sociological Review* 23:455–78.

Ostrander, Susan A. 1993. "Surely You're Not in This Just to Be Helpful: Access, Rapport and
Interviews in Three Studies of Elites." *Journal of Contemporary Ethnography* 22:7–27.

Pallister-Wilkins, Polly. 2015. "The Humanitarian Politics of European Border Policing: Frontex
and Border Police in Evros." *International Political Sociology* 9 (1): 53–69.

Patler, Caitlin. 2018. " 'Citizens but for Papers': Undocumented Youth Organizations,
Anti-deportation Campaigns, and the Reframing of Citizenship." *Social Problems* 65 (1):
96–115.

Pérez, Gina M. 2015. *Citizen, Student, Soldier: Latina/o Youth, JROTC, and the American Dream.*
New York: New York University Press.

Phillips, S., J. M. Hagan, and N. Rodriguez. 2006. "Brutal Borders? Examining the Treatment
of Deportees during Arrest and Detention." *Social Forces* 85 (1): 93–109.

Plascencia, Luis F., Allise Waterston, and Gina Pérez. 2015. "Latinos, Militarism, and Militarization." *Latino Studies* 13:150–61.

Portillo, Shannon. 2012. "The Paradox of Rules: Rules as Resources and Constraints." *Administration and Society* 44 (1): 87–108.

Presser, Lois. 2013. *Why We Harm.* New Brunswick, NJ: Rutgers University Press.

Prieto, Greg. 2015. " 'Traitors' to Race, 'Traitors' to Nation: Latina/o Immigration Enforcement
Agents, Identification and the Racial State." *Latino Studies* 13 (4): 501–22.

———. 2018. *Immigrants under Threat: Risk and Resistance in Deportation Nation.* New York:
New York University Press.

Provine, Doris Marie, and Roxanne Lynn Doty. 2011. "The Criminalization of Immigrants as a
Racial Project." *Journal of Contemporary Criminal Justice* 27 (3): 261–77.

Pugh, Allison J. 2013. "What Good Are Interviews for Thinking about Culture? Demystifying
Interpretive Analysis." *American Journal of Cultural Sociology* 1:42–68.

Rabin, Nina. 2013. "Victims or Criminals—Discretion, Sorting, and Bureaucratic Culture in the
US Immigration System." *Review of Law and Social Justice* 23 (2): 195.

———. 2019. "Searching for Humanitarian Discretion in Immigration Enforcement: Reflections on a Year as an Immigration Attorney in the Trump Era." *University of Michigan Journal
of Law Reform* 53:139–71.

Raganella, Anthony J., and Michael D. White. 2004. "Race, Gender, and Motivation for Becoming a Police Officer: Implications for Building a Representative Police Department." *Journal
of Criminal Justice* 32 (6): 501–13.

Rahr, S., and S. K. Rice. 2015. *From Warriors to Guardians: Recommitting American Police Culture
to Democratic Ideals.* Washington, DC: US Department of Justice, Office of Justice Programs,
National Institute of Justice.

Ray, Victor. 2019. "A Theory of Racialized Organizations." *American Sociological Review* 84 (1): 26–53.

Ray, Victor, Pamela Herd, and Donald Moynihan. 2023. "Racialized Burdens: Applying Racialized Organization Theory to the Administrative State." *Journal of Public Administration Research and Theory* 33 (1): 139–52.

Reagan, Ronald. 1986. "Statement on Signing the Immigration Reform and Control Act of 1986." November 6. https://www.reaganlibrary.gov/archives/speech/statement-signing-immigration-reform-and-control-act-1986.

Riley, Jason. 2022. " 'Hunting of Man' Quote Used in Warrant Training for Louisville Police." https://www.wdrb.com/wdrb-investigates/hunting-of-man-quote-used-in-warrant-training-for-louisville-police/article_27540c9c-02ef-11ed-8805-bf6155d98224.html.

Rios, Victor M., Greg Prieto, and Jonathan M. Ibarra. 2020. "Mano Suave-Mano Dura: Legitimacy Policing and Latino Stop-and-Frisk." *American Sociological Review* 85 (1): 58–75.

Rivera, C. 2014. "The Brown Threat: Post-9/11 Conflations of Latina/os and Middle Eastern Muslims in the US American Imagination." *Latino Studies* 12:44–64.

Rivera, Kendra Dyanne, and Sarah J. Tracy. 2014. "Embodying Emotional Dirty Work: A Messy Text of Patrolling the Border." *Qualitative Research in Organizations and Management: An International Journal* 9 (3): 201–22.

Rodríguez, Nestor, and Cristian Paredes. 2014. "Coercive Immigration Enforcement and Bureaucratic Ideology." In *Constructing Immigration "Illegality": Critiques, Experiences, and Responses*, edited by C. Menjívar and D. Kanstroom, 63–83. Cambridge: Cambridge University Press.

Rodríguez-Muñiz, Michael. 2021. *Figures of the Future: Latino Civil Rights and the Politics of Demographic Change*. Princeton, NJ: Princeton University Press, 2021.

Rojek, Jeff, V. M. Manjarrez, Scott Wolfe, and A. Rojek. 2017. "El Paso Sector Border Patrol Agent Survey Report." *Journal of Criminal Justice* 54:20–29.

Rowe, Mike, and Michael Rowe. 2021. "Understanding the Quiet Times: The Role of Periods of 'Nothing Much Happening' in Police Work." *Journal of Contemporary Ethnography* 50 (6): 751–74.

Rumbaut, R. G. 2016. "Zombie Ideas and Moral Panics: Framing Immigrants as Criminal and Cultural Threats." Russell Sage Foundation Blog Series. https://www.russellsage.org/zombie-ideas-and-moral-panics-framing-immigrants-criminal-and-cultural-threats.

Ryo, Emily. 2013. "Deciding to Cross: Norms and Economics of Unauthorized Migration." *American Sociological Review* 78 (4): 574–603.

———. 2017. "Legal Attitudes of Immigrant Detainees." *Law and Society Review* 51 (1): 99–131.

———. 2019. "Predicting Danger in Immigration Courts." *Law and Social Inquiry* 44 (1): 227–56.

Ryo, Emily, and Ian Peacock. 2018. "The Landscape of Immigration Detention in the United States." American Immigration Council. https://www.immigrationresearch.org/system/files/the_landscape_of_immigration_detention_in_the_united_states.pdf.

Schuck, Amie M. 2021. "Motivations for a Career in Policing: Social Group Differences and Occupational Satisfaction." *Police Practice and Research* 22 (5): 1507–23.

Scott, James C. 2020. *Seeing Like a State: How Certain Schemes to Improve the Human Condition Have Failed*. New Haven, CT: Yale University Press.

Scott, Marvin B., and Stanford M. Lyman. 1968. "Accounts." *American Sociological Review* 33:46–62.

Shapira, Harel. 2013. *Waiting for José: The Minutemen's Pursuit of America*. Princeton, NJ: Princeton University Press.

Shiff, Talia. 2021. "A Sociology of Discordance: Negotiating Schemas of Deservingness and Codified Law in US Asylum Status Determinations." *American Journal of Sociology* 127 (2): 337–75.

Sierra-Arévalo, Michael. 2021. "American Policing and the Danger Imperative." *Law and Society Review* 55 (1): 70–103.

Simon, Jonathan. 2007. *Governing through Crime: How the War on Crime Transformed American Democracy and Created a Culture of Fear*. Oxford: Oxford University Press.

Skolnick, Jerome H. 1966. *Justice without Trial: Law Enforcement in a Democratic Society*. New York: Wiley.

Skrentny, John D. 2013. "Have We Moved beyond the Civil Rights Revolution." *Yale Law Journal* 123:3002–24.

Slack, Jeremy, Daniel Martínez, and Scott Whiteford, eds. 2018. *In the Shadow of the Wall: Family Separation, Immigration Enforcement and Security*. Tucson: University of Arizona Press.

Small, Mario L. 2015. "De-exoticizing Ghetto Poverty: On the Ethics of Representation in Urban Ethnography." *City and Community* 14 (4): 352–58.

Souris, R. N. 2024. " 'The Cruelty Is the Point': Virtue Ethics and Immigration." *Polity* 56 (3): 355–521.

Souter, J. 2011. "A Culture of Disbelief or Denial? Critiquing Refugee Status Determination in the United Kingdom." *Oxford Monitor of Forced Migration* 1 (1): 48–59.

Sowatey, Emmanuel A., and Justice Tankebe. 2018. "Doing Research with Police Elites in Ghana." *Criminology and Criminal Justice* 19 (5): 537–53.

Sprunt, Barbara. 2020. "Biden Would End Border Wall Construction, but Wouldn't Tear Down Trump's Additions." NPR. https://www.npr.org/2020/08/05/899266045/biden-would-end-border-wall-construction-but-wont-tear-down-trump-s-additions.

Stel, Nora. 2016. "The Agnotology of Eviction in South Lebanon's Palestinian Gatherings: How Institutional Ambiguity and Deliberate Ignorance Shape Sensitive Spaces; The Agnotology of Eviction." *Antipode* 48 (5): 1400–1419.

Stets, Jan E., and Michael J. Carter. 2011. "The Moral Self: Applying Identity Theory." *Social Psychology Quarterly* 74 (2): 192–215.

Stumpf, Juliet. 2006. "The Crimmigration Crisis: Immigrants, Crime, and Sovereign Power." *American University Law Review* 56:367.

———. 2020. "Justifying Family Separation: Constructing the Criminal Alien and the Alien Mother." *Wake Forest Law Review* 55:1037.

———. 2023. "Crimmigration and the Legitimacy of Immigration Law." *Arizona Law Review* 65:113.

Swidler, Ann. 1986. "Culture in Action: Symbols and Strategies." *American Sociological Review* 51 (2): 273–86.

Thuesen, Frederik. 2011. "Navigating between Dialogue and Confrontation: Phronesis and Emotions in Interviewing Elites on Ethnic Discrimination." *Qualitative Inquiry* 17 (7): 613–22.

Thumala, Angélica, Benjamin Goold, and Ian Loader. 2011. "A Tainted Trade? Moral Ambivalence and Legitimation Work in the Private Security Industry." *British Journal of Sociology* 62 (2): 283–303.

Todak, Natalie, Jessica Huff, and Lois James. 2018. "Investigating Perceptions of Race and Ethnic Diversity among Prospective Police Officers." *Police Practice and Research* 19 (5): 490–504.

Tosh, Sarah. 2019. "Drugs, Crime, and Aggravated Felony Deportations: Moral Panic Theory and the Legal Construction of the 'Criminal Alien.'" *Critical Criminology* 27:329–45.

TRAC Immigration. 2016. "Historical Data: Immigration and Customs Enforcement Removals—ICE Data through January 2016." Syracuse University. https://trac.syr.edu/phptools/immigration/removehistory/.

———. 2017. "ICE Immigration Raids: A Primer." Syracuse University. https://trac.syr.edu/immigration/reports/459/.

Tuckett, Anna. 2018. *Rules, Paper, Status: Migrants and Precarious Bureaucracy in Contemporary Italy*. Stanford, CA: Stanford University Press.

Turner, Jonathan H., and Jan E. Stets. 2006. "Moral Emotions." In *Handbook of the Sociology of Emotions*, edited by Jan E. Stets and Jonathan H. Turner, 544–66. New York: Springer.

Tyler, T. 2017. "Procedural Justice and Policing: A Rush to Judgement?" *Annual Review of Law and Social Science* 13:29–53.

Ugelvik, Thomas. 2016. "Techniques of Legitimation: The Narrative Construction of Legitimacy among Immigration Detention Officers." *Crime, Media, Culture* 12 (2): 215–32.

US Commission on Civil Rights. 2019. "Trauma at the Border: The Human Cost of Inhumane Immigration Policies." https://www.usccr.gov/files/pubs/2019/10-24-Trauma-at-the-Border.pdf.

US Customs and Border Protection. 2015. "National Standards on Transport, Escort, Detention, and Search." https://www.cbp.gov/sites/default/files/assets/documents/2020-Feb/cbp-teds-policy-october2015.pdf.

———. 2021. "CBP Use of Force Policy." https://www.cbp.gov/sites/default/files/assets/documents/2021-Jul/cbp-use-of-force-policy_4500-002A.pdf.

———. n.d. (a). "Careers: U.S. Border Patrol." https://careers.cbp.gov/s/career-paths/usbp. Accessed September 17, 2024.

———. n.d. (b). U.S. Customs and Border Protection. "The United States Border Patrol Academy." https://www.youtube.com/watch?v=D99GXFSyWpg. Accessed September 17, 2024.

———. n.d. (c). U.S. Customs and Border Protection. "Preparing for the Border Patrol Academy—Hiring Process Deep Dive." https://www.youtube.com/watch?v=7ovjN_v6Haw. Accessed September 17, 2024.

———. n.d. (d). CBP "Law Enforcement Explorer Program." https://careers.cbp.gov/s/career-paths/cbp-explorer-program.

US Equal Employment Opportunity Commission. 2016. "Advancing Diversity in Law Enforcement." https://www.justice.gov/d9/advancing_diversity_in_law_enforcement_report_october_2016.pdf.

US Immigration and Customs Enforcement. 2014. "ICE Enforcement and Removal Operations Report." chrome-extension://efaidnbmnnnibpcajpcglclefindmkaj/https://www.ice.gov/doclib/about/offices/ero/pdf/2014-ice-immigration-removals.pdf.

———. 2015. "ICE Enforcement and Removal Operations Report." chrome-extension://efaid nbmnnnibpcajpcglclefindmkaj/https://www.ice.gov/sites/default/files/documents /Report/2016/fy2015removalStats.pdf.

———. 2016. "Fiscal Year 2016 ICE Enforcement and Removal Operations Report." chrome-e xtension://efaidnbmnnnibpcajpcglclefindmkaj/https://www.ice.gov/sites/default/files /documents/Report/2016/removal-stats-2016.pdf.

———. 2018. "ICE Academy Instructors Teach Potential Deportation Officers." https://www .ice.gov/news/releases/ice-academy-instructors-teach-prospective-deportation-officers.

———. 2020. "Immigration Enforcement Actions: 2019." https://ohss.dhs.gov/sites/default /files/2023-12/enforcement_actions_2019.pdf.

———. n.d. (a). "Career Frequently Asked Questions (FAQs) | ICE." https://www.ice.gov /careers/faqs. Accessed December 2, 2023.

———. n.d. (b). "Episode 2: Physical Fitness and Mental Challenges | ICE." https://www.ice.gov /podcasts/episode-2-physical-fitness-and-mental-challenges. Accessed December 2, 2023.

———. n.d. (c) "Fact Sheet: ICE Fugitive Operations Program." https://www.ice.gov/doclib /news/library/factsheets/pdf/fugops.pdf. Accessed September 11, 2024.

Vaisey, Stephen. 2009. "Motivation and Justification: A Dual-Process Model of Culture in Action." *American Journal of Sociology* 114:1675–715.

van der Woude, Maartje, and Joanne van der Leun. 2017. "Crimmigration Checks in the Internal Border Areas of the EU: Finding the Discretion That Matters." *European Journal of Criminology* 14 (1): 27–45.

Van Maanen, John. 1973. "Observations on the Making of Policemen." *Human Organization* 32:407–18.

———. 1975. "Police Socialization: A Longitudinal Examination of Job Attitudes in an Urban Police Department." *Administrative Science Quarterly* 20:207–28.

Vega, Irene I. 2014. "Conservative Rationales, Racial Boundaries: A Case Study of Restrictionist Mexican Americans." *American Behavioral Scientist* 58 (13): 1764–83.

———. 2018. "Empathy, Morality, and Criminality: The Legitimation Narratives of US Border Patrol Agents." *Journal of Ethnic and Migration Studies* 44 (15): 2544–61.

———. 2019. "Toward a Cultural Sociology of Immigration Control: A Call for Research." *American Behavioral Scientist* 63 (9): 1172–84.

———. 2022. "'Reasonable' Force at the US-Mexico Border." *Social Problems* 69 (4): 1154–69.

Vega, Irene I., and V. Ortiz. 2018. "Mexican Americans and Immigration Attitudes: A Cohort Analysis of Assimilation and Group Consciousness." *Social Problems* 65 (2): 137–53.

Vega, Irene I., and Maartje van der Woude. 2023. "Colourblindness across Borders: The Deracialized Logics of Dutch and American Border Agents." *Theoretical Criminology* 28 (3): 309–27.

Vila, P. 2005. *Border Identifications: Narratives of Religion, Gender, and Class on the US-Mexico Border*. Austin: University of Texas Press.

Vitus, Kathrine. 2008. "The Agonistic Approach: Reframing Resistance in Qualitative Research." *Qualitative Inquiry* 14 (3): 466–88.

Waddington, Peter A. J. 1999. "Police (Canteen) Sub-culture: An Appreciation." *British Journal of Criminology* 39 (2): 287–309.

Wadhia, Shoba Sivaprasad. 2019. "Banned: Immigration Enforcement in the Time of Trump." New York: New York University Press.

Ward, Geoff K. 2006. "Race and the Justice Workforce." In *The Many Colors of Crime: Inequalities of Race, Ethnicity, and Crime in America*. Edited by J. K. Lauren, D. P. Ruth, and H. John, 67–87. New York: New York University Press.

———. 2015. "The Slow Violence of State Organized Race Crime." *Theoretical Criminology* 19(3): 299–314.

Ward, Geoff, and Peter A. Hanink. 2016. "Deliberating Racial Justice: Toward Racially Democratic Crime Control." In *The Routledge Handbook of Criminal Justice Ethics*, edited by Jonathan Jacobs and Jonathan Jackson, 282–300. New York: Routledge.

Ward, Geoff, and Aaron Kupchik. 2009. "Accountable to What? Professional Orientations towards Accountability-Based Juvenile Justice." *Punishment and Society* 11 (1): 85–109.

Watkins-Hayes, Celeste. 2009. *The New Welfare Bureaucrats: Entanglements of Race, Class, and Policy Reform*. Chicago: University of Chicago Press.

———. 2011. "Race, Respect, and Red tape: Inside the Black Box of Racially Representative Bureaucracies." *Journal of Public Administration Research and Theory* 21 (2): i233–i251.

Weber, M. 1978. *Economy and Society*. Vols. 1 and 2. Edited by G. Roth and C. Wittich. Berkeley: University California Press.

Weichselbaum, Simone, and Beth Schwartzapfel. 2017. "When Warriors Put On the Badge." The Marshall Project. https://www.themarshallproject.org/2017/03/30/when-warriors-put-on-the-badge.

Weissinger, George. 2017. *Law Enforcement and the INS: A Participant Observation Study of Control Agents*. New York: Rowman and Littlefield.

Weitzer, Ronald. 2000. "White, Black, or Blue Cops? Race and Citizen Assessments of Police Officers." *Journal of Criminal Justice* 28 (4): 313–24.

———. 2014. The Puzzling Neglect of Hispanic Americans in Research on Police-Citizen Relations. *Ethnic and Racial Studies* 37, 1995–2013.

———. 2017. "Recent Trends in Police-Citizen Relations and Police Reform in the United States." In *Police-Citizen Relations across the World*, 28–45. New York: Routledge.

Westley, William A. 1970. *Violence and the Police: A Sociological Study of Law, Custom, and Morality*. Cambridge, MA: MIT Press.

Wettergren, Asa. 2010. "Managing Unlawful Feelings: The Emotional Regime of the Swedish Migration Board." *International Journal of Work Organisation and Emotion* 3 (4): 400–419.

White, Michael D., Jonathon A. Cooper, Jessica Saunders, and Anthony J. Raganella. 2010. "Motivations for Becoming a Police Officer: Re-assessing Officer Attitudes and Job Satisfaction after Six Years on the Street." *Journal of Criminal Justice* 38 (4): 520–30.

The White House. 2002. "President Bush Signs Homeland Security Act: Remarks by the President at the Signing of H.R. 5005 the Homeland Security Act of 2002." News release, November 15. https://georgewbush-whitehouse.archives.gov/news/releases/2002/11/20021125-6.html.

———. 2014a. "Fact Sheet on the Immigration Accountability Executive Action." November 24. https://obamawhitehouse.archives.gov/the-press-office/2014/11/20/fact-sheet-immigration-accountability-executive-action.

———. 2014b. "Remarks by the President in Address to the Nation on Immigration." News release, November 20. https://obamawhitehouse.archives.gov/the-press-office/2014/11/20/remarks-President-address-nation-immigration.

Wilson, James Q. 1989. *Bureaucracy: What Government Agencies Do and Why They Do It.* London: Hachette.

Wimmer, Andreas. 2008. "The Making and Unmaking of Ethnic Boundaries: A Multilevel Process Theory." *American Journal of Sociology* 113 (4): 970–1022.

Wingfield, Adia Harvey. 2010. "Are Some Emotions Marked 'Whites Only'? Racialized Feeling Rules in Professional Workplaces." *Social Problems* 57 (2): 251–68.

———. 2021. "The (Un)Managed Heart: Racial Contours of Emotion Work in Gendered Occupations." *Annual Review of Sociology* 47:197–212.

Wingfield, Adia Harvey, and Renée Skeete Alston. 2014. "Maintaining Hierarchies in Predominantly White Organizations: A Theory of Racial Tasks." *American Behavioral Scientist* 58 (2): 274–87.

Wingfield, Adia Harvey, and Koji Chavez. 2020. "Getting In, Getting Hired, Getting Sideways Looks: Organizational Hierarchy and Perceptions of Racial Discrimination." *American Sociological Review* 85 (1): 31–57.

Wittock, Nathan, Laura Cleton, Robin Vandevoordt, and Gert Verschraegen. 2023. "Legitimising Detention and Deportation of Illegalised Migrant Families: Reconstructing Public Controversies in Belgium and the Netherlands." *Journal of Ethnic and Migration Studies* 49 (7): 1589–609.

Wyllie, Doug. 2018. "How the Bond between Cops and Kids Might Help Solve the Police Recruitment Crisis." *Police Magazine*, September 21, 2018. https://www.policemag.com/blogs/careers/blog/15317158/how-the-bond-between-cops-and-kids-might-help-solve-the-police-recruitment-crisis.

Zacka, Bernardo. 2017. *When the State Meets the Street: Public Service and Moral Agency.* Cambridge, MA: Belknap Press of Harvard University Press.

Zamora, Sylvia. 2022. *Racial Baggage: Mexican Immigrants and Race across the Border.* Stanford, CA: Stanford University Press.

Zepeda-Millán, Chris. 2017. *Latino Mass Mobilization: Immigration, Racialization, and Activism.* Cambridge: Cambridge University Press.

A NOTE ON THE TYPE

This book has been composed in Arno, an Old-style serif typeface in the classic Venetian tradition, designed by Robert Slimbach at Adobe.

GPSR Authorized Representative: Easy Access System Europe - Mustamäe tee 50, 10621 Tallinn, Estonia, gpsr.requests@easproject.com